CAREFULLY TEAR THIS PAGE OUT AND RETURN RECEIPT

> **Package Contents recently sent to your attention:**
> - 1 copy of course book: IMAN 100, Beliefs of a Muslim

Dear Tayba Student,

As an active and registered student, we ask that you please fill out this Return Receipt form and send it back to us as soon as you receive your course material. This receipt is so that we can verify if and when you have received the course materials we have recently mailed to you.

<u>Please mail to:</u>

Tayba Foundation

PO BOX 1154 Portsmouth

NH 03802

Alternatively, you may choose to send this form or receipt confirmation through your appointed Chaplain. We can be reached at the above mailing address or by email at <u>instructors@taybafoundation.org</u> or by phone at <u>(510) 491-7859</u>.

Student Name: _____ ID: _____

Facility Name: _____

Facility Address: _____

City: _____ State _____

Date your book(s) were received: _____

Did you receive your package with the contents listed above? [ ] Yes [ ] No

If you received all of the items, please skip to the next question. If not, please identify what you are missing:

_____
_____
_____

Did your facility have any issues with the material, the contents of the package or the packaging?
[ ] Yes [ ] No

If yes, please describe:

_____
_____
_____

Have you ensured that you are authorized to receive books from Tayba, and that Tayba is considered as an approved "vendor" at your facility? [ ] Yes [ ] No

This page has been left blank

IMAN 100:
BELIEFS OF A MUSLIM

TAYBA

TAYBA FOUNDATION
Freedom Through Education

IMAN 100: Beliefs of a Muslim
ISBN: 978-1075399909
Imprint: Independently published by Tayba Foundation

© 2024 TAYBA FOUNDATION
First edition published in December 2018 by Tayba Foundation.
Current edition revised and re-published in January 2024 by Tayba Foundation.

All rights reserved. No part of this publication may be reproduced, stored in a retrieval system, or transmitted in any form or in any means - by electronic, mechanical, photocopying, recording or otherwise - without prior written permission of the publisher.

TAYBA

Tayba Foundation
PO Box 1154
Portsmouth, NH 03802-1154
United States of America

Tayba Foundation is a registered non-profit 501(c)3 educational and charitable organisation located in the San Francisco Bay Area, but serving all states.

Phone number: 510-491-7859 | 510-641-8881 | 510-491-6165
Website: taybafoundation.org

IMAN 100:
BELIEFS OF A MUSLIM
AN INTRODUCTION TO ISLAMIC FAITH

TAYBA

A Tayba Foundation Publication

Author: Shaykh Rami Nsour al-Idrisi
Contributors: Abdul Muhaymin Al Salim (Eugene Priester III)

TAYBA FOUNDATION
Freedom Through Education

IMAN 100
Beliefs of a Muslim, *Version 6*

Student Handbook	p. 1
Beliefs of a Muslim	p. 10
Outline Summary for Beliefs of A Muslim	p. 143
Understanding the Angels	p. 165
Our Beloved Prophets	p. 183
Multiple Choice Exam and Assignments	p. 219
Multiple Choice Exam Answer Bubble Sheet	p. 237
Extra Student Application Form	P. 245

TAYBA FOUNDATION
Freedom Through Education

STUDENT HANDBOOK

IMAN 100, Beliefs of a Muslim
Version 6

Instructors: Tayba Faculty

At the Tayba Foundation, we believe that all people contain a wellspring of goodness within them, and we believe in the power of human potential.

Even when individuals encounter dramatic setbacks in life, lasting change is possible.

Tayba Foundation is a non-profit organization dedicated to serving individuals and families impacted by incarceration. We believe in the power of human change through holistic education, guidance, and support. Our work is organized into two interrelated program areas: Education and Life Skills.

This handbook contains the information you need to complete this course. It is split into three sections, please read them all carefully:

1. Course information
2. Assignments and grades

Course Information

IMAN 100 is a correspondence course. To succeed in this course, you must go through the material carefully and ask questions when you need to.

Course Description

Īmān, or faith, is what makes a person a Muslim. Islām, or practice, completes the faith but as long as someone holds the essentials of faith, that person is a Muslim. Thus, the magnitude of faith is something never to be underestimated and is one of the most important, if not the most important subject to be studied in Islām.

The core text of this course is designed to ensure that a student will know their essentials (farḍ ʿayn) in regards to knowledge of the beliefs of Islām. The text draws from the work of many scholars who have come before us.

Course Objectives

Upon successful completion of the course, the student will:

- Understand the essential beliefs related to the Islamic faith.

The student will meet the following learning objectives:
- Demonstrate knowledge and sound understanding of the essentials related to the Islamic faith (Īmān).
- Achieving this objective will be assessed through the multiple choice exam and essay assignment.

Textbook and study materials

The textbook used for this course will be "IMAN 100, Beliefs of a Muslim" by Shaykh Rami Nsour al-Idrisi and Abdul Muhaymin Al Salim (Eugene Priester III). You will be provided with a copy of the original Arabic text, translation and commentary.

Instructors

A number of instructors contributed to the development of this course. Those instructors are available to answer questions during semester time, as well as grade your assignments at the end of the semester.

How to contact your Instructor

You can contact Tayba instructors by email, phone (collect call), or by written letter. We expect all students to keep in contact with their instructors throughout the semester, as far as possible.

We encourage you to send in your questions during the semester by phone, mail or email. Please note that <u>questions about the course should **not** be submitted with your course assignments</u>. However, if you have difficulty sending mail, you may send in questions along with your coursework submission. However, they may not be answered at the same time your coursework is graded.

By email: For questions regarding the course material or assignments, you can email <u>instructors@taybafoundation.org</u> via CorrLinks, ConnectNetwork, GettingOut, JPay, JailFunds, Securus, or SmartJailMail, if those services are available to you. When sending email, always include "IMAN 100, Beliefs of a Muslim" in the subject or first line of the message. We will not answer messages from unapproved sources so please do not try to contact us via Facebook Messenger, SMS, or Gmail while you are incarcerated.

By letter: Please be sure to write your **name and ID number** on all communication with Tayba Foundation, particularly on all of your assignments.

By phone: Phone access has always been part of the package of services provided with every course, so please call us collect. Please see the contact list of phone numbers below.

You may also consider giving the message to a Chaplain, family member, or friend with whom you are in contact. That person could then email us or phone us and we can answer an inquiry if you give them permission to receive information on your behalf about your studies.

Academic Dishonesty

The Tayba Foundation's Student Code of Conduct and Honor Code strictly prohibits any form of academic misconduct, such as plagiarism or cheating on exams. Academic misconduct is an unacceptable activity in scholarship and is in conflict with academic and professional ethics and morals. Academic misconduct may result in a failing grade and/ or expulsion from the program.

Semester schedule

A key to success in a correspondence class is to keep up and not get behind. You are free to submit your work before the final deadline, however please note that tests and papers will <u>not</u> start to be graded until the deadline. Submit all tests and the term paper together.

Suggested timeline to keep up with the coursework:

Spring Term (March 1 - June 30)	**Fall Term** (September 1 - December 31)
March: Lessons 1-4	September: Lessons 1-4
April: Lessons 5-7	October: Lessons 5-7
May: Lessons 8-11	November: Lessons 8-11
May/June: Lessons 12-14, plus review the material	November/December: Lessons 12-14, plus review the material
June: Submit all assignments together	December: Submit all assignments together

The final deadline to submit the exam and all assignments is <u>June 30th</u> for the Spring Term and <u>December 31st</u> for the Fall Term.

If, for any reason, you are unable to submit the coursework on time, please provide a brief note in advance of the due date, explaining the reason for late submission.

Course assignments and grades

Assignments that you must complete

There are **two assignments** that you must complete. Details are found **at the end** of this course book.

1. One multiple choice exam. There are 100 questions and the exam is worth 100 points.
2. 7x Short Answer Questions.

Assignment deadline

The final deadline to submit the exam and the writing assignments is **June 30th** for the Spring Term and **December 31st** for the Fall Term.

Please note that any assignment received after the due date will NOT be graded until the following semester.

If, for any reason, you are unable to submit the coursework on time, please provide a brief note to your instructor, before the deadline, explaining the reason for late submission. Your instructor will make a decision as to whether an extension can be offered to you.

You are free to submit your work before the final deadline, however please note that assignments will usually not be graded before the deadline.

A reminder that any questions you have must be submitted throughout the course term and not sent in with your assignments.

Essay Writing Made Easy - a Student Guide

All essays should have an **introduction**, a **body**, and a **conclusion.** A balance of these 3 sections is important. A good rule of thumb is:

Introduction: 10 % **Body:** 80 % **Conclusion:** 10 %

Helpful Tip: Before you begin your essay, create an outline to help organize your thoughts.

Step1:

The first thing you need to do is answer your topic or research question.

For example: **How has the knowledge you have learned from "The Abridgement of Al-Akhdari," affected your personal, family, and community life?**

- Ask yourself what topics, from the text, will you reflect on? Wuḍūʼ, Tawba, Ghusl, Prayer etc.
- Think about how the knowledge you have learned has affected your personal, family, and community life.
- Ask yourself some specific questions: (for example)
    o How has the act of Tawba changed my life with my parents?
    o After learning the importance of ghusl, how has it changed my understanding of cleanliness?
    o How has the act of promoting good and forbidding evil affected my relationship with the brothers in my community?

Step 2:

In this step you want to narrow your ideas further. An average essay will make a general statement of what was learned and briefly mention what effect(s) it had on your life. A _strong_ reflective essay will:

- State what was learned
- State how it has affected an area of your life
- Provide personal examples
- Give an insight to the outcome

(Example)
- Promoting Good and Forbidding Evil
    - Give a brief statement on what this means
    - Discuss how you tried to implement what you learned
    - Give examples of the success or obstacles you encountered
    - Provide an insight as to why you encountered problems
    - Talk about how it made you feel

Step 3:

Create a topic sentence.

This is probably the most important part of the essay. Every essay must have a topic statement. The topic statement is one or two sentences, in your **introduction**, that contains the focus of your essay and tells the reader what the essay is going to be about. You want to make sure your topic piques the interest of the reader.

(Example of Average topic sentence)

1. *"For the purpose of this essay I will talk about wuḍū, tawba, and ghusl and how they have affected me in my personal, family, and community life."*

This topic sentence is correct. But it is also unimaginative.

(Example of an interesting topic statement)

1. *"Knowledge is the key to freedom," is a statement I have heard throughout my life. I have never truly understood its meaning until I began studying sacred knowledge. What I have learned has had a profound effect on all areas of my life.* **(Then you can list the topics you will discuss)**

This topic pulls the reader into wanting to read further to find out what the author has to say. Don't worry if a topic statement extends a little beyond the two sentence norm. Sometimes you need to build up to what you want to talk about.

Important Note: Now that you've organized what your thoughts and ideas are you can start your essay.

Introduction

The introduction is the first paragraph and the point of entry for your essay. It is where you will introduce your topic sentence.

Body of the essay

The body of the essay is where you will discuss your three points. Each paragraph will focus on one topic. To make your paragraphs effective follow these guidelines:

Paragraph 1, 2, & 3

1. **Topic sentence** - The topic sentence introduces the point you will talk about.
2. **Supporting sentences** - The supporting sentences provide details to support the topic. Use examples, your opinion or personal accounts to give more value to your topic.
3. **Concluding sentence** - The concluding sentences sum up what you've said in the paragraph and pave the way for your next topic sentence.

Conclusion

Your conclusion is your last chance to highlight your point of view to your readers. The impression you create in your conclusion will leave a long lasting effect with your reader long after they've finished the essay. The end of an essay should bring a sense of completeness and closure to your discussion.

IMAN 100:
BELIEFS OF A MUSLIM

Beliefs of a Muslim

Compiled by

Rami Nsour[1]

---

[1] Shaykh Rami wrote the main text, while the footnotes have been added throughout the years by Tayba instructors in response to recurring questions that have been raised since IMAN 100 was initially completed. Additionally, Ustadh Abdul Muhaymin Al Salim wrote the final two chapters expanding upon our beliefs about the Angels and the Prophets.

بِسْمِ اللَّهِ الرَّحْمَٰنِ الرَّحِيمِ

Introduction

It is with great pleasure that I am able to present to you the work that you have in your hands. It is a work that I feel honored to have been a part of as it is something that is drawn from the work of many scholars who have come before us. It is a text that is designed to ensure that a student will know their essentials (farḍ 'ayn) in regards to knowledge of the beliefs of Islam. In this introduction, I would like to briefly address the importance of the study of Iman, where we take our sources from, and how this text was compiled.

Iman, or faith, is what makes a person a Muslim. Islam, or practice, completes the faith but as long as someone holds the essentials of Iman, that person is a Muslim. Thus, the magnitude of Iman is something never to be underestimated. When discussing this, I often ask my students the following question; "What would the Muslim community (Umma) do if the Ka'bah were to be desecrated or destroyed (God forbid) by someone?" The answer is always that the Muslims would never sit silent as that happens.

I then ask, "What would be the reaction if a believer were to be harmed or killed (God forbid)?" The answer is not usually as emphatic as it was to the first question. Sometimes I would ask my students which they thought was better, themselves or the Ka'bah, with the answer usually coming back that the Ka'bah is better. I then relate the story of the Prophet (peace and blessings be upon him) speaking to the Ka'ba. He was making tawaaf and looked at the Ka'ba and said, "By Allah, how grand you are and how grand you are with Allah, but by Allah, one believer is greater to Allah than you." At this point, I often see a realization come into the eyes of the student. Once we realize the value of this faith that we have within us, we will put more effort into learning about it and adhering to it.

INTRODUCTION

وعن ابن عباس رضي الله عنه قال: نظر رسول الله ﷺ إلى الكعبة، فقال: "ما أعظم حُرْمَتَك." وفي رواية أبي حازم: "ما نظر رسول الله ﷺ إلى الكعبة، قال": "مرحباً بك من بيت، ما أعظمك وأعظم حُرْمَتَك، وللمؤمن أعظم حُرْمَة عند الله منكِ، إنَّ الله حرَّم منكِ واحدة، وحرَّم من المؤمن ثلاثاً: دمه، وماله، وأن يُظنَّ به ظنَّ السُّوء."

On the authority of Ibn 'Abbas (radiy Allahu anhuma) who said, "The Messenger of Allah ﷺ looked at the Ka'ba and said, **"How grand is your sanctity."** In a narration according to Abi Hazim, "When the Messenger of Allah ﷺ looked at the Ka'bah, he said, **'Welcome to you O House, how grand you are and how grand is your sanctity, verily a believer has a greater sanctity with Allah than you. Allah has protected for the believer three matters: his blood, his wealth and that people have a bad opinion of him.'"** (Bayhaqi, *Shu'ub al-Iman*).

To learn the faith, we have to go back to the primary sources of Iman. The subject of Iman covers aspects that are from the matters of the unseen world (ghayb). The only way to know about the unseen world is through Revelation (wahy). Thus, the only valid source for learning about Iman is the Book of Allah (Quran) and the teachings (Sunna) of the Prophet Muhammad ﷺ.

For each individual Muslim to try and extract the necessary sections of the Quran and Sunna to learn the essentials of the faith would be very difficult. It would be similar to a sick person having to go back to the medicinal sources to extract the ingredients to make his own medicine. If the person is not trained, then they will not be able to make the medicine in time and will suffer or perish. Allah is Merciful to us in that he has given us people who master many different disciplines so that they may provide us with a finished product.

We have people who have mastered the study of medicine and provide us with life-saving extracts in the form of medicine. In the same way, we have people who have mastered the sciences of the deen to provide us with texts to save our faith. These texts, or mutun, are studied so as to ensure that knowledge of their faith is complete and correct. The texts give the opportunity for a student to study comprehensively the science of Iman. Then, when the student goes back to the primary sources, they will able to see and understand, in context, the verses or Hadith that deal with matters of the faith.

This gives a person the ability to have a closer relationship with their Lord while reading the sources of revelation, the Quran and Sunna. This is especially important in building a relationship with the Quran as the majority of the verses deal with faith while the minority deal with specific rulings (ahkam). When choosing what to study, one chooses the texts that have

INTRODUCTION

been accepted by the overwhelming majority of the Muslim community (ummah) and then studies that text with a teacher possessing a license to teach (ijaza) and an unbroken chain of transmitters (sanad) back to the Prophet Muhammad ﷺ.

Over the years in my experience of teaching Iman, I have used various mutun that are used in institutions around the Muslim world. These mutun are designed to allow for incremental learning of Iman. So, by the time a student graduates, they have covered a few mutun and thus have completed the study of the essentials of Iman. If the learning environment set up for a student allows for the study of multiple mutun, then there is not a need for an additional text such as this one that I have compiled. The issue that is faced by many students is that there are so many subjects to be covered in the course of one day that it makes it difficult to spend the time needed to cover multiple mutun on a single subject. In an attempt to work towards a solution to this problem, I have compiled the work before you.

I have used the word 'compiled' as it reflects more accurately what I have done. I began by choosing nine texts that are studied currently throughout the ummah. The titles of these texts are listed below. I then began a detailed systematic analysis of each text listing the contents in outline format. I then created a new outline that includes the core of each text while removing any repetitions of points. What this final compilation allows for is a student to study the core of all nine texts without having to go through each one individually. The main outline is very detailed and designed for the teacher to use and comprises the material that should be mastered by the student. The outline material is what a student would need to show proficiency in by completing an assessment. Once a student is proficient based on this outline, they will be able to go through many of the basic mutun easily without having to spend time explaining the concepts.

Serious students should study at least one or two basic texts to give them the opportunity to experience the traditional way of learning and be connected to a scholar with a sanad. The first suggested text would be *Aqidatul Awaam* which is a short poem outlining the very basic tenets of faith. The second suggested text is the section on Iman from the *Risala* of Ibn Abi Zayd, the content of which has been included in this compilation. The *Risala* is around 1,200 years old and is still studied to this day making it one of the oldest continuously studied children's books on the tenets of faith. This compilation will also prepare the students for the study of an intermediate text, such as *Al-'Aqīdah aṭ-Ṭaḥāwiyya* (the Aqida of Imam al-Tahawi). The text of Imam al-Tahawi is also one of the oldest continuously studied texts on Iman in institutions around the world. It has been translated a number of times into English and has both written and audio commentaries in English, making the study of it accessible to the English speaking Muslim. For those who have studied the book of Al-Tahawi, this current course will fill in a lot of areas that are not covered in that course. It will also act as a tool to

INTRODUCTION

show you how to teach Aqida to a new student, as the Tahawiyya is quite advanced for someone new to studying aqida.

If a student knows the content of this course well, then they will have completed their fard ayn requirements of the study of Iman. And Allah knows best. Any other specific questions they have about faith should be directed towards scholars as they come up. To get a more solid grounding in the study of Iman, a student should complete the *Aqida* of Imam al Tahawi, which Tayba Foundation offers as their IMAN 101 course.

The text of Imam al Tahawi is beneficial for a number of reasons:

- It is one of the most accepted texts on Iman.
- The format is very clearly laid out.
- The Arabic is something that can be understood by non-native speakers if they are pursuing a serious study of Arabic.
- It has been translated a number of times and these translations should all be acquired by the student.
- There have been a number of commentaries written in English thus allowing the student to pursue a scholarly study of the text in the English medium.
- There are a number of Arabic commentaries on the text.
- Due to the number of resources available in both English and Arabic, the text can be studied multiple times at varying levels to gain a solid foundation in the study of Iman.
- There are a number of recorded audio commentaries available on the text.

As long as a student knows the content of the outline below, they would not necessarily need to cover the Tahawiyya to complete their fard al-ayn studies of Aqida. When they move on in their studies, and their ability to comprehend difficult matters of faith increases, they should study the Tahawiyya. What the study of the Tahawiyya will give them is a firm foundation in the Aqida so that they are prepared to deal with the issues that they will face when being exposed to people of other faiths and people who may question or criticize their beliefs.

The books used for this compilation are listed below. It should be noted that each of these books covers subjects besides Iman, thus only the respective sections where used:

1. *The Risala* by Ibn Abi Zayd
2. *The Helpful Guide* (*Al-Murshid al-Mu'in*) by Abdul Wahid Ibn Ashir

INTRODUCTION

3. *The Lamp of the Traveller* (*Siraj al-Salik*) by Sayyid Uthman ibn Hasanayn Al Ju'li
4. *The Foundations of Deen* by Uthman dan Fodio
5. *The Maqasid* of Imam Nawawi
6. *Teaching the Truth* (*Taleemul Haqq*) Edited by Shabbir Ahmed E. Desai
7. *Teaching the Deen* (*Taleemul Deen*) by A.H. Ilyas
8. *The Essentials of the Beginner* (*Kafaf al-Mubtadi*) by Muhammad Mawlud
9. *The Creed of the Masses* (*Aqidat al-'Awaam*) by Shaykh Al-Marzuqi

Lesson Overview

Lesson 1: The Shahada
Lesson 2: Allah
Lesson 3: Prophets and Messengers
Lesson 4: Prophets and Messengers (cont'd)
Lesson 5: Angels
Lesson 6: The Books
Lesson 7: The Final Hour and the Afterlife
Lesson 8: Akhira, Death, the Barzakh and the 'Araf
Lesson 9: Resurrection
Lesson 10: Qadr
Lesson 11: the Unseen
Lesson 12: Other tenets of our Faith
Outline Summary for Beliefs of a Muslim
Belief in Angels
Belief in Our Beloved Prophets

The Shahada: Testimony of Faith

<u>When does a person become Muslim?</u>

I would like to begin this course by speaking about the Shahada, or the testimony of faith. The reason I begin with this is that the Shahada is the intersection between faith (Iman) and practice (Islam). In other words, the window into the world of faith for us to see the belief of a person is through their outward testimony of faith. This is very important in all times, but especially in ours when we have people who have resorted to takfir (accusation of apostasy) of other Muslims or defining who is or is not a Muslim in ways that are not sound. The cure to these issues is to understand the "Sign of Faith" as Abdul Wahid ibn Ashir refers to the Shahada in his book *Al-Murshid al-Mu'in* (The Helpful Guide). We want to know: Who is a Muslim? What does it take to become a Muslim? And at what point is a person a Muslim? So let us begin.

I think that one of the most powerful lessons I learned throughout my studies was finding out at what point a person becomes Muslim. I remember this came through one of the very first lessons that I studied in the *Mukhtasar of Khalil* in the section on ghusl (the full shower). As is well-known, a person who becomes Muslim should take a ghusl after their Shahada, and this can be seen in stories from the time of the Prophet Muhammad ﷺ. But what if a person takes the shower before he or she publicly announces the Shahada? The answer, according to the *Mukhtasar* is that as long as the person was firmly resolved in the belief that they are Muslim, then the ghusl is correct. In other words, the person became Muslim at the point of their accepting they were Muslim, not when they publicly announced it. Now, this may seem like a random point of fiqh, but let me show you the impact it can, and did, have in my experience.

I remember once speaking with a fellow student and dear friend who I studied side-by-side with in the Mahdara (*def.* "religious school" [primarily in Mauritania]) of Ahl Fahfu (i.e., "The Tribe of Fahfu") where Murabit al-Hajj was the main teacher. The student was from the United Kingdom (Britain to be exact) and would visit his family from time to time. After one of his returns, he was sharing with us how much he wanted his parents to be Muslim. He also shared a conversation where his father said that he believed in one God and the teachings of Islam, but just had never become Muslim. As soon as I heard that, the lesson from the section of ghusl came to mind. I told my friend that his father had the basis of Islam and just needed to acknowledge it. He was so happy to know that and could not wait to call his

The Shahada

father. I remember clearly that phone call, and I can describe exactly how and where my friend was sitting when he was talking to his father. I remember him saying, "Dad, you remember that conversation where you told me such and such?" Then there was a short pause. "Dad, I just want to tell you that you are Muslim."

That is the power of knowledge. You don't have to change a person. You just have to show a person what they already know. Many times since then, I have found people who hold the belief, but just need someone to show them that they have it. They were Muslim the instance they acknowledged Islam to be true. The only exception would be if a person acknowledges it to be true but when asked if they were a Muslim said, "No." In other words, a person has to have faith and acknowledge their submission to that faith. But even that acknowledgment can happen internally. The outward expression of faith (Shahada) is only to let others around them know they are Muslim. If we did not know they were Muslim and they died, then they would not be buried in a Muslim cemetery, we would not inherit their wealth, and we would not make dua for them. We have to know a person is Muslim based on their outward state. This is based on a **Hadith**, *"I was ordered to judge based on the outward state of people."* Going back to my friend's father, if he had passed before we knew he was Muslim, he would still be Muslim, it's just that we would not have given him all the rites of a Muslim when he passed.

Time and time again, I have met people and when I asked them, "Do you believe this, this and this (the pillars of faith)?" They say yes. But they don't see themselves as being Muslim. But once pointed out to them, they don't reject it. So think of how many people out there accept the tenets of faith of Islam, but don't consider themselves Muslim and others don't consider them Muslim either? This is not to say that "everyone is Muslim" (which some people like to say as a convenient tagline), but it is to say that there are more Muslims out there than we are counting. A proof for this can be found in the Hadith which is counted in the 40 Hadith of Imam Nawawi that discusses that deeds are by their final actions:

> By Allah, other than Whom there is no deity, verily one of you performs the actions of the people of Paradise until there is but an arm's length between him and it, and that which has been written overtakes him, and so he acts with the actions of the people of the Hellfire and thus enters it; and verily one of you performs the actions of the people of the Hellfire until there is but an arm's length between him and it, and that which has been written overtakes him and so he acts with the actions of the people of Paradise and thus he enters it.

Imam Nawawi has his own commentary on the 40 Hadith and there he explains this Hadith saying:

The Shahada

This is a figure of speech for clarification. What is meant is 'a portion of time from the end of his life' and not literally an arm span's amount of time. So, if a non-believer says 'Lā ilāha ill Allāh Muhammadur Rasūlullāh' he will go to Paradise and if a Muslim makes a statement of disbelief at the end of his life he will go to Hell. In this hadith, there is proof that one cannot be certain about entering Paradise or Hell regardless of how many good or bad actions were done.

So we can see from this Hadith and the commentary by Imam Nawawi, that there will be people who outwardly are not known to be Muslim but in reality are. This is what I want you to get out of this discussion. Shahada does not make a person Muslim, faith (Iman) makes a person Muslim. The Shahada is just so other people know him or her to be Muslim. It also serves to allow the person to realize, acknowledge, and accept that they are Muslim. I will end this discussion with a very special story.

Years ago, I taught in a Muslim homeschooling co-op (ILM Tree) that had pre-K through 8th grade. It was actually in ILM Tree that I began the development of this course, as I mentioned in the introduction. My daughter Sumaya (named after the great Sahabiya and first martyr) attended pre-K there and was about 4 years old. Over the summer, she told me that she missed her friends and named them. One of the people she named was a lady who was not Muslim. But this lady had worked in the school for a number of years and spent a lot of time with the Muslim community of the school. She even had her granddaughter (who was not from a Muslim family) attend the school, which included learning the Quran and praying dhuhr. So the lady was very much a part of the community and no one pushed Islam on her or pushed her to become Muslim. She was allowed the freedom to grow at her own pace within the comfort and security of a very loving community. I remember once asking one of the teachers if anyone had asked her about taking the Shahada, and that teacher told me that no one had.

So when we returned to school in the fall, I had just finished making wudu for dhuhr and was about to head to the congregational prayer when I saw the lady in the school hallway. I told her what my daughter had said over the summer and that she had counted her as a friend. The lady was very touched by that and then shared with me a conversation that she had with my daughter earlier that day. She said that they had both levels of the Pre-K in a room and were doing a project. One of the children sneezed and said "Alhamdulillah." The lady told the child, "Yarhamuk Allah." At which point she said my daughter looked up and said, "Aunty, are you Muslim like us?" She responded by saying, "I am kind of like you." So I then asked her, "What do you mean by that?" And I proceeded to ask her about the pillars of faith, to which she responded yes to them all. But when I asked, "Do you believe that Jesus is not the son of

God?" She hesitated. When I saw that hesitation, I clarified by saying, "And by that we mean begotten son of God, like a man and a woman have a child, but not 'son of God' meant as a term of respect for a holy person?" She said, "O, of course I do not believe him to be the *begotten* son of God." I told her, "You are Muslim. Did you realize that?" She said, "No." I said, "You were Muslim the instant that you accepted this set of beliefs as being true." I told her if she would like to say it in Arabic I can walk her through it and she did. My daughter was so proud that she was the cause for a person to accept Islam.

As a note about the term "son of God," I must credit a friend of mine who explained what it may mean to some converts or potential converts. We were standing on Silva Ave near the old location of Zaytuna Institute (now Zaytuna College) and he was sharing with me how he converted. One of the things he mentioned was that he came from a Baptist background and did not like some of the "fire and brimstone" preaching that he encountered. He appreciated the Muslims he met who did not use that type of preaching. But what stood out for me about his conversion story was what he said about the term "son of God." He told me that before his conversion to Islam, he never believed that Jesus (alayhis salam) was literally the son of God, as in the begotten son of God. He said that to him, it was a term of respect given to any holy person. In the same way that a person may call a group the "Children of God" if they are committed to believing in and serving God. So while he used the term "son of God" he never meant it in the way some Christians believe it.

This was the first time I heard someone explain their view in this way to me, and it helped put things in context. Since that time, when speaking to Christians, I have made sure to keep this in mind and not merely tell a person that they cannot be Muslim unless they reject that Jesus is the son of God. I ask them what they mean by their use of the term "son of God" and what their beliefs are about it. Now, it is true that we should not, as Muslims, use that term since there is so much ambiguity about it, but we should dig deeper when we are speaking with others who use it. This is why, when I spoke with the lady at my daughter's school, I asked her what she meant by the use of the term. I once asked a man who was Mexican and brought up Catholic what he meant by the term "son of God" and he said, "All prophets are the son of God. Moses is a son of God, Muhammad is a son of God." He was using it as a title of respect, not in the way the Church may have intended it to be used as in the Trinity belief. So when speaking with people about the pillars of our faith, and specifically about our belief in Jesus (alayhis salam), let us take some time to go beyond the words that a person uses, and look at what their belief is. In the same way, let's go beyond whether or not a person has publicly announced a Shahada in Arabic and look to see if they are already holding the beliefs of Islam.

The Shahada

What does the Shahada mean?

Let's look at the word Shahada and what it means. Then I will mention another story where I learned from a convert to Islam what the Shahada meant to him. If we look at the structure of the Shahada, there is both a negation and an affirmation in the first part speaking about Allah, and then an affirmation when speaking about the Prophet Muhammad ﷺ. The Arabic states, "La ilaha illa Allah Muhammadun Rasul Allah." There is no god except Allah and Muhammad is the Messenger of Allah. For the negation aspect, we are essentially negating anything that cannot be attributed to Allah and affirm the opposite of each of those aspects (Quranic references in parenthesis):

We negate that Allah has the attributes of:	We affirm that Allah has the attributes of:
Non-existence	Existence (6:101-102)
Having a beginning	Being Pre-eternal (57:3)
Having an end	Infiniteness (55:27)
Being Dependent	Absolute independence (35:15)
Resembling His creation in *any* way	Completely different from His creation (42:11)
Multiplicity	Oneness in His Essence, Attributes, and Actions (2:133), (2:163)
Incapacity	Power (57:2)
Being forced	Will (85:13-16), (28:68)
Ignorance	Knowledge (64:4)
Death	Life (2:255), (25:58)
Deafness	Hearing (20:46), (31:28), (6:103)
Muteness	Speech (4:164)

The Shahada

Blindness	Sight (20:46), (31:28), (6:103)[1]

There was an older gentleman in our community and he became Muslim a long time ago. I first met him while taking an introduction to Arabic class at a local community college. Years later, I went to his house to purchase some calligraphy that was done by a Chinese Muslim man (Hajj Noor Deen) who combines Arabic and Chinese calligraphy. The older gentlemen walked me to my car afterward and as we stood there on the street, he told me what the Shahada meant to him.

He said that the word Shahada means "a witnessing" or "a testimony" and that the only way to bear testimony is for a person to actually have seen something. You can't bear witness to something that you have not witnessed. He went on to explain that for him, the Shahada was more than just belief. And as proof of this, the testimony of faith (Shahada) is not a statement of "I believe that there is no god except Allah and Muhammad is the Messenger of Allah," it is a statement of "I bear witness there is no god except Allah and Muhammad is the Messenger of Allah." So it is faith and more. He told me that for him, this was very profound. He would look all around him and see, witness, proof for the oneness of Allah. Once you have witnessed the signs of the oneness of Allah, now you can bear witness and proclaim the Shahada.

Here is some artwork of the kalima by Hajj Noor Deen:

---

[1] Pay close attention to this chart and remember that it is here. Many of you will not realize the significance of this chart until much later. Shaykh Rami has done a wonderful service creating this seemingly simple chart, especially because of the Qur'anic references.

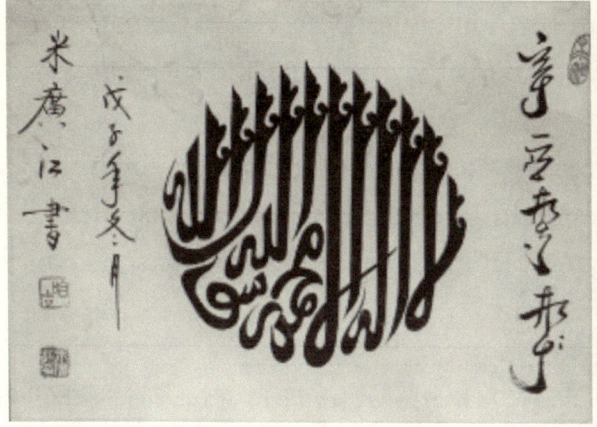

The Shahada

23

Another very important point is the idea of "taqlid in faith." The discussion about taqlid in aqida is found in intermediate books such as *Jawharat al-Tawhid* and *Ida'at al-Dujannah*. What taqlid in aqida means is that a person "believes what he hears of the matters of aqida without having proof", kind of like a blind following. So if it is not sufficient for a person to say the Shahada without knowing the meaning and not having proof, then what about a person not understanding what it means?[3] Just merely repeating the words is not enough. If a person says, "I just repeated what I learned from my parents," this would not be sufficient as a Shahada. But once a person knows what they are bearing witness to, then they can bear that testimony. Just like in a court of law, you cannot bear witness to something that you yourself have not seen and say, "I heard others say they saw such and such happen and I bear witness along with them."

I remember once being at an Islamic center when a non-Muslim came to visit. He sat down and enjoyed a conversation about Islam with a teacher there. Towards the end, the teacher asked him to repeat the Shahada in Arabic after him, which the person did. The

---

[2] All of these pieces and more can be viewed at "http://www.hajinoordeen.com/"

[3] NOTE: Taqlid in matters of beliefs (aqida) and taqlid in matters are law (fiqh) of two completely different things. Taqlid in aqida, generally speaking, is unlawful. While taqlid in fiqh is initially obligatory, but becomes unlawful once you reach a certain level of scholarship. Taqlid as it relates to fiqh will be discussed in much more detail in FIQH 100.

teacher was happy that the person had "become Muslim" but I and another Muslim present realized that the person did not know what he was saying and was merely being courteous and repeating the statement after the teacher. In another story I heard from a friend of mine, he was going through a toll booth and the attendant asked if he was a holy man (the brother was a shaykh and was wearing a thobe, turban, and beard). The attendant asked to be taught a prayer, to which the shaykh had her repeat the Shahada in Arabic. There is no doubt the person will benefit from saying the Shahada, but without knowing what it means, that is not enough to enter the fold of Islam. In another instance where I was present, a man was instructed on saying the Shahada and then told he was Muslim. He later said that he was deeply offended at having been forcibly converted. Needless to say, the man never identified himself as being Muslim.

Once a person makes a positive, informed statement of faith in Islam, it is not our duty to investigate and figure out if in fact the person is "truly" Muslim. What is sufficient is for the person to answer "Yes" if they were asked, "Are you Muslim?" Once a person answers in the affirmative, that is enough for us to treat them as a Muslim and offer them all the rights owed to a fellow Believer. According to the opinion of Imam Muhammad of the Hanafi scholars, even performing an action of the Muslims, such as praying, is enough for us to consider them Muslim (although this is a weak opinion).[4] Which brings us to the next question, "Does the Shahada have to be stated in Arabic?" But before going into that, I would like to mention two points about witnessing and testimony.

The first is that the signs of the oneness of Allah are all around us. Everything in creation is a sign (ayah). Each sign is pointing to the lesson that the Creator is One. I saw an amazing video on YouTube of an Australian convert to Islam named Ruben Abu Bakr. There are also some articles online about his story:

If one had told Abu Bakr earlier, that he would one day become a Muslim, his reply would most probably have been, "Nah! No way!!!" for like many Australians his perception of Muslims was that they were terrorists. However, there is no accounting for the Mercy and Graciousness of Allah who leads to His Path those whom He wills from all peoples upon the earth; and Abu Bakr was to find this in due course.

When asked what had triggered his search to find the true meaning of life, for that was the primary aim of his quest, his response was this: "There were a couple of things. It was the year my

---

[4] In the context that Imam Muhammad found himself where religious affiliation was considered a political act, his opinion was perfectly valid. But this opinion should not be applied indiscriminately, especially in prison where many people may join the prayer out of comradery or while holding beliefs that keep them outside of the fold of Islam. In these situations, what is said in the section below "What about a person who holds beliefs contradictory to Islam?" applies.

parents said they were going to separate. It was not the year they formally divorced, but it was the year my Dad moved out of the house. I went a little off the rails. I (even) had trouble with the police... I was drinking a lot." It may be seen that this was a painful time for this young man. This was to be further compounded, for it was in this year that one of his friends died. Of this event, he said: "That led me to think, 'There's my mate. He just died, and he is only eighteen years old! Is he just worm food?' You know what I mean. That's when I started relating it to my life, thinking, 'If I died tomorrow what would it matter? What would it matter except to the few who know me among the billions on this Earth?' So I started thinking, 'No! There has to be more. There has to be more than just this!'"

It was with these questions in mind that Abu Bakr commenced his journey, looking to religion for the meaning of existence. He describes his experiences in this way:

"First, I mean, logically, I'm an Aussie, so I went straight to Christianity, and I thought I'd have that fish sticker on the back of my car, and "I love Jesus". I was thinking I'd go buy them and see if they did something for my parking fine!" his waggish sense of humour bubbling to the fore. Then seriously he explains, "Honestly I went through all the (Christian) religions; well not all the religions, but the ones I had access to I investigated. Christianity, including Catholicism, I investigated quite a bit. But the problem was I just couldn't find the answer. While they were all nice, I couldn't sit there and say, 'This is the religion for me!' and 'This sounds beautiful!'" His search continued.

"I looked at Hinduism when I was working in a service station with some Hindu friends. We had conversations all the time. We didn't argue because we were pretty good friends. One would say, 'You have to believe in this god about this, and this god of that.' I would go, 'Come on man! What if they argue?' He was not to know it, but his argument was one already mentioned in the Qur'an: **(Allah hath not chosen any son, nor is there any god along with Him; else would each god have assuredly championed that which he created, and some of them would assuredly have overcome others. Glorified be Allah above all that they allege.)** (Surah 23:91)

Then I looked at Judaism. Again it didn't get me in the way that I thought it would! However, what started to get me was Buddhism. I thought, 'This is really nice you know!' But nowhere could I read or see that Buddha was actually talking about himself. Not (other than) as a person that you follow - not as a deity! And this was a religion. So you know what I mean, it was just a nice way to be. It's not 'This is the purpose of why you are here.' And while it was nice I thought, 'This can't be it either.'

My friend, a Christian who had earlier said to 'vow to God', said, 'Why don't you try Islam?' I said, 'Naah man! They're terrorists! I'm not going near a mosque. No way!'

But I found myself near a mosque, Preston Mosque. I went in and started to ask questions. And basically every question I asked, no-one would answer from their minds, everyone was pulling out a Qur'an and saying, 'Here it is.' And that really surprised me because (almost)

The Shahada

every time I went to a priest, I did not see the Bible once. They almost never pulled out the Bible, they were just, 'Here's your answer.' This was the same with almost every religion. There were some who did read from the Bible a couple of times. But in the mosque, every single time - out came the Qur'an, and that got me. This is not about these people, it's about the Book, and that's when I started reading the Qur'an. It took months and months though, six to seven months. I had a lot of questions!"

At the end of these months, how did this young man, now twenty years of age, decide to become Muslim? The crucial moment of his conversion came one night, as he explained:

"One night I had just been speaking to a couple of Australian brothers at the mosque. They told me to take the Qur'an home and read it. I had already taken one, but they gave me this one with big letters - the other one I had was little and was harder to read. That night I sat in bed and lit a candle. I had the window open. It was a nice summer's night. It had this atmosphere, this religious atmosphere. I was set, and I was sitting there thinking, 'This is beautiful and very sacred!'

"Everything was really good and I started reading Qur'an and thinking, 'This is very beautiful, it says exactly what I think it should say.' It feels like it's right you know, but I'm not quite there, you know! I just need a bit of a hand. And I sat back, Qur'an in hand, and said, 'O God, give me a sign! But it has to be pretty good - like lightning,' - and it was a clear summer's night. 'If you do lightning, I'm yours - I'm your servant. And maybe if you can't do lightning - something like a crack or something; or a flash of light; or the candle! I would be pretty impressed if the candle just blew up to about two feet high, you know, like in the movies!"
"And I'm sitting there waiting!"......

"Nothing at all happened! Like I couldn't even say a creak in the wall was my sign! So I'm sitting there pretty disappointed, and I'm angry .. Right? And I'm like, 'God, I'm asking you. You're supposed to be All-Powerful! Alright - I'm going to give you a second chance.' Like that was a fair bit to ask - summer, lightning! 'Okay, maybe like, a car can just backfire that goes past - that's something that happens all the time, but at least I'll know it's for me.' So I lowered my levels .. Right?

"Subhan'Allah!" (Exalted is Allah) he exclaims, shaking his head at the very thought of it. "And I'm sitting there thinking, 'Alright!' So I look around again - Nothing! All is so silent.. I could have been in space. Not even an ant made a noise, and by this time I was shattered, because this was the moment! I had thought, 'This is it!' you know, 'This is my time!'... And nothing happened!"

"So I'm sitting there, pretty disappointed, and I thought, 'I may as well keep on reading Qur'an". So I looked down and turned the page, and the very next ayat (verse) was something to the effect: "For those of you who ask for signs, have I not shown you enough already? Look around at the sky, the trees, the water, these are your signs. These are the Signs for those who know!"

(Lo! In the creation of the heavens and the earth, and the difference of night and day, and the ships which run upon the sea with that which is of use to men, and the water which Allah sendeth down from the sky, thereby reviving the earth after its death, and dispersing all kinds of beasts therein, and (in) the ordinance of the winds, and the clouds obedient between heaven and earth: are signs (of Allah's Sovereignty) for people who have sense.) (Surah 2:164)]

"I was sitting down; I freaked out! I closed the Qur'an and chucked the quilt over my head. I was freaking out because here it was! You know what I mean?"

"So the next morning I went straight to the mosque and told them I wanted to become Muslim because I had had my sign. I had it, even though it was not my sign. I shouldn't be arrogant and think I have a sign. Isn't the water my sign and all these things around me are signs, you know, that there is a Creator!"

Subhan Allah! This is an amazing story that really touched me. One thing that also stood out was his reaction after realizing the Quran was speaking to him. Go back and look at his reaction. What does that remind you of? Who else had the same reaction when first experiencing revelation? Why is that? Is that something in the human fitra?

Here are some other verses that speak about signs:

(And they say, 'Why does he not bring us a sign from his Lord?' Has there not come to them evidence of what was in the former scriptures?) (Quran 20:133)

(Indeed, within the heavens and earth are signs for the believers; and in the creation of yourselves and what He disperses of moving creatures are signs for people who are certain [in faith]; and [in] the alternation of night and day and [in] what Allah sends down from the sky of provision and gives life thereby to the earth after its lifelessness and [in His] directing of the winds are signs for a people who reason—these are the verses of Allah which We recite to you in truth. Then in what statement after Allah and His verses will they believe?) (Qur'an 45:3-6)

(And He has subjected for you the night and day and the sun and moon, and the stars are subjected by His command. Indeed in that are signs for a people who reason.) (Qur'an 16:12)

The Shahada

(Those who do not know say, "Why does Allah not speak to us or there come to us a sign?" Thus spoke those before them like their words. Their hearts resemble each other. We have shown clearly the signs to a people who are certain [in faith].) (Qur'an 2:118)

(We will show them Our signs in the horizons and within themselves until it becomes clear to them that it is the truth. But is it not sufficient concerning your Lord that He is, over all things, a Witness?) (Qur'an 41:53)

There are other verses, but these are a few.

The second point about signs (ayahs) is that the experience of those signs will differ from person to person. This is something I learned from reading a commentary of the great Maliki scholar Shaykh Muhammad 'Illish who served as a Shaykh of Azhar during his time over 150 years ago. In his commentary on a book of aqida, he discusses how various people will experience signs according to their nature and disposition. So, for example, the person inclined toward the study of language will see the Oneness and Greatness of Allah through the signs of language. He mentioned how they will notice, for example, that the Arabic word for "honey (عسل)" spelled backward in Arabic is the word for "sting (لسع)." The linguist will see Divine perfection in the languages he studies. Take this idea and apply it now to any person who has an inclination towards something. The doctor and surgeon will appreciate and notice things in his or her field pointing them to the Oneness of Allah through what they witness in the creation. The geologist will see things in his or her field. And so on and so forth. So in your journey, look for the signs that are all around you and the ones your eyes and your heart point you to look.

Does the Shahada have to be stated in Arabic?

Over the years, some of the most common misperceptions that I have found about the Shahada is that it has to be stated in Arabic and that it must be done in a masjid. The short answer is that it can be said in any language and it can be done in any place. There is the condition that it has to be actually stated by the tongue of a person who is able to speak, and through a sign (hand gesture or nod of the head) for the person who is unable to speak. But let's first look at where the idea that it has to be stated in Arabic may have come from.

We find many Hadith that speak about a person doing the Shahada in a verbal form. Some of the scholars have mentioned that the Shahada must be stated in Arabic and be done in the proper order, for it to be an official Shahada. So because this opinion exists, we should be on the safe side and have people do the Shahada in Arabic (as I did when the lady at my daughter's school announced her Islam). But we should know that the majority of scholars have not mentioned this as a condition to becoming Muslim, so we should realize that there are people who have already stated their Shahada before making their public Arabic Shahada announcement.

A proof that the scholars use that the Shahada can be made in a form other than the typical form of "Ash-hadu an lā ilāha ill Allāh wa ash-hadu anna Muhammadar Rasūlullāh" is the story of Khalid ibn Walid and the tribe of Jadhima narrated by Ibn Umar (Radiy Allahu anhuma):

> The Prophet sent Khalid bin Al-Walid to the tribe of Jadhima and Khalid invited them to Islam but they could not express themselves by saying, "Aslamna (*i.e.*, we have embraced Islam)," but they started saying "Saba'na! Saba'na (*i.e.*, we have come out of one religion to another)." Khalid kept on killing (some of) them and taking (some of) them as captives and gave every one of us a captive. When there came the day then Khalid ordered that each man (*i.e.*, Muslim soldier) should kill his captive, I [Abdullah Ibn Umar] said, "By God, I will not kill my captive, and none of my companions will kill his captive!" When we reached the Prophet, we mentioned to him the whole story. On that, the Prophet raised both his hands and said twice, **"O God! I am free from what Khalid has done."** (*Sahih al-Bukhari,* Volume 5, Book 59, Number 628)

So we see from this instance that the Prophet ﷺ considered them to be Muslim even though they did not use the word "Islam" or "Ash-hadu." From this Hadith, the scholars have derived the ruling that any verbal affirmation of Islam, in any form, is acceptable as a Shahada. So, if a person is asked, "Do you believe in One God, His Messengers, His Books, His Angels, the Last Day, Qadr, that Jesus is not the son of God, and that Muhammad of Arabia is the last and final Messenger?" And the person says, "Yes." That verbal affirmation is sufficient as a Shahada. If a person is not able to speak, then a simple nod of the head or "thumbs up" or any gesture of agreement is sufficient for a Shahada. This discussion can be found at length in the ghusl section of the commentaries of the *Mukhtasar of Khalil*.

What about a person who holds beliefs contradictory to Islam?

We have discussed internal belief, outward affirmation, and in what language the Shahada can be said. But what happens if a person outwardly professes the Shahada, and let's say he or she does it in Arabic, and yet holds a belief that contradicts Islam? Is that a valid Shahada? The short answer is no, but let's look at this with some examples.

The Shahada

A person states the Shahada, knowing full well what it means, but harbors some belief that contradicts Islam. Maybe a Christian with trinitarian beliefs still believes Jesus to be God, yet states the Shahada. Or maybe a person believes in most of the pillars of Islamic faith but denies the afterlife. Or maybe a person believes in all the pillars and the afterlife but denies portions of the Quran. In all three of these cases, that person would not be Muslim, even though they stated the Shahada. But going back to an earlier discussion we had about not taking it upon ourselves to interrogate Muslims, we may or may not know they are not in fact Muslims. The only way for us to know that is for them to make a statement that contradicts the Shahada.

In the same way that we only know their Islam through a statement and testimony, we also do not negate their Shahada except through a statement or a clear action that contradicts Islam. So could there be Muslims in our community that are not in fact Muslim? Yes, that was also the case at the time of the Prophet Muhammad ﷺ. But did he root out all those people and excommunicate them? No, in fact, he avoided that because he did not want people to say, "Muhammad kills his companions" because the greater community sees the Muslims as one body and would not understand the concept of the Munafiq.

As a final example of Shahada with kufr, there is a modern-day phenomenon among some communities which is called "Perennialism." In this belief-system, they say that all major religions are correct, that they are all from God, so anyone who follows any of them can attain Paradise. Even though many of them claim to be Muslim, they believe that the Hindu who may worship idols, the Christian who believes in the Trinity, or the Jew who denies both Jesus and Muhammad ﷺ, all will be given Paradise because they all allegedly affirm "perennial wisdom." We know that this particular claim of Perennialism contradicts Islam because the only way Allah will accept belief is within the parameters of Islam. As is stated in the Quran, Allah says, **(The religion with Allah is Islam)** (Quran 3:19). For a person to believe that other religions are true as well, would contradict the Shahada, even if the person stated it, prays, fasts, and pays zakat.

This principle is best known to us through what are called the Wars of Apostasy (ridda), when Abu Bakr ordered military campaigns against the people who left Islam. This was the case even though they held onto parts of Islam, including the Shahada and the prayer. But they rejected the pillar of zakat.

What is the difference between Iman, Islam, and Ihsan?

The Shahada

One of the most famous Hadith that is taught in learning circles (halaqas), is what is referred to as "The Hadith of Jibreel." It is narrated on the authority of Umar (radiy Allahu anhu):

While we were one day sitting with the Messenger of Allah ﷺ, there appeared before us a man dressed in extremely white clothes and with very black hair. No traces of journeying were visible on him, and none of us knew him. He sat down close by the Prophet ﷺ, he put his knees to his knees and his hands on his thighs, and said, "O Muhammad! Inform me about Islam."

The Messenger of Allah ﷺ said, **"Islam is that you should testify that there is no deity except Allah and that Muhammad is His Messenger, that you should perform salah, pay the Zakah, fast during Ramadan, and perform Hajj to the House if you are able to do so."**

The man said, "You have spoken truly." We were astonished at his questioning him (the Messenger) and telling him that he was right, but he went on to say, "Inform me about iman."

He (the Messenger of Allah) answered, **"It is that you believe in Allah and His angels and His Books and His Messengers and in the Last Day, and in qadr (fate), both in its good and in its evil aspects."** He said, "You have spoken truly."

Then he (the man) said, "Inform me about Ihsan." He (the Messenger of Allah) answered, **"It is that you should serve Allah as though you could see Him, for though you cannot see Him yet (know that) He sees you."**

He said, "Inform me about the Hour." He (the Messenger of Allah) said, **"About that, the one questioned knows no more than the questioner."** So he said, "Well, inform me about the signs thereof." He said, **"They are that the slave-girl will give birth to her mistress, that you will see the barefooted, naked, destitute, the herdsmen of the sheep (competing with each other) in raising lofty buildings."** Thereupon the man went off. I waited a while, and then he (the Messenger of Allah) said, **"O Umar, do you know who that questioner was?"** I replied, "Allah and His Messenger know better." He said, **"That was Jibril (the Angel Gabriel). He came to teach you your religion."**

There are so many lessons that we can derive from this Hadith. The structure of the Hadith and breaking down the various aspects of faith is what I used to structure this current course.

The Hadith mentions Islam, Iman, and Ihsan. Knowing these concepts is very important, especially when it comes to understanding the Shahada. If you notice, the Shahada is mentioned in the category of Islam and not in the section on Iman. To me, I see this as the link between faith and practice. While the faith is inward, it cannot be complete until there is an outward profession. Ibn Abi Zayd, in his book the *Risala* (written over 1,200 years ago), says "Belief consists of what you say with the tongue, what you believe sincerely in the heart, and what you do with the limbs." Thus, there cannot be faith that is accepted by the Muslim community until there is a profession on the tongue. This is the bridge between inward faith and outward expression. We are not able to see what is in the hearts of people, so while a person may hold proper faith (iman) in their hearts, and if they died would be considered a believer by Allah, we can only accept a person as a believer once they profess their faith. But the Shahada is the only one of the pillars that must be done for a person to be considered Muslim by other people. For the other pillars of Islam, they act to complete the Shahada, but they are not a requirement for the Shahada. Ibn Abi Zayd says about this that:

The statement of belief is not complete without action. Neither the statement nor action are complete without intention. And neither the statement nor intention are complete unless they are in accordance with the Sunna.

Keep these points in mind when you find a person who may say, "I am a Mu'min but not a Muslim." The reality is that anyone who has faith and professes it is a Muslim, regardless of whether they practice or not. They should not make a statement like that. In the same way, a person should not say, "I practice Ihsan but not Islam." There cannot be any Ihsan without Islam and Iman. So if there are people, which there are, who claim to practice Islamic spirituality but not practice or believe in Islam, then that is not sufficient to allow them to attain salvation and Paradise.

A person begins with having Iman (faith), they then profess that faith (Islam) and then work on perfecting their practice and belief (ihsan). They are all part of a process of development and you cannot have a higher stage without the previous stage.

Can a person be a believer and not pray?

Over the years, in speaking with people who are thinking about embracing Islam, a common reservation I hear is, "But I am not ready to practice everything." What I tell them is that they must realize that faith and practice are separate. The only condition is that the person must believe the action to be an obligation even if they fall short in performing the obligation. Whereas if a person were to deny an obligation of the deen, then this would contradict Islam. Yes, a Muslim should practice the faith, but faith is not dependent on practice. This is not to belittle the importance of practicing Islam, but at the same time, imperfect practice should not overshadow the grandness of Iman. Think back to the Hadith about the Ka'ba and what it is that makes a person greater than the Ka'ba.

Ibn Ashir is his text *Al-Murshid Al-Mu'in* (which is part of Tayba's FIQH 102 course), says that the Shahada is "ra's al-maal" which is Arabic for "financial capital." Your actions, then, are your profit. Think of it in terms of a business; what is more important to establish first, the funds that you will start the business with or the profit that you will make in the business? In the same way, start with Iman and the Shahada and from there work on your profit. And in any case, as long as you have your profit, you have the basis of a successful business. A person may be taken to account for not practicing, but as long as he or she left the world with the Shahada, they are guaranteed paradise.

Another thing to remember is that at times, a person needs to be allowed room to grow in their practice of Islam. Not everyone is like Umar ibn Al Khattab, who went from being an enemy of Islam 100% to a supporter and one who practiced Islam 100% with the utterance of the Shahada. Other people need time to grow in their practice. This is not to say that they are excused for not practicing, but it is to say that we should not discourage people from entering merely because they say they cannot pray, fast, wear Hijab, etc.

But let's also take a look specifically at the question I used to head this section: can a person be a believer and not pray? This discussion stems from multiple Hadiths of the Messenger of Allah ﷺ that imply, in one form or another, that leaving the prayer is kufr (disbelief). Here is one narration: "The Messenger of Allah ﷺ said, **'The covenant that distinguishes between us and them is the prayer, and whoever neglects it [or "leaves it"] has disbelieved (become a kāfir).'"** (*Nasai* 1/231, *Tirmidhi* 2621)

While there were some scholars of the Salaf al-Salih (*def.* "the first three generations of righteous Muslims") who understood these to mean that simply missing the prayer is an act of kufr, the majority of scholars understood these Hadith to be either: (a) rhetorical statements likening missing the prayer to kufr or (b) a reference to abandoning the prayer outright.[5] Of

---

[5] What we mean by rhetorical statements is that they are intentional exaggerations that stress the seriousness of the sin that aren't meant to be taken literally. This is very common in the Arabic language. Therefore, the dominant opinion of all Four Schools, including the Hanbali School, is that failing to perform the obligatory prayer is a major sin, but is not automatically kufr. Missing the prayer is only considered kufr when the obligation of the prayer is denied. Properly understanding this issue requires knowledge of Arabic and legal methodology (usul al-fiqh), something that very few people reading this have at this time. Many students read the hadith in Tirmidhi and falsely think that what is at stake is whether or not we accept the Prophet ﷺ at his word. That is not the case. This hadith can legitimately be interpreted two different ways as reflected in the translation above. The second way, which the overwhelming majority of scholars prefer, is supported by numerous other pieces of evidence and is objectively the stronger opinion. This is what Shaykh Rami is explaining, while avoiding all of the technical discussion so as not to overly complicate the issue. But we will

the scholars who held it to be literally kufr is Ahmad Ibn Hanbal, but even his view has many conditions that need to be in place before that ruling takes effect, according to Shaykh Muhammad 'Illish. In any case, it is not the job of the average Muslim to attribute kufr to the community and especially in this case where the majority of scholars have not taken the Hadith literally. In fact, there are several Sahih Hadith which proves their interpretation. Below are two along with commentary:

The Hadith of Ubadah Ibn Sāmit (may Allah be pleased with him) who narrates that the Messenger of Allah ﷺ said, **"Allah has ordained upon his servant five daily prayers. Whoever performs them and does not abandon them (out of belittling their obligation), then for him is Allah's promise to enter Paradise. Whoever doesn't perform them then he doesn't have that promise from Allah. Thus, if Allah wills, He will punish him. If He wills, he will forgive him."** (*Muwatta* 320, *Abu Dawud* 1420)

Al-Zurqāni stated in his commentary on *Muwatta*, "In this Hadith [is proof] that a person who does not perform the prayer does not commit apostasy, and (secondly) that there is no certainty that he will be punished. In fact, he is left to Allah's decision." (Sharh Al-Zurqāni 1/358) Why? Because like we said in ISLAM 99, the fact that Allah's will decided to punish or forgive this individual means necessarily that the one who committed this sin is not guilty of apostasy. If they were guilty of apostasy through this action alone, the option of forgiveness would not be available.

There is also the Hadith of Abu Hurairah (may Allah be pleased with him):

The Messenger of Allah ﷺ said, **"Verily, the first things a person will be taken to task for, on the day of Judgment, are his obligatory prayers. Either he will have fulfilled them, otherwise it will be said 'See if he has performed any supererogatory!' If he has performed some, then his [missed] obligatory prayers will be completed with his supererogatory prayers.** (Nasai 1/233, Abu Dawud 864, Tirmidhi 413, Ibn Majah 1425)

Keep these Hadith and the principle from them in mind when you speak to people who are thinking about Islam and are stopping because they feel they are not ready to practice.

The person may say, "I don't want to be a hypocrite and I want to practice fully if I become Muslim." Tell them, first of all, you will not be a hypocrite (munafiq). The definition of a munafiq is the one who outwardly professes and practices Islam, but inwardly denies it.

---

return to this subject in more detail in sha Allah in FIQH 102/112/122 where we will go over the more technical points once everyone has acquired a little better grasp of the way fiqh works.

The Shahada

This is different from a person who inwardly accepts Islam, outwardly professes it, and yet has some struggles in practicing the tenets of Islam. Encourage them that with the baraka (*def.* "spiritual blessing") of their pronouncing faith, they will be given the strength to practice. Also remind them that we never know when our life will end, and it is better to end in a state of professing Islam. If they then choose Islam while not practicing, the community around them must be careful not to then badger them until they leave Islam altogether.

A number of years ago, I heard a story told to me directly by the Imam of Masjid Santa Clara. He said that he took the Shahada of a woman who then asked about the Islamic ruling on makeup for women. He said he told her not to worry about that now. People who attended that gathering criticized him for not telling her it was prohibited for a women to wear makeup in public in front of men. He responded by saying, "This woman literally just became Muslim and there are more important things for her to focus on now, like learning the prayer and proper aqida." He then told me that the woman was eventually chased out of Islam.

I was once sitting with one of my teachers, Murabit Muhammad Al-Amin (also known as 'Haddamin') and told him the above story. He told me that telling the sister to not worry about it was the sunna and he related to me a Hadith in which a man wished to become Muslim but had a drinking problem. The Prophet ﷺ allowed him to become Muslim and then work on changing his habit of drinking. The principle here is that a person should not be discouraged from becoming Muslim due to a habit, and also that we can give a person time to change that habit. It does not mean that the habit is permissible, it is just that we, the community around the person, allow them the time they need to change.

In another instance, a friend of mine took the Shahada of his mother who was still married to her non-Muslim husband. The son told his mother that it was not permissible for a Muslim woman to be married to a non-Muslim man. The mother responded by saying, "If I have to leave your father, then I will leave Islam." At that point, a person should look at what is the lesser of the two harms: (a) a Muslim woman remaining married to a non-Muslim man or (b) the woman leaving Islam? The answer is clear. It is this balancing and assessment that a person must make when interacting with others. If enjoining righteousness will lead to a greater harm, we do not enjoin that matter. Doing so is in fact prohibited. This was discussed in ISLAM 99 briefly and you will learn more about the rules of this in ADAB 102.

To end, we ask the same question: Can a person be a believer and not pray? As long as they recognize it is an obligation, then whether or not they perform the prayer, they are Muslim. They have to deal with the sin of leaving the prayer and perform tawbah (discussed in FIQH 101), but they are nonetheless Muslim. This is a similar situation that almost all of us find ourselves in. While we may not struggle with the prayer, many of us stubbornly refuse to refrain from backbiting people who have insulted us, will not lower our gaze when in the presence of the opposite sex, or continue to cut ties with close family members because they have wrong us. Like the prayer, all of these things are mentioned in the Qur'an as clearly prohibited. And like the prayer, failing to act on them is a major sin while refusing to accept they are obligatory is an act of kufr. So we all have to be honest with ourselves and not forget that we all have things we need to work on as individuals. And while we always encourage others to be better, we also need to be on guard against allowing Shaytan to deceive us into becoming satisfied with our current level of practice because we might not be struggling with the same things that other people are having difficulty with.

Who is responsible to state the Shahada?

One of the points about the Shahada I think is important to note is the discussion of the scholars in terms of who will be taken to account for not stating the Shahada. We go through life and we see many people around us who are not Muslim. Some of them have learned about Islam and some have not. Who will be taken to account for not being Muslim? We find in the Quran that Allah says:

(And never would We punish until We sent a messenger) (Quran 17:15)

From this, the scholars have stated that a person is not taken to account for refusing Islam until they have received the message of Islam. Those who have not received the message of Islam are considered to be like the people of the fatrah. The people of fatrah (ahl al-fatrah/أهل الفترة) are those who were in between two Messengers. In Sura Mai'dah, verse 19 it states:

(O People of the Scripture, there has come to you Our Messenger to make clear to you [the religion] after a period [of suspension] of messengers, lest you say, "There came not to us any bringer of good tidings or a warner." But there has come to you a bringer of good tidings and a warner. And Allah is over all things competent.)

Once the Messenger ﷺ came, they no longer had an excuse for not believing. But what about the people of the fatrah? So, for example, the Christians who came after Isa alayhis salam and before the Prophet Muhammad ﷺ, are not taken to account for what they did not know. It is mentioned in the tafsir of these verses that the Christians who changed the religion and included shirk in their belief system, will not be taken to account because they were never sent a Messenger.

The Shahada

When we look around us in our times, we don't have to look far to find people who have not yet received the message of Islam. I used to use as an example of people who have not heard about Islam, the example of people in the middle of the rainforest who have little contact with the outside world. It was not until I was sitting in a retail store that I used to own a few years ago in a mall (clothing and skateboards), that this realization changed for me.

A person came into our store and said that he tried to come to the store a number of times but the gates were locked every time. I told him that we have to close a few times so that I can go and pray (when I was alone in the store). I then told him I am Muslim and that we pray five times a day. I asked him if he ever heard about Islam or Muslims and he said, "No." And that was right here in the middle of the San Francisco Bay Area in 2007! You don't have to go to the rainforest to find people who have not heard about Islam.

In another similar example, there was a person who told me his conversion story. He said that in 2003 (two years after 9/11) he used to walk to his university and every day he would pass by a masjid. He came from a very devout and practicing Catholic family but his sister decided to take a comparative religion class in college. She liked it a lot and advised her brother to take it as well, which he did. In the class, the last religion to be covered was Islam. When the professor mentioned the word "Quran," this brother raised his hand and said, "What is that?" The professor said, "The book of the Muslims." The brother said, "The Muslims? Who are they?" He said, "They follow Islam." The brother said, "What is Islam?" He later went on to embrace Islam and study Arabic and Islam seriously. But up until then, he was living in a major metropolitan U.S. city, at a university, passing by a masjid every day, and this is all two years after 9/11 when everyone is supposedly supposed to have heard about Islam.

Once the message does reach a person, then they are obliged to follow it and are responsible if they reject the message. This is as long as they are a mukallaf, also known as baligh. The mukallaf is the person who has physically reached adulthood (defined as puberty by the Shariah) and has a functioning intellect.

The definition of intellect would be if a person were spoken to in a reasonable manner, they could respond appropriately. So, for example, if you asked a person, "What is the weather like today?" and they say, "Blue moons are better than lions," that would be a sign they do not have intellect. The person without intellect is not responsible, and the proof for this is the following Hadith:

The Pen has been lifted from three: from the sleeping person until he awakens, from the minor until he grows up, and from the insane person until he comes to his senses. (Narrated by Abu Dawud and Ibn Majah)

The Shahada

Also for the child, until he reaches puberty, he is not accountable. Puberty, or bulugh, is defined by any of the following:

- Wet dream
- Menstruation
- Coarse pubic hair

Once a person has a sign of puberty and a functioning intellect, they are now a mukallaf (responsible person) and have the duty to accept and follow Islam once the message reaches them. If a person dies before reaching puberty, then they are not accountable, even if they had heard and understood the message. However, if a child were to state the Shahada, that would be a valid entering into Islam.

Why the Shahada is the Sign of Faith?

Ibn Ashir, in his book *Al-Murshid Al-Mu'in* (Tayba's FIQH 102 course) said: "The statement, 'There is no god except Allah, Muhammad was sent by Allah' contains all the meanings of faith. It is for that reason that it is the sign ('alamah) of faith." If we look at the Shahada, we see an affirmation of Allah and that Muhammad is His Messenger ﷺ. As you go through the rest of this book, you will see that every point can fit in either "There is no god except Allah" or "Muhammad is the Messenger of Allah ﷺ."

Take for example all the discussion about what we believe Allah to be and what we believe Him not to be. When we look at our affirmation of the only god being Allah, we are essentially denying every attribute that cannot belong to Allah (like there being multiple gods) and we are affirming that Allah must have certain attributes to be the One True God (such as being All-Powerful and Everlasting).

When we look at the affirmation of belief in the Books, Angels, and Last Day, these are all aspects that have been brought to us through the Messenger of Allah ﷺ. When we affirm him as being the "Messenger of Allah," we are by default affirming everything he taught to us. When we affirm him being the Messenger of Allah ﷺ, we are also affirming the fact that Allah has sent messengers and prophets and that we believe in all of them.

So, as you go through these lessons, try to see how you can fit each section into the statement of faith; the Shahada.

Can a person delay the Shahada?

The Shahada

The last point I will make in this section about the Shahada is the importance of not delaying it once a person understands the message of Islam. This is important for the individual who has yet to declare the Shahada, as well as the people around him or her.

For the individual, he or she should not delay the Shahada since none of us know when we are going to die. A person may think about pronouncing their faith, and then delay it and then meet an unexpected death.

For those around the person, they should not say things like, "Wait and think it over" or "Give yourself a couple of weeks." Once a person is willing to pronounce the Shahada after understanding what it entails, no one should encourage him or her to delay it. Asking a person to delay the Shahada is essentially like saying, "You should remain in kufr for a little longer." It is for this reason that Imam Nawawi lists in the section on apostasy (ridda) in his book *Rawdatul Talibeen* that one form of apostasy is to tell a person to delay their Shahada.[6]

May Allah guide us all to live a life of the Shahada and help guide all those around us to the Shahada. May Allah give us a seal of the Shahada when our souls are taken from our bodies.

---

[6] As we mentioned in ISLAM 99, this includes telling the person to wait on the Imam so that he can talk to them. When someone takes their Shahada, we are witnessing it, not "giving it to them" as many Muslims commonly say. So if they want to declare it in front of the community, we should witness their Shahada immediately and then they can meet with the Imam and go through whatever formal process has been put in place. But refusing to witness their Shahada and telling them to wait a couple hours or days to take their Shahadah with the Imam falls under Imam Nawawi's examples of the things that are considered apostasy. THis is even if this is the "rule" that has been put in place.

Allah ﷻ

✦ Allah Exists.

Before we begin talking about who we believe Allah to be, we must affirm that He exists. There are many logical proofs that a person may use to come to the conclusion that Allah exists, but ultimately it is faith that gives us that firm belief in His existence. As I discussed in the section of the shahada, each person will have his or her own method to witness the existence of Allah. For the person who loves nature, they will see proof in nature. For the mathematician, they will see proof in mathematics. For the linguist, they will see proof in languages. For the social conscious person, they will see proof in society. For the person who loves studying about people, they will see proof in people. Ask yourself this question; What are the proofs, signs, or evidence that I see that allows me to be firm in my belief that Allah exists? This is a question that is posed numerous times in the Quran in various forms and is encouraging us to think, reflect, and understand that Allah exists.

One of the rational proofs is about the creation that we all see around us and does not require any faith to believe in. If a person denied the existence of the creation around us, that person would be considered insane. Once we have established that creation exists, and we know that every created thing requires a creator, then we know that it must be Allah who created things. Otherwise, we are forced to accept the illogical notion that everything came into being on its own. Here is a story about Abu Hanifa (Allah have mercy upon him) using this principle in a debate with an Atheist:

Long ago in the city of Baghdad, there was a Muslim empire. On one side of the River Tigris were the royal palaces and on the other side was the city. The Muslims were gathered in the Royal Palace when an Atheist approached them. He said to them, 'I don't believe in God, there cannot be a God, you cannot hear Him or see Him, you're wasting your time! Bring me your best debater and I will debate this issue with him.'

The best debater at the time was Imam Abu Hanifah (Rahimuhullah). A messenger from amongst the Muslims was sent over the River Tigris to the city, where Abu Hanifah Rahimullah was, in order to tell him about the Atheist who was awaiting him. On crossing the River Tigris, the messenger conveyed the message to Abu Hanifah Rahimullah saying, 'Oh Abu Hanifah, an Atheist is waiting for you, to debate you, please come!' Abu Hanifah Rahimullah told the messenger that he would be on his way.

The messenger went over the River Tigris once again and to the Royal Palaces, where everyone including the Atheist awaited the arrival of Abu Hanifah Rahimullah. It was sunset at the time and one hour had passed, but Abu Hanifah Rahimullah still hadn't arrived. Another hour had passed,

ALLAH

but still there was no sign of him. The Muslims started to become tense and worried about his late arrival. They did not want the Atheist to think that they were too scared to debate him, yet they did not want to take up the challenge themselves as Abu Hanifah Rahimullah was the best of Debaters from amongst the Muslims. Another hour passed, and suddenly the Atheist started laughing and said, ' Your best debater is too scared! He knows he's wrong, he is too frightened to come and debate with me. I guarantee he will not turn up today.'

The Muslims increased in apprehension and eventually it had passed midnight, and the Atheist had a smile on his face. The clock ticked on, and finally, Abu Hanifah Rahimullah had arrived. The Muslims inquired about his lateness and remarked, 'Oh Abu Hanifah, a messenger sent for you hours ago, and you arrive now, explain your lateness to us.'

Abu Hanifah Rahimullah apologized for his lateness and begins to explain, while the Atheist listens to his story.

"Once the messenger delivered the message to me, I began to make my way to the River Tigris, and on reaching the river bank I realized there was no boat, in order to cross the river. It was getting dark, and I looked around, there was no boat anywhere nor was there a navigator or a sailor in order for me to cross the river to get to the Royal Palaces. I continued to look around for a boat, as I did not want the Atheist to think I was running away and did not want to debate with him.

I was standing on the river bank looking for a navigator or a boat when something caught my attention in the middle of the river. I looked forward, and to my amazement, I saw planks of wood rising to the surface from the sea bed. I was shocked, amazed, I couldn't believe what I was seeing. Ready-made planks of wood were rising up to the surface and joining together. They were all the same width and length, I was astounded at what I saw.

I continued to look into the middle of the river, and then I saw nails coming up from the seafloor. They positioned themselves onto the boat and held the planks together, without them being banged. I stood in amazement and thought to myself, 'Oh Allah, how can this happen, planks of wood rising to the surface by itself, and then nails positioning themselves onto the boat without being banged?' I could not understand what was happening before my eyes."

The Atheist meanwhile was listening with a smile on his face. Abu Hanifah Rahimullah continued, "I was still standing on the river bank watching these planks of wood join together with nails. I could see water seeping through the gaps in the wood, and suddenly I saw a sealant appear from the river and it began sealing the gaps without someone having poured it, again I thought, 'Ya Allah, how is this possible, how can sealant appear and seal the gaps without someone having poured it, and nails appear without someone having banged them.' I looked closer and I could see a boat forming before my eyes, I stood in amazement and was filled with shock. All of a sudden a sail appeared and I thought to myself, 'How is this happening, a boat has appeared before my eyes by itself, planks of wood, nails, sealant and now a sail, but how can I use this boat in order to cross the river to the Royal Palaces?' I stood staring in wonderment and suddenly the boat began to move. It came towards me against the current. It stood floating beside me while I was on the river bank as if telling me to embark on it. I went on the boat and yet again it began to move. There was no

ALLAH

navigator or sailor on the boat, and the boat began to travel towards the direction of the royal palaces, without anyone having programmed it as to where to go. I could not understand what was happening, and how this boat had formed and was taking me to my destination against the flow of water. The boat eventually reached the other side of the River Tigris and I disembarked. I turned around and the boat had disappeared, and that is why I am late."

At this moment, the Atheist burst out laughing and remarked, "Oh Abu Hanifah, I heard that you were the best debater from amongst the Muslims, I heard that you were the wisest, the most knowledgeable from amongst your people. From seeing you today, I can say that you show none of these qualities. You speak of a boat appearing from nowhere, without someone having built it. Nails positioning themselves without someone having banged them, sealant being poured without someone having poured it, and the boat taking you to your destination without a navigator against the tide, your talking childish, your talking ridiculous, I swear I do not believe a word of it!"

Abu Hanifah Rahimullah turned to the Atheist and replied, "You don't believe a word of it? You don't believe that nails can appear by themselves? You don't believe sealant can be poured by itself? You don't believe that a boat can move without a navigator, hence you don't believe that a boat can appear without a boat maker?" The Atheist remarked defiantly, 'Yes I don't believe a word of it!'

Abu Hanifah Rahimullah replied, "If you cannot believe that a boat came into being without a boat maker, then this is only a boat, how can you believe that the whole world, the universe, the stars, the oceans, and the planets came into being without a creator!?" The Atheist astonished at his reply got up and fled.

You can use the above story as well as developing your own proofs to be used to politely debate people who deny the existence of Allah, or even for your own belief. There are Muslims who struggle with believing whether or not there really is a God, and they need to work through their own rejections, why they are there, and how to counter those thoughts.

An example that I use for my students is I take out my phone and place it on the ground. If you don't have a phone, you can just tell the listener to imagine that you have a phone or camera. Then I tell them that imagine that this phone was a pile of sand, metal, and whatever else is needed to build a phone. Then, in one million years, it became this phone which I can use to call people, email, take pictures and videos, and more. No one would believe that. So how can we believe that the human eye, just the eye, came together on its own? The entire world today cannot create a working human eye, and even if they did, they would only be manipulating currently existing matter (genes, stem cells, etc). They cannot create something from nothing.

My father once used math when discussing the existence of God with a fellow engineer. My father and the other man were professors of engineering at Santa Clara University. The

ALLAH

other man said he was an Atheist. My father asked him, "How can you deny the existence of a creator when you know that it is impossible for things to come together on their own?" He then used the idea of the factorial of any number as a base to show that things cannot come together on their own. The factorial is that you take any number and multiply all of its parts. So, the factorial of 2 is 2, because 1x2=2. The factorial of 3 is 6 because 1x2x3=6. The factorial of 4 is 1x2x3x4=24. The factorial of 5 is 120 because 1x2x3x4x5=120. The symbol for factorial is "!" so 2!=2 and 4!=24 and 5!=120.

One of the ways that the factorial is used is for determining chance. So if you had 5 different colored blocks and place them in a random order, and you were trying to get the combination of black-blue-red-green-yellow (for example), the chance that they would be in that order is 1 in 120 (since the factorial of 5 is 120). Using the concept of factorials a person can even figure out the chance of rolling snake eyes, twice or more (but since this is not a math test, we will stop here).

So my father told the other engineer that imagine a leaf on a tree only has 7 characteristics (even though we know that there are more) but he said let's just assume that there are only 7. This would include the height, width, color, weight, smell, taste, and thickness (for example). The chance that these 7 characteristics came together on their own in the way that they did is a 1 in 5,040 chance. This is because the factorial of 7 (7!) is 1x2x3x4x5x6x7=5040. Then he told him that we know there are many more characteristics per leaf than just 7, there are hundreds. Multiply this by all the leaves on a tree and all the trees in the world. What is the chance that they all came together in the way that they did? To give you an idea, you get to the factorial of 20 which is 2,432,902,008,176,640,000. That means that just 20 characteristics coming together by chance is 1 in 2,432,902,008,176,640,000! And according to statisticians, when the probability gets too big, then they consider it impossible to occur. So here is statistics, a branch of math, proving to an engineer that it is impossible for everything to come together on its own, and yet the man remained an Atheist. That is kufr; denying what is plain to see.

A question that should be posed to those who deny a creator is the question in Sura 52:35: **(Were they created from nothing, or are they the creators?)** So if there is no Creator, then how did things come into existence? If they respond by saying that all matter was created from previous matter, then this leads to an argument of infinite regression ("tasalsul" in Arabic). If they say that one thing created the other which was created by the first, then this is a circular argument ("dawr" in Arabic). In either case, the argument is flawed.

A Muslim at any time should be confident in proofs to show the existence of Allah, but I feel that is especially true in our day and age with the rise of Atheism. People from all religions are dealing with the attacks on faith by Atheists. The Atheists are doing this from the pulpits of politics (especially in Europe), in the media, literature, comedy, acting, etc. There is a mockery of religion in the rhetoric of these people and it is subtly placed in popular shows and even children's cartoons. Just as Iblis (may Allah curse him) promised that he would lay in ambush at every location, the Atheists are doing just the same. We have to be aware of their strategies and proofs and be able to refute them. During the Ramadan of this year (1437/2016), I gave two lectures on this very point. After each lecture, Muslims came up to me and told me of their struggles with Atheism. In one case, a young Muslim who was born and raised Muslim and he told me, "I retook my Shahada last night after struggling with the existence of God for one whole year." Another brother told me that he was over his struggle with evolution and is now practicing Islam.

✦ Allah is One.

This seemingly simple statement is the basis of understanding Tawheed (Oneness of Allah) properly. We must realize that Allah is One in His Essence, Attributes, and Actions. His Oneness is completely different from our understanding of the number one. He is "Ahad" in that His being One is indivisible and unlike creation. When we say that we believe Allah is One, we must also reject anything that negates that Oneness, such as:

- Him having partners
- He is not made up of parts nor does He have limbs
- Him having children or a wife

Sura Ikhlas (Chapter 112 of the Quran) is a Sura that sums up the lessons of Oneness.

I heard a story of a man who went to do da'wah to some Bedouins. The man was a convert to Islam from Christianity. When speaking with two Bedouins, one of them asked what he believed in before becoming Muslim. The man said, "That Jesus was the son of God." The Bedouin man responded by saying, "That makes sense since Jesus did not have a father." The other Bedouin man took his shepherd stick and hit the first Bedouin who made that comment and then scolded him saying, "He does not give birth nor was He given birth to" (quoting the verse from Sura Ikhlas). This shows how the understanding of a seemingly simple and short Sura (Ikhlas) can have a profound effect on one's understanding of Allah (Tawheed).

A fellow student and friend of mine told me a very amazing story about when he studied with the Mauritanian scholar Shaykh Muhammad Al-Ma'moon. The Shaykh told him that he would not teach him the aqida section from the book of Ibn Ashir (*Al-Murshid Al-Mu'in*) and that Sura Ikhlas was sufficient for Tawheed.

ALLAH

I will digress here a little and tell you about Shaykh Muhammad Al-Ma'moon. I had heard about him a lot while I was in Mauritania from the student I mentioned above who studied with him while in Medina. The shaykh had left Mauritania after studying for many years with Murabit Al Hajj. Murabit Al-Hajj really loved him and would always be so happy to hear news about him or that he sent his salam. Shaykh Muhammad Al-Ma'moon only left Mauritania because he wanted to live and die in the city of the Messenger of Allah ﷺ. I heard so much about him from my dear friend, that upon my first visit to Medina I made it a point to try and visit him.

When I was in Medina, I was asking around and yet could not find someone to take me to visit him. As I was literally leaving Medina to make umrah and I was walking towards our next stop, the adhan for Maghrib was given. I was traveling with one of my teachers and we had planned to join Maghrib and Isha at our next destination since we were travelers. But since the adhan was given and we were close to the masjid, we went back to pray. As we approached the masjid, the teacher I was with walked into the masjid which was fully packed. Right after he walked in, the guard closed the entrance and when I tried to enter, he told me that the masjid was at capacity and that I would have to pray outside. I then went to the lines of the congregation that were forming outside the masjid. After we were done praying, I saw a young man I had met while studying in Mauritania. This young man, Ibrahim, was one of the nicest people I have ever met. Maybe later in the text I will find a place to tell you about him. Ibrahim and I greeted each other as we had not seen each other in four years. Now remember, we are meeting each other "randomly" in a masjid where hundreds of thousands of people pray. What are the chances of that?

I told Ibrahim that one of the things I wanted to do was visit Shaykh Muhammad al-Ma'moon. He told me (and I will never forget the way he said it), "I know exactly where he lives and I have a car and can take you there right now!" I waited for my teacher to come out of the masjid and then introduced him to Ibrahim. And we proceeded to visit Shaykh Muhammad Al-Ma'moon who lives in a very simple house. One thing that the Shaykh kept telling us during his visit was that he was friends with the father of the teacher I was with, Shaykh Salek. He told Shaykh Salek the Hadith, "From the best acts of birr is to visit the friends of your father once your father passes away." This is a beautiful example of a lesson that you will cover in ADAB 101 (Rights of Parents). Although Shaykh Muhammad al-Ma'moon lives in poverty, he emphatically and happily told us that he is proud to be a student of Murabit al-Hajj, to live in Medina and that he is waiting for a home in the Baqi'. The Baqi' is the cemetery of Medina. He, like many others who go to Medina or Mecca, are trying to fulfill the command of the Hadith, **"Whoever is able to die in one of the two Sacred Precincts**

ALLAH

(Haramayn) [i.e., Makka or Madina] then he should do so." Shaykh Muhammad al Ma'moon later got his wish. May Allah have mercy on him.

You must excuse the digression, but I felt it was important that you know who this man is, especially since I mentioned his view of Sura Ikhlas being enough to teach aqida. And that was to emphasize the idea of this point, which is "Allah is One."

◆ Allah exists pre-eternally.

We must believe that Allah was always in existence and has no beginning. He existed even before creation was in existence. He is The First, without a beginning, and He is The Last, without an end. So His being The First is different than what we conceive as the idea of first. When we think of "first" we think of a timeline and that there was something there before the "first" of whatever we are thinking about. His being First is different because He is not bound by time and not preceded by nonexistence.

(He is The First and The Last, The Manifest and The Hidden, and He is All-Knowing about everything.) (Quran 57:3)

This verse that has the proof for Allah being The First, is a verse that I used to hear quite often from the Muadh-dhin of the Masjid of Murabit Al-Hajj. The muadhdhin's name is Shaykh Muhammad Ali and he was always in a humorous mood making jokes. Whenever people would ask if he needed to get some medical attention, he would say, "All I need is the best injection!" Then he would make his finger like it was a syringe, touch his skin and recite the ayah above.

Anyone who visited Murabit al-Hajj's school would be quite familiar with Shaykh Muhammad Ali. He was always at the masjid reciting or teaching Quran and waiting to give the adhan after looking at the stars, shadows, or the other signs in the sky (which we will cover in FIQH 101 and ASTR 101). In fact, I learned the Islamic Astronomy of constellations from him outside the masjid with him pointing out the stars, but I couldn't keep up at first. He would point things out so fast as he was intimately familiar with the sky, whereas to me I couldn't make things out at first. But once I became familiar with the sky, looking up at the heavens has now become like looking at the roads in my neighborhood, but with much, much more awe. Shaykh Muhammad Ali is also known as being one of the foremost Hafiz of the Quran and teachers of the Quran. His students are well-known for having great memorization. His teacher was Shaykh Muhammad Ahmed ould Bayba who was my first teacher when I was in Mauritania.

ALLAH

✦ Allah is perfect in all ways.

We cannot attribute any deficiency to Allah in either His Essence, Attributes, Speech, and Actions. One of the proofs of His perfection is how well He made the creation that we see around us. Our minds cannot fully conceive Allah, but we can conceive and understand the creation around us. So when we look at the perfection in creation, then we know that it was made by a perfect Creator.

(Who made well whatever He created, and started the creation of man from clay.) (Quran 32:7)

Being able to witness the creation around us are blessings that Allah has given us so that we can reflect on them. <u>We can't think about Allah, so we think about His creation.</u> And look at the ayah again. After He tells us that He created everything in a perfect way, He reminds us of who we are and what we were created from. It should humble us. So rather than assuming that our intellect is the greatest thing in the universe and if our intellect can't figure it out then it must not exist (as some Atheists get lead into believing), we should humble ourselves by reminding it that we are made from dirt. One of the Mauritanian shuyukh (*pl.* of "shaykh") once picked up some dirt and told a student, "Don't forget where you came from."

Another blessing that we have been given is the Quran. A perfect book to remind us of the perfect Creator who sent it to us through the most blessed Messenger of Allah, a man who was perfect as a human can be, in both his form (khalq) and his character (khuluq). May Allah send peace and blessings on the perfect man, Muhammad ﷺ.

✦ Any imperfection is not attributed to Allah.

If there was imperfection with Allah, He would not have been able to create this universe around us that we see moving and growing in order.

✦ Allah is without need.

Allah exists without the need of anything. He is Al-Ghani in that he does not need anything to exist. Creation, on the other hand, needs a lot of things to exist. They need to be created and sustained by Allah. Allah does not need anyone to create Him nor sustain Him.

ALLAH

(O mankind, it is you who are in need of Allah, but Allah is The Self-Sufficient (Al-Ghani), Worthy of All Praise (Al-Hameed).) (Qur'an 35:15)

✦ Allah does not exist in time, place, or direction.

Time, place and direction are all created matters. Allah is completely different from His creation. He is not bound by anything in His creation. He existed before creation and thus He existed before there was even something called time, place, or direction. If we attribute time, place, or direction to Allah then we have either made Allah resemble His creation or we have declared that His creation exists without beginning. Both are impossible. Let's look at how Ali ibn Abi Talib (Allah ennoble his face) addressed the issue:

Nu'man ibn Sa'd said "Once I was in Kufa at the abode of the government, which was the house of Ali ibn Abi Talib (karama Allahu wajhahu), when Nawf ibn Abdullah came in and said, 'O Commander of the Believers, there is a group of 40 Jewish men here at the door.' Ali said, 'Let me meet them.' When they stood before him, they said, 'O Ali, describe to us this Lord of yours who is in the Heavens, How is He? And how was He? When was He? And upon which thing was He?"

There was a long speech that 'Ali gave as an answer, and it is a complete and eloquent explanation of our belief. The point I wanted to mention that relates to this point is when 'Ali said:

Glory be to Him, He spoke to Musa with Speech but without the use of limbs, tools, lips, or uvula. Glory and Elevated is He beyond being given limitations to His Attributes. Whoever believes that our Lord has limits, is ignorant of the Creator Who is worshipped. Whoever mentions that places confine Him, will always be baffled and confused. Rather, Allah encompasses all places. So if you are truthful, O you who is going out of his way to describe The Merciful One in contrast to what has been mentioned in the Revelation and Proof [i.e. The Quran], then describe to me Jibreel, Mika'eel, and Israfeel! You will not be able to! Are you unable to describe a created thing which is a creation just like you but you try to describe the Creator who is worshipped?! (Taken from *Hilyat al-Awliya*)

✦ One without father, son, friend, spouse, or partner.

There are many verses in the Quran that mention this. Sura Ikhlas is one. Other verses include 2:116, 4:171, 6:101, 9:30, 10:68, 17:111, 18:4, 1935, 19:88-92, 21:26, 23:91, 25:2, 37:152, 39:4, 43:81-82, 72:3.

ALLAH

✦ First without beginning.

See the discussion above about verse 57:3.

✦ Last without End.

(And the Horn (Sūr) will be blown, and all those in the heavens and all those in the earth will faint, except the one whom Allah wills (otherwise). Thereafter, it will be blown once again, and suddenly they will stand up, looking around.) (Quran 39:68)

In a Hadith narrated that explains this verse it states:

It has been narrated from a Hadith of Anas that the Prophet ﷺ recited the verse **(And Horn (Sūr) will be blown, and all those in the heavens and all those in the earth will faint, except the one whom Allah wills.)** The companions said, 'Who are the ones which Allah has made an exception for?' He said, 'They are Jibril, Mika'il, Israfil and the Angel of Death. Then Allah says to the Angel of Death, 'O Angel of Death, who remains from My creation?' And He is Well-Aware. The Angel of Death says, 'Jibril, Mika'il, Israfil and your weak slave, the Angel of Death.' Allah then says, 'O Angel of Death, take the souls of Israfil and Mika'il.' And they fall dead like two giant mountains. Then Allah says, 'O Angel of death, die!' And then he dies. Then Allah says to Jibril, 'Who remains?' Jibril says, 'Blessed and Elevated are you O Possessor of Grandness and Honor! Your Blessed Wajh which is Everlasting and Jibril, the finite dead one.' Allah then says, 'O Jibril, you must die.' And so he falls in prostration with his limbs trembling and says, 'Glory be to you my Lord, Blessed and Elevated are you O Possessor of Grandness and Honor!

Then only Allah will remain.

✦ Totally independent and not in need of anything.

Studying the 99 Names of Allah is a great way to learn who Allah is. All over the Muslim world, there is a focus to have children memorize the 99 Names. There is a Hadith about memorizing them and that the person who does so will enter Jannah. If you have not already memorized those names, I would suggest that you begin reciting them regularly and work on memorizing them and then understanding the meaning of each Name. There are some good CDs with recitations of the 99 Names. One of those names is Al-Ghani, which means "The Independent."

You may see Al Ghani translated as "The Rich," but I think "Independent" is more fitting. The reason is that when we think of richness, we usually think of a person who has a lot. That could be money, land, jewels, etc. But there is a problem with this idea of "Richness," or in Arabic "Ghinaa." That problem is that the person is only rich because he has those things and thus his richness is dependent on those things. Imam Shafi'i once said, "وَلَيْسَ الغِنَى إِلَا عَنْ الشَيءِ لَابِهِ (Wealth is only being independent of something, not [independent] with it)."

Let's think for a moment about a millionaire. He or she has a lot of wealth, and so people may think that the person is independent by having that wealth. But in reality, that person is dependent on that wealth. So he or she may be independent of certain things, like bills (because they can be paid with the money), but they are still dependent on the money.

When we think about Allah and His being Independent, He is absolutely free of having any need for anything. He does not need anything in His creation and He does not need us to do anything for Him. He reminds us of this in the Quran when He says:

(Yes, you are such that you are called upon to spend in Allah's way, but some of you withhold in miserliness—and he who withholds in miserliness withholds against himself—and Allah is the Free-of-Need (Al-Ghani), and you are the needy. And if you turn away, He will replace you by some other people, then they will not be like you.) (Quran 47:38)

We must remind ourselves of this Attribute of Allah when we give charity for His cause (fi sabili-Llah) or when we do any act of worship ('ibadah) or good interaction with others (mu'amalah). We must remind ourselves of this because we have to be certain that Allah is not in need of anything that we put forward. Rather, He is giving the opportunity for us to help ourselves by giving in His path and serving Him.

◆ Totally different than His creation.

We must believe that Allah is completely different than anything in His creation. This includes everything from the throne to the earth (min al-'arsh illa al-farsh). The verse from the Quran that we should keep in the forefront of our mind at all times, and especially when we get thoughts of making Allah resemble something in His creation is (لَيْسَ كَمِثْلِهِ شَيْءٌ) **(There is**

nothing like unto Him) [laysa ka-mithlihi shay]) (Quran 42:11). Anything you can imagine, Allah is completely different than that.

Allah is not a body having a whole body or parts of a body. He does not breathe, sleep, eat, drink, rest, grow, change, die, etc. He is not like anything in creation.
One of the things that distinguishes Islam from other religions is that we have this principle. If you open most books of other faiths, they do not have an issue with even conceptualizing and drawing what they believe the Divine to be.

✦ He speaks, but His Speech is different than creation.

We believe that Allah possesses the attribute of Speech which is an attribute that is pre-eternal just like His Essence (Dhat), Attributes (Sifat), and Actions (Af'al). Shaykh Ibrāhīm ibn Muhammad Al-Bayjūrī in his commentary on *Jawahara al-Tawhid* says:

> And know that the phrase 'Kalām Allah' (Allah's Word or Speech) is applied to the beginningless unuttered speech (kalām nafsī qadīm), which happens to be a quality (sifa) present with His being (Dhat)—High is He.

We will go into more depth about the Speech of Allah in the course IMAN 101.

We believe that Allah speaks to His prophets and His angels. We know that He can convey revelation through an angel (Jibril), through a dream, or by speaking directly to the prophet, as He did with Musa (alayhis salam). Allah says in the Quran:

([We have sent] some Messengers We have already told you about, and some other Messengers We did not tell you about, and Allah has spoken to Mūsā directly.) (Quran 4:164)

It is for this direct Speech of Allah that Musa (alayhis salam) gained the title Al-Kaleem (The One Who was Spoken To). We must affirm that Musa was spoken to and at the same time we affirm that the Speech of Allah is nothing like His creation. The Speech of Allah is an Attribute of Allah, so it is not bound by time and has existed before the creation, time, and space all began. We do not need to know how this occurred to affirm that it took place. Part of our being Muslim is to submit. We submit our limbs and our intellect. So when we accept that Allah has pre-eternal Speech and spoke to Musa directly, we know it to be true and submit our intellects to that truth, even if our intellects cannot comprehend how it occurred. I will end this section with an interesting narration mentioned by Al-Qurtubi in his tafsir of the above ayah:

> The use of the masdar (i.e., "takleeman") is used for emphasis and it is a proof to refute the one who says, "Allah created speech for Himself and placed it in the tree and Musa heard it." Rather, it is the True Speech that allows for the Speaker to be a Speaker. Al-Nahhas said, "The grammarians are in consensus that if you stress a verb by using the masdar, then it is not metaphorical...." Wahab ibn Munabbih said, "Musa alayhis salam said, 'O My Lord, for what reason did you take me as the One Who was Spoken To (Al-Kaleem)?' He asked for the action that pleased Allah so that he could do a lot of it. So Allah the Exalted said, 'Do you remember when a baby goat (kid) ran away from your flock and you followed it for most of the day and it tired you out? Then you took it, kissed it and held it close to your chest, and said to it, 'You tired me out and you tired yourself out.' And you didn't become angry with it. It is for that reason that I took you as a Kaleem."

May Allah make us from among those who can control their anger and get the reward of those who control their anger.

✦ He hears everything, but His Hearing is different than that of creation. He sees everything, but His Sight is different than the seeing of His creation.

In the same way that the Speech of Allah is completely different than His creation, the same is the case for the Hearing and Sight of Allah. He sees and hears everything, but His Hearing and Sight are completely different from His creation. He does not need to process sound so He can hear and He does not need to collect light through a lens so that He can see. He is completely different than His creation, and He is not in need of anything to allow Him to hear and see.

Someone may ask, "Yes, but how does he see in a way that is different than us?" The simple answer is that we must submit our intellect to the fact that He is completely different than us and that He hears and sees. But, if we want to convince ourselves using proof, we do not have to look further than ourselves. And we are ordered to reflect on our own selves (Quran 41:53). When we close our eyes and go to sleep, we may see dreams. In those dreams, we "see" and "hear" things that are not really happening. How does that occur? It happens and we believe it. So we have a concept of seeing and hearing right here before us that goes beyond the conventional way of seeing and hearing. Allah is completely different than His creation, He is Powerful and able to do all things, and He Sees and He Hears.

ALLAH

Going back to the idea of thinking about ourselves, there is a saying "Whoever knows their own self will know his Lord." Some attribute this as being a Hadith, but Imam Nawawi and others refuted that it is a Hadith. But we can see that there is wisdom that can be derived from it. Basically, if you understand who you are, then you can know that Allah is different than that. If we realize that we are in need, then we know that Allah is free of need. If we know our limits and powerlessness, then we know that Allah has no limits and has full power. If we know that we sleep, eat, and drink, then we know that Allah does not sleep, eat, or drink.

✦ He knows everything and nothing can escape His knowledge.

(Allah made people, their thoughts, and knows everything that enters their hearts.) (Quran 50:16). (He knows all dry things and wet, all leaves and grains.) (Quran 6:59). (He knows everything before it happened.) (Quran 67:14).

(Do not take the verses of Allah in jest, and remember the grace of Allah on you and what He has revealed to you of the Book and the wisdom, giving you good counsel thereby, and fear Allah, and be sure that Allah is the One Who knows everything.) (Quran 2:231)

(Indeed We have created man, and We know whatever thoughts his inner self develops, and We are closer to him than (his) jugular vein.) (Qur'an 50:16)

In this last verse mentioned (Qur'an 50:16) we must remember that Allah is not physically closer to us than our jugular vein. If that was the case, then that would mean that Allah is bound by place and time and that He resembles creation. But He is closer to us than our jugular vein in that He is close in the sense that He knows everything about us. Al-Qurtubi mentions in the tafsir of this ayah that:

The means (We are closer to Him than his jugular vein), but this is not a proximity of distance... Another explanation is that 'We have more knowledge of what his soul whispers to him than his jugular vein knows' because the jugular vein is one that is directly connected to the heart. So the knowledge of The Lord is closer than the knowledge the heart has. This meaning has been narrated from Muqatil who said, 'The jugular vein is one that is connected to the heart, and this proximity is one of knowledge and power.' Some people can hide things from others, but nothing is hidden from the Knowledge of Allah.

This last part of the tafsir really made me think. There are things that we can hide from others and there are even things that we can hide from ourselves. We can convince ourselves of a feeling or a reason for doing something, but deep down in our souls, the reality of that feeling or the reason for doing something is different from what we know. There are things that we can hide so deeply we forget them, such as repressed memories.[1] But Allah knows all this, that which we hide from others and even that which we hide from ourselves. Part of the Ihsan of our Deen is to go deep within to try and uncover those things that we have hidden from ourselves. Call it introspection, inward journey, or whatever you would like, but the point is that we must do it. We must go on that inward journey to uncover the secrets of our souls. We will discuss this process more in IHSN 101.

◆ He has absolute power (Qudra).

We believe that Allah has Absolute Power and that He controls everything. (Quran 10:3, 51:58)

◆ He does whatever He wants (Irada).

Allah does whatever He wants and no one can compel Him to do anything or to refrain from doing something. Whether we understand the action or not, whether we agree with the action or not, it does not affect His Irada (Complete Free Will). This is one Attribute of Allah that helps me get through understanding difficult situations. Whenever something very bad occurs, like when little children or innocent people are hurt and hearing the news is very difficult, I recite the following verse a number of times to remind me that Allah does whatever He wills:

(فَعَّالٌ لِمَا يُرِيدُ **He is ever doer of what He intends).**) (Quran 85:16)

This reminds me that He does whatever He wants and that all things are coming from His choice. There is not an alternate force in creation that does things. We do not believe that only good things come from Allah and that evil comes from the Devil. This idea creates an image similar to Greek mythology where there are two or multiple gods each with power to do things that are constantly in a struggle. No. All things come from Allah and He does whatever He wills.

If you look at the Hadith of Jibril, you will see that one of the pillars of faith mentioned is that we believe in the Qadr (Divine Ordainment) of Allah. And more specifically, if you look

---

[1] Not only that, but we often change our memories to fit what we wanted to happen and so deceive ourselves even about things we have witnessed with our own eyes and ears.

at the Hadith, is that we accept both the good that happens and the bad that happens as being part of the Qadr. And if we begin to question "why" Allah did something, we should remember the verse:

(He is not questioned of what He does, and they are questioned.) (Quran 21:23)

So we do not have a "right" to know "why" Allah did something. And we cannot feel as though we are entitled to ask why He did something and to get an answer. Rather, we should not worry about asking Allah why He did or did not do something but focus on what we will be asked about; our actions.

A final note about the Will of Allah is that we must remember that Allah does not have an opposite. He is in control of everything and He is doing everything. So there is not a power out there, such as the Devil, who controls evil, and Allah only controls good. Allah is in control of *everything*.

✦ He can create or leave things uncreated based on His choice.

Allah is the Creator whether or not He creates something. He was the Creator pre-eternally even before He brought creation into existence. No one can force Him to create or uncreate.

✦ No one can force Him to do anything.

There is nobody or nothing which can compel Allah to do anything or to stop Him from doing something.

✦ He is Living and never dies. He was never born nor does He have children.

Ayah Al-Kursi and Sura al-Ikhlas contain these lessons. They are both powerful sources of understanding who Allah is. They should be learned and committed to memory and taught to those who are new to Islam or learning about Islam.

ALLAH

✦ **We deny the opposites of the above-mentioned matters, in that we reject that Allah:**

- Is more than One;
- Has a beginning or an end;
- Needs anything from us;
- Has similarities to creation in speech, sight, knowledge, or any other attribute;
- Is forced to do something;
- Can cease to exist or die;
- Is incapable.

✦ **Our minds and thoughts cannot imagine His true essence.**

One of the best sayings that sum up one of the core concepts of Tawheed (Oneness of Allah) is the following:

كُلُّ مَا يَخْطُرُ بِبَالِكَ فَاللهُ بِخِلَافِ ذَلِكَ

(Everything that you can imagine, Allah is other than that)
[Kullu ma yakhturu bi-balik, fa Allahu bi khilafi dhalik]

While this is not something taken from a Hadith, the lesson is found in the Quran.[2] We know that **(There is nothing like unto Him)** and so anything that we can try to imagine Allah as being, then Allah is completely different than that. So we should not try to imagine what Allah is, rather, we should think about His creation. In a Hadith narrated in the *Mu'jim* of Al-Tabarani on the authority of Ibn 'Umar (radiya Allahu anhuma) who said: The Messenger of Allah ﷺ said, **"Think about the blessings of Allah and do not think about Allah."**

This does not mean that we cannot think about Allah in general, but that we should not try and visualize what He "looks" like. We can think about Allah in general and His Attributes and His Actions, and what He has created.[3] Ibn Abi Zayd, in the *Risala*, said:

---

[2] This statement is commonly attributed to Imam Ahmad ibn Hanbal.

[3] And this is because our minds only think about things in relation to each other, while Allah is beyond all comparisons. We know what "hot" is by comparing it to something that is "cold" or what "sharp" by comparing it to something that is "dull." So the way our minds think make them utterly incapable of understanding Allah as He truly is. This is why the basis of our understanding of Tawheed is negation rooted in the cosmic reality that Allah is Al-Ahad (The Utterly Unique).

ALLAH

His Essence cannot be encompassed by those who describe Him, He will not be encompassed by those who reflect. Those who reflect should think about his signs but not think about the reality of His Essence.

Imam al-Tahawi said in his book (which is covered in Tayba's IMAN 101 course): "Thoughts cannot reach Him, Understanding cannot grasp Him. He does not resemble creation." To complete this point, look up and reflect on the following verses: 6:103, 42:11, 30:8, 7:185. Then write them out here in your book:

✦ Allah does not have a body nor an attribute of a body.

We do not believe that Allah has a body, as that is a concept known as "Tajseem" (anthropomorphism). Allah is unlike His creation.

✦ Only Allah creates and He is Al-Khaliq.

Only Allah can create and only He is Al-Khaliq. When we make things we are just manipulating the creation. We are taking things that are in creation and changing their form. But in terms of originating creation, that belongs only to Allah. This is why one of His Names is Al Fatir, which means "The Originator." He is the Original Creator. When we "create" things, we are only changing the form of things. That is why the challenge to mankind is to create something from nothing. Even if they take carbon and make something amazing out of it, or take some cells and clone something, they are still only manipulating something which is already in existence. Let's see them make something from nothing. They can't.

ALLAH

There is an interesting story about the word Al-Fatir, which has an entire Sura named after that Attribute (Sura 35):

> Ibn Abbas, may Allah be pleased with him, said 'I did not know what **(Fatir as-samawati wa-l-ard)** meant until two Bedouins came to me disputing over a well. One of them said to his companion "Ana fatartuha" meaning "I started it."

So imagine the two men, one who dug the well in the first place and maybe the other one came later and re-dug it. The second said that he "made" it but the first said, "I originated it" (fatartuha). And just like only Allah can originate creation, only He can sustain it (Al-Qayyum) and only He can annihilate it. While we may destroy something, we cannot take something out of existence. Only Allah can do that.

I will end this section with a tribute to someone who articulated Tawheed in an eloquent manner in English. When I initially finished the above notes, I thought to myself that this section deserved a closing, but I could not think of what to write and then moved on to type the notes for the next section. This was on June 4, 2016, the day after Muhammad Ali (the famous boxer) passed away. My wife showed me a video of him talking about his "bodyguard." I thought it was a great exposition of Tawheed and decided to use it to end this section. I also am considering the inclusion of it in this text as a sadaqa jariya (ongoing charity), the reward of which will go back to Muhammad Ali. That is my tribute to a man who did so much for the deen of Islam by conveying the Message through the public platform that Allah gave him. A man who did so much for humanity.

> *Interviewer*: You don't hide from your public. You walk around, you talk to people, you meet people.
> *Muhammad Ali*: (motions and sounds as if a gun went off)
> *Interviewer*: That's right, have you ever thought about being assassinated?
> *Muhammad Ali*: Didn't I read your mind?
> *Interviewer*: You did.
> *Muhammad Ali*: See? If I get shot, or something happens to me, it would have to be because someone doesn't like me for what I believe... and I'd die for that.
> *Interviewer*: You would?
> *Muhammad Ali*: And let me tell you, if somebody wants to get you. See in the Holy Quran, the Islamic Bible, it says, "Not one soul comes on earth without the permission of Allah (God), not one soul leaves without the permission. When you die, it's time. So, I don't believe that it's time for me to die in that way. If it is, then I welcome it. If it happens, it happens. It's God's will.
> *Interviewer*: Do you have a bodyguard?

ALLAH

Muhammad Ali: (counts on his fingers to seven then laughs and says) No, I got one bodyguard. He has no eyes, though He sees. He has no ears though He hears. He remembers everything without the aid of mind or memory. When He wishes to create a thing, He just orders it be and it comes into existence. But this order is not conveyed in words which takes a tongue to formulate or sound carried to ears. He hears the secrets of those and their quiet thoughts. That's God, Allah. He's my bodyguard. He's your bodyguard. He's the Supreme.
-END-

May Allah enshroud him with His Mercy.

The Prophets & Messengers

The following are the four necessary qualities of all prophets:

- Sidq (Truthfulness)
- Amanah (Trustworthiness)
- Tabligh (Conveying the Message)
- Fatana (Intelligence)

Of all the lessons in this section, this is the most important for you as a Muslim to understand and believe. We will go through each point one by one.

✦ Sidq: Truthful in all that they speak.

The prophets have to be known as truthful people so that when they bring the message, they are not doubted. One of the amazing things about the Prophet Muhammad ﷺ is that his people believed him because they knew him to be truthful. He was so truthful that he was given the title "Al-Ameen" by Quraysh and that's how they referred to him. Here is a story that illustrates the trust they had in him:

> Then, as commanded, the Prophet took his preaching to his own clan. One day he climbed on top of Mount Safa, in Mecca, and called out: **"O people of Quraysh! O people of Quraysh!"** Hearing his call, the people of Quraysh gathered around him and asked what the matter was. The Prophet said: **"If I told you that there was an army behind this hill, would you believe me?"** They all replied: "Indeed, for we trust you, and we have never known you to tell a lie." The Prophet then said: **"Know then that I am a Warner and I warn you of a severe punishment. O Banu Abdul Muttalib! O Banu Abd Manaf! O Banu Zuhra! O Banu Taym! O Banu Makhzum! O Banu Asad! God has commanded me to warn my nearest kinsmen, that I can guarantee to you no good on the earth or in heaven unless you witness that there is none worthy of worship except God."** Hearing this, the Prophet's uncle, Abu Lahab, got up and said: "Perish thou this very day! was it for this that thou assembled us here?"

✦ Amanah: Trustworthy in all that is entrusted to them from Allah, angels, or the people.

Not only do they have to be people who speak the truth, but they also have to be people who are trustworthy and who fulfill trusts. The reason for this is so that people do not have doubts in their minds about whether or not the person actually told them everything they were entrusted to by Allah.

✦ Tabligh: They convey all that they were ordered to convey from Allah.

They have to convey the message. It is inconceivable that a prophet would hide a portion of what he was ordered to convey. Look at the Final Hajj Sermon and reflect on what the Prophet Muhammad ﷺ said. He told them he conveyed the message. This was important for him to emphasize.

To compare this with a non-prophet, we can look at the example of a scholar or anyone with some knowledge. The law states that they have to convey the knowledge they have if they are asked or need to teach. But it is conceivable for a scholar or someone with some knowledge to conceal that knowledge. They would be sinning if they did that, but it could happen. In the case of a prophet, it is inconceivable for it to occur. It is impossible to occur.

✦ Fatana: They are very smart and can debate with their people.

Some scholars have mentioned this as a specific point of belief about all the prophets. The reason is that the prophets have to discuss matters of faith with people who may have arguments to support their disbelief. The prophet would then have to logically refute those claims and arguments. To do this, he would have to be a very intelligent person. When we look at the story of Ibrahim alayhis salam with Nimrod (Quran 2:258), we see the example of an eloquent and intelligent debater in Ibrahim alayhis salam.

Now that we have affirmed the four positive traits necessary for all prophets, let's take a look at the opposite of these four which are the four negative traits that we deny their possibility with any prophet. The following four attributes are impossible for all prophets:

- Kadhib (Lying)
- Khiyana (Abuse of trust)
- Kitman (Hiding the revelation, or a portion, they were ordered to convey)
- Being feeble-minded

✦ Kadhib: Lying

This is the opposite of the necessary attribute of truth. For the same reason why the prophets must be truthful so that their people know they are conveying the message truthfully is the same reason that it is impossible for them to ever lie.

THE PROPHETS & MESSENGERS

We can take a moment here to discuss a story mentioned in the Hadith about the "lies" of Ibrahim alayhis salam.

> Ibn Sirin narrates from Abu Hurayra that the Prophet ﷺ said, **"Ibrahim, (PBUH), never lied except three times, two were for the sake of God, the Almighty, when He said, 'I am sick' and 'The biggest of them did it.' And one was about Sarah. He went by the land of one of the tyrants with Sarah, who was very beautiful. He said to Sarah 'This is a tyrant person, if he knows that you are my wife he will overcome me (kill me) because of you. So if he asks you, tell him that you are my sister. You are indeed my sister in Islam, and I do not know any Muslims on the face of the earth except myself and you."** (Muslim, 2371)

I discussed this in the course ADAB 102 (Prohibitions of the Tongue) which is part of the coursework which you will be going through, in sha Allah:

> In the next story that Shaykh Muhammad Mawlud is referring to in saying, the big one did it, this is a reference to a story that happened to Ibrahim alayhis salam. Ibrahim alayhis salam in the well-known story, he did not want to worship the idols of his people and he hated the idols of his people. When his people went out to their festival he went and destroyed the idols. But he left the largest idol standing and he put the axe that he had destroyed the other idols with, he put it with that idol. When the people came back they asked Ibrahim alayhis salam, "Who did this?" and Ibrahim (alayhis salam) said, "The big one did it, the big idol did it." So this might seem as if it's a "lie" because the big one didn't actually in fact break the idols, it was Ibrahim alayhis salam doing it. But he's stating this to clarify the truth because as soon as he said that, the people realized, "Well the big one can't do it. He can't do anything." It's as if Ibrahim alayhis salam is saying, "Exactly, he cannot do anything, so why are you worshipping them?" He did that to clarify the truth.
>
> Now we also know that the prophets cannot lie, so even though this seems as if it's a lie and in a Hadith the Prophet ﷺ actually referred to this as one of the "lies" that Ibrahim (alayhis salam) said, it's not really a lie[1] because if we look at the story with an understanding that the prophets cannot lie, then how did Ibrahim alayhis salam say that the big one meaning the big idol did this? One explanation is that it means that it was the hate for the idols that caused Ibrahim alayhis salam to destroy them, and he had an especially high hatred for the large idol. It was the big

---

[1] The word "kadhib (كذب)" in Arabic is used whenever someone says something that is not true, whether or not it was said or unintentionally, innocently or with an aim to harm. However, in English, we generally only refer to someting as a "lie" when it is said intentionally and with malice. So perhaps a better translation of the hadith referenced above is **"[Prophet] Ibrahim (peace be upon him) never said anything literally untrue except three times..."** and each of the examples are situations where: (a) there was either a justifiable reason for Ibrahim to be deceptive using what is known as equivocation (ta`reed) or (b) it was clear to everyone involved that what was said wasn't actually true. That being the case, referring to them as "lies" is both incorrect and inappropriate.

idol that caused his hatred to well up and make Ibrahim alayhis salam break the idols. Essentially it was the big one that did it, meaning it was the big one that caused him to break the idols so he was not lying. When we look at the Hadith that the Prophet (Sall Allahu alayhi wa sallam) said that Ibrahim (alayhis salam) made three lies; one is when he told his people when they went out to the festival that he's sick, one is when the big one did it and one is when he told the ruler of Egypt about his wife Sarah that this is my sister.

If we look at all of those there's an explanation for all of those situations. When his people went out to the festival and they asked him to join them he said "Inni saqeem (I am sick)." One of the understandings is that what it means is that he felt sick in his heart and so he was not lying. He was not physically sick but he was telling the people Inni saqeem, and they understood ok he can't go with us.

Another tafsir is that at that time of Ibrahim (alayhis salam) people had a very deep understanding of the stars. What would be considered astrology now was something that was a verified science at that time and Ibrahim (alayhis salam) knew it. So people knew that there were certain times where they would look at the stars and this would be a good time for planting or this would be a good time for marriage, the marriage will be successful if you do this when the stars are aligned in such and such way. The people also knew that there were certain times that would be indicated by the movement of the stars where if a person traveled, he would get sick. So Ibrahim (alayhis salam) was living at a time where the people had this knowledge of the stars. He himself had this knowledge of the stars and so he told them "Inni saqeem," meaning, "If I go out with you, I would go out at a time that the stars are saying I would get sick." They understood this, they accepted it and they let him be. By Ibrahim (alayhis salam) saying, "Inni saqeem," he was essentially saying, "I will get sick if I go out with you right now," so they accepted it.

In any case, any of the explanations that are given all lead to the point that Ibrahim (alayhis salam) was not actually lying in that he was telling something that was not true. He was just stating something in a different way. So when he says, "The big one did it," they understood that he's saying the big one actually physically did it. Ibrahim alayhis salam's intention was, and Allah knows best, that it was the big one that caused his anger to be so great that he destroyed the idols or what I just mentioned about his statement, "I am sick."

In the third situation where he said to the ruler in the land of Egypt. "This is my sister," talking about his wife, he meant this is my sister in Islam, so it was not truly a lie. Imam Qustalani says about this, about the hadith where the Prophet ﷺ said, **"Ibrahim (alayhis salam) only told three lies, two of them for the sake of Allah,"** meaning in his saying **(Inni saqeem (I am sick))** and saying **(The big one did it.)** And one of them about the situation with his wife Sara in saying she was his sister. Imam Qustalani says this is not actual lying that would be a cause of criticism for he is beyond doing something like that. The Prophet ﷺ used the word lying metaphorically as what Ibrahim (alayhis salam) did was an illusion that could have two meanings, and he did it for a valid purpose, meaning to clarify the truth.

THE PROPHETS & MESSENGERS

Ibn Aqil said the intellectual proofs avert the apparent meaning of using the word "lying" when discussing Ibrahim (alayhis salam), meaning that we can use intellectual proof to show that Ibrahim (alayhis salam) was not actually lying. It was referred to as a "lie" by the Prophet ﷺ and also Ibrahim (alayhis salam) himself in the "Hadith of the Intercession" where he said, "I only told three lies." In the "Hadith of the Intercession" he was saying this out of a state of extreme fear because he has a high station. He was saying it out of humility. Only three times did he say something that appeared to be a lie. He himself referred to it as a lie but we know that the prophets are trustworthy. One of their characteristics is that they all have amanah and they do not do khiyana, they do not deceive people. So this cannot be believed to be an actual lie that Ibrahim (alayhis salam) said.

✦ Khiyana: Abuse of trust

Just as we believe that all the prophets must be people who fulfill the trusts given to them, we also believe that it is impossible for them to ever abuse a trust. In the case of the Prophet Muhammad ﷺ, he was known for his trustworthiness long before he was sent as a prophet. It was this trustworthiness that Khadija (radiy Allahu anha) noticed and one of the reasons why she wanted to marry him. It was also this trustworthiness that she reminded him of when the Revelation first came to him. When he came down from the mountain and was afraid of what occurred and that he feared it may not be something good, she told him in her beautiful words: "Never! By God, God will never disgrace you. You keep good relations with your relatives, help the poor, serve your guests generously, and assist those hit with calamities." (*Sahih Al-Bukhari*)

Another proof that he never abused a trust is the fact that after he left Mecca, he left his cousin Ali (radiy Allahu anhu) to distribute all the trusts that were left in his possession. It took him three days to distribute everything. That is a sign that he was given a lot of items to care for.

✦ Kitman: Hiding the revelation, or a portion, they were ordered to convey.

It is impossible for the prophets to conceal the revelation that they were given and ordered to convey. As an example of how this might be believed by a deviant person, there is an example of people claiming they were taught things by the Prophet ﷺ after his passing that he did not teach other people. There is one such example in West Africa where some people follow the teachings of a person who claimed to have been taught a prayer by the Prophet ﷺ. They claim this prayer was something that was not given by the Prophet ﷺ to his companions and that reading it has the reward of reciting the Quran multiple times. When I asked one of my teachers about this belief, he said that it is like claiming the Prophet ﷺ did kitman by not conveying this prayer to his Companions.

✦ Wasa: Being feeble-minded

In the section about what is necessary for a prophet, it was mentioned that being intelligent was an obligation. This means that the opposite of intelligence, which is being feeble-minded, is impossible. And this concludes the section about the necessary and impossible traits for a prophet to have. This only leaves the section of what is possible for them to do.

✦ Normal human states are possible for the Prophets

Since we discussed the issues that are necessary and impossible for a prophet and that they are perfect human beings, some may feel that this means that nothing bad can happen to them. The following are possible for a prophet:

- Light sickness. A wisdom (hikma) of this is that it makes us feel better when we experience similar situations by saying, "Well, so and so prophet experienced such and such." This is called tasalli.
- Eating and drinking;
- Marriage;
- Human emotions such as sadness.

The following are impossible states (ahwal) for a prophet to have:

- Disbelief. They all believed in Allah both before and after their prophethood.
    - The story of Ibrahim (alayhis salam) has to be clarified. The story of him saying that **(The moon is my Lord...)** is a tactic of debate that he employed. It was as if he was saying, "What if I were to say, 'The moon is my Lord..'" but he just dropped the supposition of "what if."
- Severe sickness being defined as anything that would cause people to detract from their status. An example is something that would repulse people. Such as:
    - Leprosy: The sickness that Ayub [Job] (alayhis salam) experienced is not as the Torah mentions. We believe he got sick but not to where his skin was peeling off or that there were worms coming out of his skin.

THE PROPHETS & MESSENGERS

- o Blindness: The event that occurred to Yaqub (Jacob) (alayhis salam) was that a whiteness covered his eyes but he could still see.
- To do the haram, or even think about it. The prophets cannot do the minor (saghira) or major (kabira) sins both before their prophethood and afterward.
  - o Adam's (alayhis salam) eating from the tree. He did not do anything haram. There are explanations about what he did:
    - He forgot the order.
    - He thought the order was mandub. Mandub meaning that it is a recommendation for an act. Performing a mandub act is rewarded while leaving a mandub act is not punished. This differs from an obligatory act in that doing an obligation will be rewarded and leaving it can be punished.
    - He was tricked by the Shaytan and couldn't imagine someone could swear by Allah and be lying. His innocence was like a child in this respect.
    - He was always meant to go into the earth (Quran 2:30). Allah always knew that Adam and his children would inhabit the earth.
  - o The story of Yusuf [Joseph] (alayhis salam) must be clarified in that he never once even thought about doing anything haram with the king's wife. There are two main points that must be understood about this incident:
    - The infatuation of the king's wife for Yusuf (alayhi salam) is described by Allah as being overwhelming her part, while Yusuf's potential interest in the king's wife was prevented from taking root.
    - The supplication Yusuf (alayhi salam) made after the king's wife propositioned him a second time in front of her friends was made because he couldn't see any way out of the situation except prison or giving in to her demands. So he begged Allah for prison as a way to safeguard him from sin.
  - o We reject the stories mentioned in the Old Testament about the prophets doing haram (like the story about Nuh alayhis salam).

Some notes about relating the stories of the Old Testament:

- There is a Hadith where the Prophet ﷺ rebuked Umar (radiy Allah anhu) for reading the Torah for religious guidance. It is understood that this may have been a prohibition during the early days of the Muslims since the religion was

67

still being formulated in terms of beliefs and practice. It could also be understood that the lesson is that Muslims should not allow reading of the previous scriptures (such as the Old and New Testament) to take precedence over reading the Quran. In either case, there is no longer any prohibition in reading the previous scriptures as other Hadith indicate.

- There are a number of Sahih Hadiths that mention the permissibility of reading the scriptures of Bani Israel. The only condition is that we use the Quran and Sunna to judge whether or not they could be true and also that we only affirm the Quran as being free from error.

- Abu Hurayra related that "The people of the Scripture (Jews) used to recite the Torah in Hebrew and they used to explain it in Arabic to the Muslims. On that Allah's Messenger said, **'Do not believe the people of the Scripture or disbelieve them, but say, (We believe in Allah and what is revealed to us .)** (Quran 2:136)'" (Bukhari)

- Abu Hurayra narrated that the Messenger of Allah ﷺ said, **"Relate traditions from the Children of Israel and there is no harm."** (Sunan Abi Dawud).

- And it is said: "There is no harm" means that it should not bother you when you hear strange stories about them (Bani Israel), since many of these events have occurred to them. In terms of how we understand the commend: **'Relate traditions from the children of Isra'il; there is no harm.'** Firstly 'Relate' indicates that it is compulsory, then he ﷺ pointed out that it is not compulsory but permissible when he said 'There is no harm,' meaning no harm in not relating their traditions. And it is said that it means relating traditions about them found in the Qur'an and authentic hadith. And Imam Shāfi'ī said: 'It is known that the Prophet ﷺ did not permit speaking lies when he said **"Relate traditions from the children of Israel,"** thus it is meant that you relate traditions that you know not to be lies: i.e., whatever you find to be compliant with your beliefs then there is no harm narrating those traditions from them. This is in obedience to the Prophet's statement **"Do not believe the people of the Scripture or disbelieve them."** He did not recommend nor prohibit relating those traditions that are known to not be lies.'" (Ibn Hajar Al Asqalani, *Fathul Bari*, Kitab: Ahaadeeth Al 'Anbiyaa', Bab: Ma Thakr 'an Bani Israel, Commentary on Hadith no. 3202)

THE PROPHETS & MESSENGERS

✦ Allah sent us the prophets from His Generosity (fadlihi).

Allah does not have to do anything for us. This rejects the notion that it is an obligation for Allah to send us prophets. We believe that Allah sent us prophets and messengers to guide us. We believe that He sent them to us from His Fadl (Generosity) and not because He had to send them. There are some deviant groups who held the belief that Allah has to do certain things. We reject this notion and belief and hold that Allah does things for us out of His Generosity and Bounty (Fadl).

✦ A prophet is a someone who was given revelation (wahy).

A messenger is a prophet who was given a specific message. A prophet continues the message of a previous prophet. All messengers are prophets, but not all prophets are messengers. The definition of a prophet is a person who was given Revelation (Wahy). This could have been in the form of directly speaking to him, conveying the revelation through the Angel Jibril, or through a Divine dream. Once the person receives this revelation, they are considered a prophet. This differs from the way a "prophet" is presented in the modern Bible (which is sometimes used for anyone who predicts the future, even fortunetellers and soothsayers) or the way people in modern times may define the word "prophet." This is very important because if we ask someone, "Do you believe that Muhammad is a prophet?" They may answer based on their own definition of what a prophet is. This can be a problem since there are some people who consider any spiritual teacher to be a prophet.

✦ A person cannot become a prophet through any means other than Allah choosing them and sending them revelation.

Thus a person cannot think that if they are very good and do a lot of reflection that they can attain the station of prophethood (maqaam an-nabuwwah). What a person can attain through work and self-reflection is the station of sainthood (maqaam al wilaya).

We believe that a person can only be a prophet through receiving revelation from Allah. A person cannot do spiritual works and reflection and achieve the station of prophethood. This is another meaning to the point we mentioned that Allah sent the prophets from his fadl. In other words, He chooses out of His generosity who gets prophethood. It is not something that can be attained (kasb) from the actions of a person. There were certain philosophers in the history of the Muslims who held this belief and considered that a person could have attained the station of prophethood. We reject this belief. What we do affirm, though, is that the station which a person can attain is the station of wilaya (protected friend). If a person does a lot of work, he or she can become a wali (protected friend). Allah can also choose to give wilaya to a person out of His Fadl, without the person having done anything.

◆ All prophets were free men.

Thus, the prophets were never slaves, women, or jinn. One of the things that we affirm is that the prophets were only men who were free. Thus, a slave could not have been a prophet, nor a woman or a jinn. It is not that a slave, woman or jinn can't be a righteous person, but their not being a prophet has to do with conveying the message. One who delivers the message must be able to move around freely in society to be able to deliver the message. A slave does not own the freedom to move around. A woman does not have the same ease of moving around as a man. A jinn would not be accepted by many people, as many people fear the spirits of the unseen. As a proof for this point, the scholars mention the following verses:

(We did not send before you (messengers) other than men from the people of the towns whom We inspired with revelation.) (Quran 12:109)

(And We sent not before you but men to whom We revealed, so ask the people of the Reminder if you do not know.) (21:7)

Many people object here saying, "What about Prophet Yusuf?" Prophet Yusuf (alayhi salam) was a unique case. Everything that happened to him was preparation for his future role. But when he was recognized as a prophet, it was when he was the chief adviser to the king, not when he was *unlawfully* sold in slavery as a child or when he was a young man in the king's household. At the point he was recognized and fully stepped into his role as a prophet, he was the second most powerful man in all of the land.

There are some scholars who accept that a woman could have been sent as a prophet and they use the verses that speak about angels speaking to Maryam alayhas salam and the mother of Musa (alayhis salam). The response to this is that an angel speaking to a person does not necessitate it being revelation (wahy).

THE PROPHETS & MESSENGERS

✦ Allah has given the prophets all human perfection and prevented them from having any human defect.

We believe that the prophets and messengers were human, but they were perfect human beings. This includes matters of their faith and practice, but also of their physical being. We will go into details and examples of these points later in this section.

✦ Allah gave them protection ('isma) from all things that are not befitting of their status.

One of the things that we believe is that they were infallible (ma'sum) and given this protection ('isma) by Allah. The reason for this is that we are ordered to follow the prophets. If the prophets were to sin, then that would be as if we are ordered to follow a sin and that would make the sin a form of worship, which is impossible.

(We did not send any Messenger but to be obeyed by the leave of Allah.) (Quran 4:64)

✦ They do not commit sin, either major (kabira) or minor (saghira) sins. They do not sin before or after their prophethood.

We believe that part of the protection ('isma) that prophets and messengers have been given is protection from committing any prohibited acts. This includes the major and minor sins. This also means that before they were sent as a prophet, they did not commit those sins. We will go into this later in this section. As a note, most prophets were given their prophethood when they were 40 years old, but there are exceptions. 'Isa alayhis salam was made a prophet while he was an infant. There is one narration that Yusuf (alayhis salam) received Revelation while he was in the well and that was when he was a child.

When this point of our belief is mentioned, some people may say, "Well what about when Musa (alayhis salam) killed the man? Or when Yusef alayhis salam thought about the wife of the Aziz?"

For the situation with Musa (alayhis salam), when he pushed the Pharaoh's man away from the Israelite he was abusing, he did not mean to kill him. Musa (alayhis salam) was a very strong man and his push caused the man to fall down and hit his head which caused him to die. So it was not murder. But due to the tense situation between the Egyptians and Jews in the city, Musa (alayhi salam) accidentally killing one of Pharaoh's guards had the potential to cause a backlash for the rest of the Jews and undermined Musa's position in Pharaoh's household.[2]

For the situation with Yusuf (alayhis salam), he never once thought about committing the haram with the wife of the Aziz. When the ayah (12:24) says [literally] that **(She inclined to him and he inclined to her)** this phrase has multiple potential interpretations and we must interpret it within the accepted lines of what is proper belief. The word translated as "inclined" or "desired" by most translators is "hamma (هَمَّ)." It does not necessarily mean "sexual desire" but "to be uneasy, preoccupied, or interested in someone or something." It also is used when you intend or plan to do something. So in this case, one tafsir is that Yusuf's thought was that he planned to hit her in order to get her away from him. The other tafsir is that he *would* have been made uneasy by her **(were it not for the proof of his Lord.)** In other words, if Allah had not given him "the proof," he would have thought about committing sin with her. But since he was protected from sin, he could not even think about doing the haram.

◆ No prophet ever experienced disbelief in Allah, even for the blink of an eye.

Continuing on with this line of belief, if we believe that the prophets cannot do sins, whether minor or major, then we also affirm that they cannot do what is worse than sinning, which is disbelief in Allah. For this reason, we believe that all prophets and messengers were believers in Allah throughout the entirety of their lives, even before they were given their prophethood. I credit my personal knowledge of this point to one of my youngest students.

Years ago, I began teaching children and it gave me one of the most blessed teaching experiences I have ever had and which is why I love teaching children. I took the advice of a friend and fellow seeker of knowledge who was a parent (at the time I did not have children of learning age). He suggested that I teach *Aqida al-Awaam* and *The Stories of the Prophets*, which I did with the 1st to 6th graders I was teaching. When we got to the following story of Ibrahim alayis salam:

(Thus We showed Ibrāhīm the kingdom of the heavens and the earth, so that he might be firm in belief. So, when the night enveloped him, he saw a star. He said, "This is my Lord." But, when it vanished, he said, "I do not like those who vanish." Later, when he saw the moon rising, he said, "This is my Lord." But, when it vanished, he said, "Had my

---

[2] And the scholars say that "The good deeds of the righteous are sins for the ones brought nigh" meaning that people are held by different standards according to their rank with Allah. Prophetic Messengers being the highest of ranks means that their doing things that are against what is best in the situation is like a non-Prophetic Messenger committing an outright sin.

THE PROPHETS & MESSENGERS

Lord not guided me, I would have been among those gone astray." Thereafter, when he saw the sun rising, he said, "This is my Lord. This is greater." Again, when it vanished, he said, "O my people, I disown whatever you associate with Allah. I have, indeed, turned my face straight towards the One who created the heavens and the earth, and I am not one of those who associate partners with Allah.) (Quran 6:75-79)

After I told the story, one little girl in the 2nd grade said, "So Ibrahim alayhis salam was a convert?" At that point I had not thought about the context of the story and what it entails, and I did not want to speak about a point of aqida unless there was a text (nass) which I could refer to as a citation. There is a Mauritanian saying which states, "The one who does not have a nass will remain in darkness flailing" (illi ma 'indahu an nass, yabqa fil dhalma yattammas). So that afternoon when I left teaching, I went to one of my teachers Shaykh Saleck and asked him about the story and whether someone could say Ibrahim alayhis salam was a "convert." Another reason for the quick return to seek out an answer is that I learned a Mauritanian saying which is "The ruling should not spend the night" (Al Hukm la yubat). Meaning, that if you need to know a ruling, you should not let it stay overnight. Go learn, ask, read, etc as soon as possible.

Shaykh Saleck told me that the conversation that Ibrahim alayhis salam had with the people was a tanzil jadali (assumption for the sake of argument). Before going into the story of Ibrahim alayhis salam, we must first understand the idea of tanzil jadali. Usually, a person would explicitly say, "Let's suppose (or assume) for the sake of argument that XYZ is true. If that is the case then ..." and they would continue with the argument showing how it would be false. Another way to begin the argument is to not explicitly state that you are assuming something for the sake of argument, as was the case in the following story about Ibrahim alayhis salam as well as the story of the 99 Ewes (Both of these Quranic stories are covered in the course ADAB 102).

Ibrahim alayhis salam was not saying that he himself actually believed those things (star, moon and sun being Lord) but rather was speaking to a people who did believe it. It was as if he was saying, "Say I were to believe that the stars, moon and sun are my Lord, how can that be, they disappear." About this story, Imam Al-Qurtubi discusses the idea that the messengers of Allah can never, at any point in their life, be other than people of monotheism, knowers of Allah and free of worshipping anything other than Allah. He says:

How can it be that a person would even think that shirk occurred from someone who has been given protection ('isma) and guidance from long ago and showed him the the kingdom so that he may be from those who have certainty. It is not permissible to describe him as not having knowledge [of Allah]. Rather, he knew The Lord at his first glance of reflection. Al Zajjaj said, "This response [that he actually did shirk as a child] is a mistake as Allah has mentioned that Ibrahim said, **(And protect me and my children from worshipping idols)** (Quran 14:35) and Allah has said **(When his Lord brought him with a sound heart)** (Quran 37:84).

I learned all this from a question from a second grader. This is why a major part of learning is teaching. We learn so much from our students and the questions they ask.

✦ There are 124,000 prophets.

There is a Hadith that states that there are 124,000 prophets who were sent. There is another that states the number as being 125,000. They don't contradict each other, as it is possible that the number is an estimation. The point of mentioning the large number of prophets is to say that there are many who we don't know who they are. So if we hear of a people claiming they were sent a prophet, then we can know that it is possible that it is true. The important thing is that we do not deny or affirm someone being a prophet unless we have revelation to support that. The revelation would be from the Quran or Hadith. Finally, let us remember that when we think about the number of the prophets and messengers, that only Allah knows their true and final number. Even the Hadith may be understood to be an approximation.

(Verily We sent messengers before thee, among them those of whom We have told thee, and some of whom We have not told thee; and it was not given to any messenger that he should bring a portent save by Allah's leave, but when Allah's commandment cometh (the cause) is judged aright, and the followers of vanity will then be lost.) (Quran 40:78)

✦ There are 314 messengers.

There is a Hadith stating that the number of the messengers are 314. This is the same number of the Muslims who were at Badr. And this is the same number of the final army of Talut (Saul) before he met Jalut (Goliath).

✦ The first prophet is Adam alayhis salam and the last is the prophet Muhammad ﷺ.

We believe that the first prophet, and the first man, was Adam alayhis salam. The last and final prophet is the Prophet Muhammad ﷺ. Any claims that there are "other final prophets" or "other prophets" after the Prophet Muhammad ﷺ are false and kufr.

THE PROPHETS & MESSENGERS

✦ We know the names of 25 prophets in the Quran.

While there are 124,000 prophets, we only know the names of 25 through the Quran (there are some others known through Hadith). The names from the Quran are also mentioned along with the term "nabiyyeen" usually and so that is how we know them to be prophets. There are other names in the Quran, but they may not have a proof of their prophethood. Below is the list of the 25 listed in the Quran. It is an obligation upon every Muslim to be familiar with the names of these 25 so that if they were to ever hear their name mentioned, they would know that person is a prophet. Memorizing them is a good way to learn them, but it is not an obligation to memorize their names.

One thing that I would suggest as an exercise is to use the index of the Quran that you have and write down the references for where each prophet is mentioned in the Quran. I have made space and lines for you to do that next to each name. You will read their stories in the book that is included as part of this packet. If you would like to learn further stories about them, read Ibn Kathir's "Stories of the Prophets." It is one that uses authentic sources for the stories. Beware of other sources as many contain false narrations about the prophets.

1. Adam_____

2. Idris (Enoch)_____

3. Nuh (Noah)_____

4. Hud_____

5. Salih_____

6. Ibrahim (Abraham)_____

7. Ismael (Ishmael)_____

8. Ishaq (Isaac)_____

9. Lut (Lot)_____

THE PROPHETS & MESSENGERS

10. Yaqub (Jacob) _____

11. Yusuf (Joseph) _____

12. Musa (Moses) _____

13. Harun (Aaron) _____

14. Shuayb _____

15. Ayyub (Job) _____

16. Yunus (Jonah) _____

17. Ilyas (Elias) _____

18. Al-Yasa' _____

19. Dhul Kifl _____

20. Dawud (David) _____

21. Sulayman (Soloman) _____

22. Zakariyya (Zackariah) _____

23. Yahya (John) _____

24. Isa (Jesus) _____

25. Muhammad ﷺ _____

As for Luqman the Wise (Quran Chapter 31) and Iskandar Dhul Qarnayn (Quran 18:83-101), they are not prophets, but rather they are from the awliya. There is a difference of opinion about Al-Khadir alayhis salam (Quran 18:65-82). We should not say definitely one way or the other.

Now that we have mentioned that there are 124,000 prophets, and that we don't know who all of them are, and that there are only 25 named specifically in the Quran, what about the people who are also mentioned in the Quran? There are others named in the Quran, such as Luqman, Iskandar and Al Khadir. There is not an additional proof that they were prophets, so most of the scholars say that they were righteous protected friends of Allah (awliya) but that they were not prophets. There are other scholars who say they were in fact prophets. The safest thing is to say "Allahu alim (Allah knows best) about their status" and neither affirm nor deny their prophethood.

✦ We affirm that the best and greatest of all the prophets and messengers is our Messenger Muhammad ﷺ.

While we recognize that there are many prophets, we know that some of the prophets are better than others. When this is mentioned sometimes, there are people who will quote the verse 3:84:

(Say (O Muhammad): We believe in Allah and that which is revealed unto us and that which was revealed unto Abraham and Ishmael and Isaac and Jacob and the tribes, and that which was vouchsafed unto Moses and Jesus and the prophets from their Lord. We make no distinction between any of them, and unto Him we have surrendered.)

The response and clarification to this verse is the verse 17:55:

(And thy Lord is Best Aware of all who are in the heavens and the earth. And we preferred some of the prophets above others, and unto David We gave the Psalms.)

What the first verse means is that we do not distinguish in the sense that we do not say one man is a prophet and another is not a prophet. An example of this would be what the Jews did by saying Musa alayhis salam is a prophet, but not 'Isa alayhis salam and Muhammad ﷺ. Or the Christians who deny the Prophet Muhammad ﷺ but affirm Sayyiduna Musa and Sayyiduna Isa alayhimus salam. So we do not distinguish in their prophethood but we can distinguish in their preference given to them by Allah, as is mentioned.

As for the proofs of the Prophet Muhammad ﷺ being the greatest of all prophets, there are many. One of the most famous is the Hadith, **"I am the master of the children of**

THE PROPHETS & MESSENGERS

Adam but no boasting." Other facts proving he is the greatest are that, Allah honored him with special gifts that He gave no other person such as:

- Al Liwa ("The Banner") on the day of Judgment;
- Al Hawd ("The Basin") on the day of judgement;
- Al Wasila ("The Means") according to a Hadith it is the highest station in Jannah which **"[I]s allowed for a slave of the slaves of Allah, and I wish that it will be me,"** said the Prophet Muhammad ﷺ;
- The Greatest Shafa'a/Intercession: Various people and Angels will be given the ability to intercede on behalf of certain numbers of people. Of all the various types of intercession, there is one that is the greatest;
- Al Fadila ("The Virtue") of being made the best of all creation;
- Isra wa-l-Mi`raj ("The Night Journey and Heavenly Ascent") which is explained later in this text.

The gifts and preference given to the Prophet Muhammad ﷺ are so many that many books of fiqh actually have sections in them called "Baab al Khasa'is" (The Chapter of Specifics). These sections list out the many things that were specific to him ﷺ.

Not only was he given things that were specific to him, but even his ummah was given things that no other ummah were given. Because this ummah is tied to the greatest of all messengers, we became the greatest of ummahs. Imam Al Busayri eloquently mentions this point in his famous poem, Al Burda. One of the things that distinguishes us is that we memorize our Book. The previous ummahs were able to preserve their book through tablets and scripture. As for us, **"Their injeels are in their hearts"** as the Hadith mentions. Other things that are specific to us are:

- Prayer does not have to be made only in the houses of worship. The entire earth has been made a masjid for us.
- We can do tayammum if we do not have water. The previous nations did not have this option.
- When a portion of our clothing gets impurity (najasa) on it, we can wash it off with water. Previous people had to cut that section out. This is what is referred to as **(The burden placed on those before us)** (Quran 2:286)

THE PROPHETS & MESSENGERS

♦ The Seal of the Messengers (the last prophet sent) is the Prophet Muhammad ﷺ. No new messenger or prophet will ever be sent after him.

We believe that there is no prophet after the Seal of the Messengers, the Prophet Muhammad ﷺ. Anyone who believes that is possible has committed disbelief (kufr). To suggest that there is a prophet after him would be to reject a clearly stated verse in the Quran:

(Muhammad is not a father of any of your men, but he is a messenger of Allah and the last of the prophets. And Allah has the Knowledge of everything.) (Quran 33:40)

Those who believe that any person after the Prophet Muhammad ﷺ are prophets have committed kufr and are not to be considered Muslims. We pray that they correct their beliefs and come to Islam; the one, true and only Islam.

♦ Isa alayhis salam will return and be from the Ummah of the Prophet ﷺ.

We believe that Isa alayhis salam will return at the end of time to slay the Imposter Christ (masih al dajjal). He will also clarify to the Christians his true status. He will show them that he is a Messenger of God, a slave of God and not the son of god. Allah (God) says in the Quran,

And he (Jesus عليه السلام) shall be a Sign (for the coming of) the Hour (of Resurrection); therefore have no doubt about it (the Hour). And follow me (Allah), this is a Straight Path." (Quran 43: 61)

Ibn Abbas has said that the meaning of this verse is that Prophet Jesus' عليه السلام descent is a sign of Qiyamah. (Musnad Ahmad) Huzaifa bin Usaid reported that Prophet Muhammad ﷺ suddenly came to us while we were talking. He asked, "What are you talking about?" We replied "We were talking about the Last Hour." Prophet ﷺ said, **"It will never come until you see ten signs before it. He then mentioned the Smoke, the Dajjal (Anti-Christ), the Daabba, the Rising of the Sun from the place of its setting, the Descent of Jesus son of Mary, Yajuj and Ma'juj (Gog & MaGog)..."** (Sahih Muslim)

Abu Huraira narrated that Prophet Muhammad ﷺ said:

There is no prophet between me and him (Jesus Christ ﷺ). He shall descend so, recognize him when you see him. He is a man of medium height, (his complexion) is between reddish and white; he will be between (or dressed in) two slightly yellowish garments; His head looks as if it is dripping water even though it is not wet. He will fight people in the cause (for the sake) of Islam, will break the Cross and kill the swine (pig) and abolish Jizya (tax on Christians and Jews); and Allah will put an end to all religious sects except Islam during his (Jesus') time. He (Jesus) will slay the Antichrist (Dajjal) and he will stay in the World for 40 years. Then, he will die and the Muslims will perform the funeral prayer for him. (Abu Dawud and Musnad Ahmad)

Prophet Muhammad ﷺ also said:

In the meantime, while the Dajjal will be busy doing this and this, Allah will send down the Messiah son of Mary (Jesus ﷺ). He (Jesus ﷺ) will descend in the eastern part of Damascus, near the white minaret (tower), dressed in the two yellow garments, with his hands resting on the arms of two angels. When he will bend down his head, water drops will appear trickling down, and when he will raise it, it will appear as though pearl-like drops are rolling down. Any disbeliever whom the air of his breath reaches, and it will reach up to the last limit of his sight, will fall dead. Then, the son of Mary will go in pursuit of the Dajjal, and will overtake him at the gate of Lud, and will kill him. (Sahih Muslim, Abu Dawud, Tirmizi, Ibn Majah).

Prophet Muhammad ﷺ said in another narration:

The Dajjal (Anti-Christ) will appear in my ummah (nation), and will live for forty. Then Allah will send Jesus son of Mary ﷺ. He (Jesus ﷺ) will closely resemble 'Urwah bin Masud (a Companion of Prophet Muhammad ﷺ). He (Jesus ﷺ) will pursue him (Anti-Christ) and kill him. Then, for seven years, the people will live in such a state that there will be no ill-will or enmity between any two individuals of them. (Sahih Muslim).

Since there are so many Hadith reporting his return, it is something that we must believe in. As a side note, I was once with a Christian relative of mine and when he learned that Muslims believe in the Second Coming of Christ, he was very surprised at first. He said that he had never learned that we believe in this. He felt that this could be a unifying factor between Muslim and Christian communities, regardless of their specific beliefs about Isa alayhis salam. Before his pointing this out to me, I only used to mention to Christians that we believe in Isa alayhis salam. Now I make it a point to mention that we not only believe in him, but we are also waiting for his return.

One thing that I point out when speaking about the return of Isa alayhis salam is the following Hadith: **"When 'Isa returns to the earth, he will marry, have a son, live for about 40 years, and die. He will be buried beside me."** (Tirmidhi, Mawahib) When 'Isa was originally here, he did not marry. But in his return he will marry. This should be a motivating factor for any parent of a girl to raise a righteous woman. Who knows? Maybe she could be the bride of a Messenger of Allah.

✦ We do not distinguish between any of the prophets in that we do not reject some and accept others (Quran 2:285).

- The Jews accept Musa alayhis salam and reject Isa alayhis salam and the Prophet Muhammad ﷺ.
- The Christians accept Musa and Isa alayhimus salam but reject the Prophet Muhammad ﷺ. We accept them all, upon them and upon our prophet be the peace and blessings of Allah.

This point was discussed earlier.

✦ We do recognize that some prophets are higher in rank than others (Quran 2:253).

There are five who are the Resolute Messengers (ulil 'azim see 46:35 and 42:13). Some of the scholars have preferred to remain silent about who exactly the five are. Others have mentioned them and their ranks. Their ranking also indicates their level:

1. Muhammad ﷺ and he is Habib Allah (The Beloved one of Allah)
2. Ibrahim (Abraham) alayhis salam and he is Khalil Allah (The Friend of Allah)
3. Musa (Moses) alayhis sala and he is Kaleem Allah (The one Allah spoke to) because Allah spoke to him with speech that does not resemble created speech.
4. Isa (Jesus) alayhis salam and he is Ruh Allah (The Spirit of Allah)
5. Nuh (Noah) alayhis salam and he is Naji Allah (The one Allah saved)

One very important thing to note about the names of the Messengers above (alayhimus salam), is that we have to consider Allah above any similarity to creation. So, when we say that

Muhammad is the Habib of Allah, we remember and affirm that Allah does not have feelings the like of His creation. His Love is not like our love. Our love is an emotion that can change and has a beginning and is created. Similarly, when we say that Ibrahim is the "Friend of Allah" we should negate any similarity of that friendship with the concept we can imagine, feel or have about friendship. Finally, and a point very relevant in our times, is that when we affirm that 'Isa is the Ruh of Allah, we are not saying that he is created from Allah, rather it is the possessive form to indicate that he belongs to Allah. This is similar to saying Baytullah for the Ka'bah in that "House of Allah" means that it belongs to Allah and not that it is His house where he resides.

After the five greatest messengers the remaining ranks are:

1. The remaining messengers. Thus, a messenger is higher in status than any prophet who is not a messenger.
2. The remaining prophets. All of the prophets supercede any other righteous person.
3. The specific angels which are the angels that are specifically mentioned and we know their names, duties and ranks. They include:
    a. Jibril
    b. Mika'il
    c. Israfil
    d. 'Izrail
4. The Sahaba. They are the ones who met the Prophet Muhammad ﷺ, believed in him and passed away with that belief. This definition is given to exclude those who became Muslim after his passing and those who apostated. You will notice the definition did not say "see" the Prophet and rather says "met" or in Arabic, literally "were with" (Ar. ijtam'a). We must make this distinction because there were Sahaba who met and believed in him, but did not actually see him because they were blind (such as Ibn Umm Maktum).[3] Also those who believed in him while he was alive but did not actually meet him are not considered to be from the Sahaba, like in the case of Uways al Qarni. There is the following ranking of virtue amongst the sahaba:
    a. The ten promised paradise
    b. The people of Badr
    c. The people of Uhud

---

[3] This also could theoretically apply to Companions who were so young that the Prophet ﷺ met them when they were infants, but passed away before they were old enough to have remembered meeting him.

THE PROPHETS & MESSENGERS

    d. The people of the Pledge of Ridwan
5. Tabi'een. They are the ones who met a Sahabi and passed away as a Muslim.
6. Tabi' at-Tab'een. Those who met a Tabi'i.
7. The remaining people of the ummah. The members of this ummah are better than the members of any previous ummah.

From amongst the women of the world, the best are:

- Khadija Al Kubra (The Great), the wife of the Prophet Muhammad ﷺ
- Maryam Al 'Adhraa (The Virgin), the mother of 'Isa alayhis salam
- A'isha, A Mother of the Believers, the wife of the Prophet Muhammad ﷺ
- Fatima Al Batul (The Chaste and Pure) and Al Zahra (The Shining One), the daughter of the Prophet Muhammad ﷺ and a "piece of him" according to the Hadith
- Aasiya, the wife of Fir'oun

Some important notes about our belief in Isa alayhis salam is that:

- He was born from Maryam the Pure and he did not have a father.
- He is not God nor is he the "son of God" as the Christians say.
- He was sent as a prophet and a messenger and given a book (Injeel).
- He was not crucified as the Christians believe. Rather, Allah made another person appear to the people as if he was Isa and they crucified that other man.
- He was saved by Allah ﷻ and then raised into the sky where he dwells now, alive, never having died.
- He will return to slay the Dajjal at the end of time.
- He will live with the Muslim ummah, marry, then pass away and be buried next to the Prophet Muhammad ﷺ.
- And his pure mother, Maryam, will be a wife of the Prophet Muhammad ﷺ, in janna.[4]

---

[4] It is mentioned in a few narrations that Lady Maryam, along with Lady Aasiya (wife of Pharaoh), will be married to the Prophet (Allah bless him and give him peace) in Paradise. For example, Abu Umama (Allah be well pleased with him) said that the Prophet (Allah bless him and give him peace) told our Mother 'A'isha, **"Verily, Allah will marry me in Paradise to Maryam the daughter of Imran, Kaltham the sister of Moses, and [Aasiah] the wife of Pharaoh."** (Tabarani) Although the narrations have some weakness in them, they are not fabricated and are mentioned by the likes of Hafiz Ibn Kathir, Allama Suyuti and Imam al-Tabarani. Due to their subject matter, they are considered to be historical reports and thus there is no obligation to either believe or reject them. We have decided to promote them since they involve a further honoring of both women

THE PROPHETS & MESSENGERS

✦ We cannot claim someone is a prophet unless there is proof from the Quran or a Hadith.

To claim that someone is a prophet when they are not really a prophet is kufr. To deny any prophet who actually is a prophet is kufr. If there is a person that could or could not be a prophet, we should just say "Allah knows best." An example of where this would be applicable is the case of Buddha or any other figure mentioned in the writings of other religions and people saying that a person was a messenger or teacher of divine truth. While we can reject the teachings which contradict Islam, we can't say for sure that he was originally a prophet or was definitely not a prophet. We can say that there is a possibility that he was a prophet and that his teachings were changed, just as the Jews and Christians changed the teachings of Musa and Isa (respectively), alayhimus salam.[5]

✦ We believe the prophets were given miracles (mu'jizat) for them to prove to their people that what they were saying was truly from Allah.

"Their miracles are as if Allah said, 'This servant has spoken the truth in all that he says.'" (Ibn 'Ashir) One of the things that we believe is that the prophets were given miracles to aid in convincing their people that they are sent by Allah with a message. The name for a miracle given to a prophet is a mu'jiza.

To use an example of a king, say a person stands up and says, "I am the messenger of the king and to prove this, the king has given me his crown to show everyone, something which he does not give to anyone normally." So the king sets a normal rule, which is that only he has the crown, and then he allows the rule to be broken to show others that this is his appointed

---

in the Afterlife and there is no evidence that obligates us to reject them. Rationally speaking, since Pharoah is without question one of the people of the Hellfire, Lady Aasiya (may Allah be well pleased with her) could not be married to him in Paradise. Similarly, the Qur'an makes no mention of Lady Maryam (may Allah be well pleased with her as well) having married anyone after she gave birth to Isa ibn Maryam (peace be upon him) and so we affirm her perpetual virginity, but only in this world. In the Afterlife, we do not believe it is unbefitting of her station to be married to someone who fits her level of righteousness and there is no one who fits her level of righteous except for the Prophets and Messengers. So we believe, as you may as well, that part of the reward for both of these noble women is the companionship of the Prophet (Allah bless him and give him peace) in Paradise for all eternity as compensation for the trial they were put through in this world. And Allah knows best.

[5] This only applies to people who lived before Prophet Muhammad alayhi salam obviously. It is not possible for anyone after Prophet Muhammad to be given that title and so we do not say "Allah knows best" for people who lived after our Prophet's earthly life. Isa ibn Maryam is an exception, but he will not have the role of a prophet when he returns.

messenger. In a similar way, Allah has rules that govern the way the world and universe operate, but He allows those rules to be changed by the prophets as miracles to show that they are Messengers sent from Allah. A good example of this is that normally, the dead don't come back to life. But in a miracle given to the prophets, He allows it to happen. In the case of the Prophet Muhammad ﷺ, he brought his parents back to life and they believed in him.[6] In the case of Isa Alayhis salam, he also brought the dead back to life as well as curing the diseased.

These miracles would sometimes come in the form similar to, but greater than, something that was common to their people at their time.

- At the time of Musa alayhis salam, magic was at a height. So, his miracle resembled some of the magic that was perfected at that time but was clearly not magic as was attested to by the experts of magic.
- At the time of Isa alayhis salam, medicine was at a height and at the forefront of people's respect. He came with miracles of healing the sick and bringing the dead to life when no other medicine could do the same.

---

[6] Although many Muslims are unaware of this incident, this occurrence is well known to the scholars of hadith. Our Mother `A'isha (Allah be infinitely well pleased with her) said,

> The Prophet ﷺ descended to Ḥaggūn in a depressed and sad mood and stayed there as long as Allah wanted him to do so. Then he came back in cheerful spirits. I asked him: "O Messenger of Allah! You descended to Ḥaggūn in a depressed and sad mood and stayed there as long as Allah wanted you to do so, then you came back in cheerful spirits. [What happened?]' He replied, "I asked my Lord - Glorified and Exalted – and He brought my mother back to life, and she believed in me. Eventually, Allah returned her back (to her former condition).'"

Even though this hadith is weak, versions of it are cited in the discussion on whether or not the Prophet's ﷺ parents are in Paradise or Hell. Among those who do are Allama Suyuti, Imam al-Qurtubi, Hafiz Ibn Kathir and Imam Sakhawi. This question was debated by the scholars because there are authentic narrations in which the Prophet ﷺ *seemed to suggest* that his parents are in the Hell, while on the other hand, an argument can be very easily made based on the Qur'an that they are from "Ahl al-Fatra" and thus "immune to prosecution" so to speak. Now is not the place to get into detail about the evidence both sides present (we discuss it in a bit more detail in IMAN 101), but suffice it to say that there are in fact strong arguments against affirming a bad end for the Prophet's ﷺ parents. Regardless, it is a difference of opinion that is not a major point of belief and therefore should not be a point of contention among the Believers. The Prophet's parents being in Paradise is the position that we uphold and the Prophet's ﷺ parents being resurrected to bear witness to their son's successful mission is a miracle that we believe happened. If anyone disagrees with us, that is fine. We have no ill-feelings towards anyone who does not believe this incident took place. But in our estimation, the Prophet's parents being in Paradise is the stronger position. That being said, since it is not an essential matter of belief, there is no need to argue over it. And while we do not condemn anyone who feels that the other position is stronger, the motivations of anyone who insist on making an issue out of this should be seriously called into question.

- At the time of Salih, alayhis salam, his people had perfected carving homes from the stone mountain. The miracle that he was given was bringing a live animal from the stone mountain.
- At the time of the Prophet Muhammad ﷺ, Arabic poetry and language was at its height. His greatest miracle was the Quran which overshadowed anything that the people had at that time.

This concludes the fundamental beliefs we all should know related to the Prophets and Messengers. Before moving on, I would like to mention that we have included a summary of the book *The Lives of the Prophets* at the very end of this coursebook. Please read that chapter as a supplement to what has been mentioned here. While this chapter has mentioned the general beliefs that we should have about all the Prophets, that final chapter discusses some of the more important points that we all should know about them individually.

The Angels

In this section I will discuss the core tenets of our belief about Angels. However, like the previous chapter on the Prophets, this chapter is also supplemented at the end of our coursebook by a summary of a unique work written about Angels by Shaykh Abdul Hamid Kishk. The summary will give you a lot more details about them. So read that summary and know its contents well! The points mentioned in this chapter will act as a guide for the bare minimum of what you should know—the skeleton if you will—while that chapter will fill in information that further adds to your understanding—or the flesh and muscles. In other words, even if you don't remember all the contents of the summary of Shaykh Abdul Hamid's work, but you know the points mentioned below, you will have covered your fard al-ayn (individual obligatory) knowledge about the Angels.

✦ Angels are a creation of Allah that were created to worship Allah.

We believe that Angels are a living creation of Allah. We reject the notion of some modernist that Angels are no more than a form of light. We believe them to have a soul and have the ability to move around just like any living creature. The only difference is that they were created to worship Allah and they do not have the ability to choose other than to fulfill the commands of Allah.

✦ They are made of light.

We believe that they are made of light. Just like humans are made from clay, but are not exactly like clay and just like jinn are made from fire but do have a form that is not exactly like fire. The original matter of each was something but the final form may differ.

One thing that Angels can do is shapeshift. It is for that reason that they can take the form of a human and may even take the form of an animal. It is mentioned by the scholars that if they take the form of an animal, they only take noble animal forms. Unlike Jinn who can shapeshift, but may take the forms of various creatures including bugs, snakes, and lizards. As a note, it is for this reason that the Prophet forbade the killing of non-poisonous snakes in Medina as they may be a visiting Jinn which is not meaning harm.

✦ They are neither male nor female. They do not have a mother or father. They do not marry nor do they have children.

We believe that the Angels are neither male nor female. They do not need to have a gender because their creation is not dependent on procreation, rather Allah creates them without the need of a mother or a father. When Allah wills to create them, they are brought into creation without the need of birth.

To believe that Angels are female is a form of disbelief (kufr). This is one thing that the kuffar of Quraysh were reprimanded for by Allah in the Quran.

(So ask them, "Does your Lord have daughters while they have sons?" Or, had We created Angels as females while they were witnessing? Beware! They are the ones who, by way of a lie of theirs, (have the audacity to) say, "Allah has children" - and they are absolute liars. Is it that Allah has chosen daughters (for Himself) instead of sons? What is the matter with you? How (arbitrarily) do you judge? Then, is it that you do not think about it? Or, is it that there is some open authority with you? Then bring your book, if you are truthful. And they have made up between Him (Allah) and the Jinns some kinship, while the Jinns already know that they are bound to be seized. Pure is Allah from what they describe!) (Quran 37:149-159)

In the same way, we should not say that Angels are males. Even though we refer to them in the masculine form (he, his, etc) in both Arabic and English, we do not believe the Angels to be males. It is just that in Arabic, there are only the masculine and feminine forms when referring to things, and so one is chosen to be used. It would be prohibited (haram) to refer to the Angels using the feminine pronouns.

Although most scholars allowed a boy to be given the name of an Angel, Imam Malik was of the opinion that using an Angel's name for a boy is makruh (disliked) because we do not want people to think that Angels are males. This ruling of Imam Malik should also make us think about being careful to not use the Latin forms of Angels that are given to girls.

✦ They do not eat food or drink water.

We believe that Angels do not need to eat or drink. Their sustenance is through glorifying Allah (tasbih). Take a look at the story of the "Guest of Ibrahim" and see at which point was it that Ibrahim realized that they were Angels. Why was it that he knew that to be a sign of Angels. Once you have found the ayah, reference it here: _____

✦ They obey all the commands of Allah and never disobey Him (reference Ayah). They cannot even think about wanting to do sin.

Allah (SWT) in the Quran says about that Angels:

(O you who believe, save yourselves and your families from a fire, the fuel of which is human beings and stones, appointed on which are Angels, stern and severe, who do not disobey Allah in what He orders them, and do whatever they are ordered to do.) (Quran 66:6)

Therefore, we reject all stories which include a reference, whether explicit or implicit, that the Angels disobeyed Allah or that they even have the ability to disobey Allah. So when we come to the story of Iblis (Satan), we do not say that he is a "fallen Angel," rather we affirm that he is from the Jinn and not from the Angels. This is explicit in the Quran:

(And (remember) when We said to the Angels; "Prostrate to Adam." So they prostrated except Iblis (Satan). *He was one of the jinns*; **he disobeyed the Command of his Lord. Will you then take him (Iblis) and his offspring as protectors and helpers rather than Me while they are enemies to you? What an evil is the exchange for the** *Zalimun* **(polytheists, and wrong-doers, etc).)** (Quran 18:50)

We even find an account of him describing what he was created from and that it was not light which the Angels were created from:

(It is We Who created you and gave you shape; then We bade the Angels prostrate to Adam, and they prostrate; not so Iblis; He refused to be of those who prostrate. (Allah) said: "What prevented thee from prostrating when I commanded thee?" He said: "I am better than he: Thou didst create me from fire, and him from clay.") (Quran, 7:11-12).

There are some verses in the Quran which say that Allah ordered the Angels to prostrate and that all but Iblis did not.

(And (remember) *when We said to the Angels*: **"Prostrate yourselves before Adam." And they prostrated** *except Iblis (Satan)*, **he refused and was proud and was one of the disbelievers (disobedient to Allah).)** (Quran 2:34)

THE ANGELS, BOOKS, AFTERLIFE, QADR & THE UNSEEN

This should not be seen as a proof that he was an Angel, as it is well-known in Arabic that you can exclude something from a group that is not from the group. As an example, it is proper to say in Arabic, "The townspeople all came except for the donkey." It would be known that the donkey is not from the townspeople, but he is included in the group because of a connection to the townspeople. So by merely having that connection, you can then be included in the group to be excluded from them. In the same way, Iblis was connected to the Angels in that he was allowed in their presence, and he worshiped in the heavens like them, but he was unlike them in that he was a jinn and had the ability to choose.

✦ We do not know how many Angels there are in total.

We do not know the total number of Angels and we know that they can be constantly created. So there is an untold number of Angels.

✦ Some Angels only worship.

We know that some Angels only have the duty to worship, and that's what they do for untold amounts of time. They are created and begin to worship and will continue that way until the Day of Judgment.

(To Him belong all those in the heavens and the earth. And those who are near to Him are not arrogant against His worship, nor are they sluggish.) (Quran 21:19)

One of the most powerful stories of this type of worship which humbles me is the following Hadith narrated in the Tafsīr of Ibn Kathir:

Verily Allah has Angels whose flanks shiver out of fear of Allah. There is not a single one of them except that if a tear flows from his eye it will fall on an Angel who is praying. And from amongst them are Angels who are in prostration from the time that Allah created the heavens and earth. They do not raise their heads, and they will not raise their heads, until the Day of Resurrection. And from amongst them are Angels who are bowing (ruku') from the time that Allah created the heavens and earth. They do not raise their heads, and they will not raise their heads, until the Day of Resurrection. Then, when they finally raise their heads, they will look to Allah (Exalted and Mighty) and say, "Glory be to You, we have not worshipped You as You deserved to be worshipped!"

THE ANGELS, BOOKS, AFTERLIFE, QADR & THE UNSEEN

The Arabic for what the Angels said is the following, in case you would like to memorize it and use it in your prayers and dhikr:

$$\text{سُبْحَانَكَ! مَا عَبَدْنَاكَ حَقَّ عِبَادَتِكَ}$$

(Glory be to You! We have not worshipped You as You deserve to be worshipped)
[Subḥānaka mā ʿabadnāka ḥaqqa ʿibādatik]

✦ Some Angels have specific duties.

While there are countless Angels only doing worship and countless others with jobs that only Allah knows who they are and what their jobs are, there are 10 Angels who we know specifically. Just like each Muslim has to know the 25 prophets mentioned in the Quran, we also must know the 10 Angels listed below.

1. Jibreel (Gabriel) عليه السلام: The Angel who brings Revelation;
2. Mika'eel (Michael) عليه السلام: The Angel who brings rain and sustenance;
   a. Sustenance is anything that you can get benefit from. So this could be food, clothing, knowledge, *etc.*;
3. Israfeel عليه السلام: The Angel who blows the Trumpet;
4. Izra'eel عليه السلام: The Angel who takes the souls at death;
5. Munkar &...
6. Nakeer عليهما السلام: The Angels who ask the initial questions in the grave;
7. Malik عليه السلام: The Keeper of the Hellfire;
8. Ridwan عليه السلام: The Keeper of Jannah;
9. Raqeeb &...
10. Ateed عليهما السلام: The general name for the Angels who record our deeds on our right and left side;
    a. The Angel who writes good deeds down writes them down immediately and the deed is multiplied 10-700 times or more.
    b. The Angel who writes the bad deeds is told by the other Angel to not write down a bad deed once it happens. The person is given 6 hours to repent (tawbah) and then if that is not done the deed is written down.
    c. We have guardian Angels that protect us (hafadha). This could be as few as two (our Noble recorders) or even 400 or more according to the Hadith.
    d. Allah does not need the Angels to protect us.

e. If we were to lose our Angelic protection even for an instant we would be crushed by unseen forces that are trying to harm us.

✦ To increase Angelic protection we have to increase the things Angels like:

We can end this section on Angels by talking about how to increase their presence around us. There are things that they like and things that they don't like. We should know these things so that we can increase the Angels who are around us. We should also know what they do not like so that we do not disrespect them. One thing to note is that the Raqeeb and Ateed (the Angels who are assigned to us), can never leave us until we pass. So when we talk about increasing the Angels presence, we are talking about the Angels other than them.

There is a Hadith that states that the Angels assigned to us either like us or they do not. If we do good actions, then they like us and will make dua for us to have a longer life so that they can be with us and write down and witness our good deeds. If we sin constantly, then they make dua for Allah to give them relief from having to be associated with us. The way that they are relieved is for us to pass away. That is not something we want an angle to be making dua for, so we should be vigilant about not sinning.

The following are things that the angles like:

- Good actions
- Dhikr
- Being properly covered with clothing
- Good smells
- Clean mouth (both in smell and not saying bad words)

And some of the things the Angels do not like are:

- Sins
- Bad smells
- Dogs[1]
- Images[2]

---

[1] When they are being used as pets or companion animals, as opposed to their being used as work animals.

[2] That is imagines of animate life. There is a difference of opinion about what "images" refers to. Some say it refers to all types of images (including photographs), while others say that it only refers to statues since the term in Arabic can mean both. But even those scholars who say that it only refers to statues agree that things like photographs should not be put in places of honor (such as being hung on the wall in a frame). On the flipside,

- Music
- Nakedness

---

those scholars who say that photographs are haram exclude things like photographs for passports and driver's licenses.

The Books

✦ Allah sent books to His messengers.

One of the pillars of faith for Muslims is to believe that Allah has sent books to us through His Messengers. There are a number of books and scriptures which were sent. We know the names of some of these, and there are others we don't know. They were sent in various languages.

✦ It is revelation (wahy) that is sent to the Messengers.

Here it is important to clarify what we mean by revelation (wahy). Wahy is considered to be a message from Allah that, when sent, the medium is not able to be corrupted by any form and is thus related to the people in the exact way that Allah sent it. Once it is received by the prophet, it is exactly as Allah sent it. Once the prophet transfers it to his people, they can corrupt or distort it and that is why we have lost all the previous revelations. The only exception to this is the Quran, since it has been protected by Allah. To give an example of something that is not wahy, let's look at dreams.

Dreams can be given to a person directly by Allah, or from an Angel, from the devil or from the self. A dream from Allah or the Angels is called a righteous dream (ru'ya saliha).

Anas bin Malik narrated that The Messenger of Allah said, **"A good dream (that comes true) of a righteous man is one of forty-six parts of prophetism (*nubuwwa*)."** (Bukhari)

Now, even though a person can receive a dream from Allah, it is not considered wahy. This is why it is only one of 46 parts of prophethood. One of the main reasons is that a person who is not a prophet is susceptible to the devil, while the prophets are protected from the devil. So when the prophets receive revelation, that communication is not hindered. Another reason is that prophets don't forget what they are given in their dreams, whereas people who are not prophets will likely forget details of their dreams. Here are two Hadith from *Sahih Al-Bukhari* about the sleep of the prophets:

Abu Salama bin `Abdur-Rahman narrated that he asked `Aisha "How was the prayer of Allah's Apostle in the month of Ramadan?" She replied, "He used not to pray more than eleven rak`at whether in Ramadan or in any other month. He used to offer four rak'at, let alone their beauty and length, and then four rak'at, let alone their beauty and length. Afterwards he would offer three rak'at. I said, 'O Allah's Apostle! Do you go to bed before offering the witr prayer?' He said, '**My eyes sleep, but my heart does not sleep.**'"

Sharik bin 'Abdullah bin Abi Namr said I heard Anas bin Malik telling us about the night when the Prophet was made to travel from the Ka'ba Mosque. Three persons (i.e. Angels) came to the Prophet before he was divinely inspired as an Apostle), while he was sleeping in Al Masjid-ul-Haram. The first (of the three Angels) said, "Which of them is he?" The second said, "He is the best of them." That was all that happened then, and he did not see them till they came at another night and he perceived their presence with his heart, for the eyes of the Prophet were closed when he was asleep, but his heart was not asleep (not unconscious). This is characteristic of all the prophets: Their eyes sleep but their hearts do not sleep. Then Gabriel took charge of the Prophet and ascended along with him to the Heaven.

So wahy is more than just receiving Divine Dreams or Divine Inspiration, that can happen to a non-prophet. But only the prophets received wahy.

The book or scripture which is sent, regardless of the language, is completely the word of Allah and does not include anything on behalf of the messenger receiving the word. So when we look at the modern version of the Bible, what we find is that it is a collection of what is claimed to be the Word of God, along with historical notes, commentary of early Christians, sayings of 'Isa Alayhis salam. Whereas when we look at the Quran, we find the Book to only have the Word of God. For commentary (tafsīr) that is another collection of information which we consider separate from the Quran. For historical notes (tarikh) that is separate. For sayings of the Prophet Muhammad ﷺ, that is found in the collections of sunna and Hadith (even though we consider it to be a form of revelation). The Modern Bible has all of these things together in one book and does not distinguish between them.

✦ There is no revelation to anyone after the Prophet Muhammad ﷺ.

Just as we believe that there is no prophet after the Prophet Muhammad ﷺ we also believe that revelation ended with him. No person now can receive revelation after him. The way that people claim revelation after him is in a number of ways. Some people will actually claim to have a book revealed to them and other people will claim to have divine revelation guiding their speeches and lessons. Some people will claim to have dreams that teach them.

One may even find Muslims who do not outright reject Islam or its core teachings, but will change things based on what they consider to be divine dreams or inspiration. The key to remember about any claim is that we weigh it on the scales of the Quran and Sunna.

✦ The book or scripture was written down, it could be read and recited but it is the Speech of Allah (*kalamul Allah*) and does not resemble the speech of humans or jinn.

We believe that the books of Allah are His Speech. Whether this is the Torah, Injil, Zabur or Quran, they are all the Speech of Allah. Thus, they are considered to be attributes of Allah and are pre-eternal. The books that we hold in our hands or read with our tongues have a connection to Allah, but we do not say that the created form that we hold in our hands is an attribute of Allah. We also must affirm that all the books, since they are the Speech of Allah, do not resemble the speech of humans or jinn.

✦ There are four books that we have to recognize were sent.

Just as we know and affirm the 25 prophets in the Quran, the 10 Angels, we also affirm the four books that we know were sent down. The following four books were sent:

- Torah (Torah) was given to Musa
- Psalms (Zabur) was sent to Dawud (David)
- Gospel (Injil) was sent to Isa alayhis salam.
- Quran (Furqan) was given to the Best of Messengers, Muhammad ﷺ

✦ All the books have been changed or lost except the Quran as Allah has promised to preserve it (Quran 15:9)

Some changed their books intentionally while some changed by mistake or portions were lost. We have the Quran preserved by isnad. Isnad is a khasiyya (special trait) only given to this ummah. Memorization of the Quran is a khasiyya of this ummah. No previous people were given a book that they memorized. They preserved their books in the written form. The ummah of Muhammad ﷺ is described in the books of the previous people as "anajeeluhum fi sudurihim" meaning "Their injeel (Holy Book) is in their hearts."

Allah also preserved the sciences needed to unlock the Quran such as Hadith, Arabic, Fiqh, Seera, Tafsīr, etc. So just as we believe the Quran to be preserved, we also believe that all the sciences needed to preserve, unlock and understand the Quran are also preserved.

✦ We believe in everything mentioned in the Quran.

One of the main beliefs that we have is that we believe in everything mentioned in the Quran. If a person says, "I believe in Allah, the prophets, the Angels and the books, but there is one ayah from the Quran I reject," that person would not be Muslim. We have to accept everything in the Quran. We may say that we don't understand something, but we cannot reject something.

I was once studying with Murabit al Hajj and was going over a section of the Quran that I was memorizing. It was a sura that mentioned the name of Egypt (Misr in Arabic). I asked him, "If someone were to deny the existence of Misr, would that take them out of Islam?" He said, "Yes, because they rejected a portion of the Quran." This is in contrast to if someone denied the existence of a land not mentioned in the Quran, like Idaho for example. Even though we would consider that person foolish, we could not say that he was not a Muslim for denying something. He only denied something established through human knowledge, whereas denying something in the Quran is to deny something established by Divine Knowledge.

There are some ayahs in the Quran that are ambiguous (mutashabih) and we do not try to explain these. The other ayahs are clear (muhkamat) and we can understand and explain these.

(He is the One who has revealed to you the Book (the Qur'ān). Out of it there are verses that are MuHkamāt (of established meaning), which are the principal verses of the Book, and some others are Mutashābihāt (whose definite meanings are unknown). Now those who have perversity in their hearts go after such part of it as is mutashābih, seeking (to create) discord, and searching for its interpretation (that meets their desires), while no one knows its interpretation except Allah; and those well-grounded in knowledge say: "We believe therein; all is from our Lord." Only the men of understanding observe the advice.) (Quran 3:7)

THE ANGELS, BOOKS, AFTERLIFE, QADR & THE UNSEEN

Ibn ʿAbbās said:

God sent down the Qurʾān according to four ways of reading (aḥruf): the lawful (ḥalāl) and the unlawful (ḥarām), ignorance of which nobody is excused; the interpretation (tafsīr) according to which the Arabs have interpreted it; the interpretation according to which scholars (ʿulamāʾ) have interpreted it; and the ambiguous (mutashābih), which none but God, Exalted is He, knows, and whoever claims knowledge of it other than God, Mighty and Majestic is He, is lying.

ʿAlī said,

[Those rooted in knowledge] are the ones whom knowledge has protected from plunging [into the interpretation of the Qurʾān] according to some whim (hawā) or with set arguments (ḥujaj maḍrūba) without [awareness of] the unseen [mysteries] (ghuyūb).' [This is] due to God's guidance of them, and His disclosing to them His unseen secrets from within the treasure chests of knowledge. Thus they said, We believe in the Book; all of it is from our Lord [3:7]. So God, Exalted is He, acknowledged them [in this verse], and made them among the people of profound and far-reaching knowledge, as an increase granted to them from Him. Just as God has said, Exalted is He, But say: 'O my Lord! Advance me in knowledge [20:114]'.

About the mutashabih, Imam Shafiʾi used to say:

I believe in what *Allah* revealed according to the meaning that *Allah* willed, and in what the Messenger of *Allah* conveyed according to the meaning that the Messenger of *Allah* willed.

THE ANGELS, BOOKS, AFTERLIFE, QADR & THE UNSEEN

Let's look at some traditional tafsīr of this verse. In the Tafsīr of Jalalayn, it says:

(He it is Who revealed to you the Book, wherein are verses [that are] clear) lucid in proof **(forming the Mother Book)** the original basis for rulings **(and others allegorical, whose meanings are not known)** such as the opening verses of some sūras. He [God] refers to the whole [Qur'ān] as: (1) 'clear' [muhkam] where He says [a Book] whose verses have been made clear [Q. 11:1], meaning that it contains no imperfections; and as (2) 'allegorical' [mutashābih], where He says a Book comsimilar [Q. 39:23], meaning that its parts resemble each other in terms of beauty and veracity. **(As for those in whose hearts is deviation, inclination away from truth, they follow the allegorical part, desiring sedition)** among the ignorant of them, throwing them into specious arguments and confusion **(and desiring its interpretation, its explanation, and none knows its interpretation)** its explanation **(save God)** Him alone. **(And those firmly rooted)** established and capable **(in knowledge)** ("al-rāsikhūna fī'l-'ilm" is the subject, the predicate of which is [what follows]) **(say, "We believe in it)** the allegorical part **(that it is from God, and we do not know its meaning; all)** of the clear and the allegorical **(is from our Lord"; yet none remembers)** (yadhdhakkar, the initial tā' [of yatadhakkar] has been assimilated with the dhāl), that is, none is admonished **(but people of pith)** possessors of intellect, who, when they see those following that [allegorical part only], also say **(Our Lord, let not our hearts deviate)**...

We will end this section with a note on who can do tafsīr. Only the people of knowledge are allowed to give explanations of the Quran and Hadith. We go to the qualified living scholars or the verified books of the scholars. For an explanation of this ruling, I will use a section from my lecture on this topic taken from ADAB 102 (Prohibitions of the Tongue):

THE ANGELS, BOOKS, AFTERLIFE, QADR & THE UNSEEN

In the next line, Muhammad Mawlud continues discussing other prohibitions of the tongue that are related to the Quran and Hadith. He says: It is prohibited to give an explanation of the Quran or Hadith based on an opinion that is not based on sound narration.

So to give tafsīr, to give explanation of the Quran or the Hadith based on your own opinion, that is not relying on a sound narration and it is considered from the prohibitions of the tongue. It is also considered haram. And the reason for this is that when you give an explanation of the Quran or Hadith you are saying 'this is what Allah meant'. You are putting yourself as a representative of Allah subhanahu wa ta'ala or his Messenger sallallahu 'alaihi wasallam, and saying this is what the ayah says and I'm going to explain exactly what he meant by this or what the Prophet sallallahu 'alaihi wasallam meant by this, so if you're not basing it on sound knowledge, on a sound narration, you could be, and most probably you would be, misrepresenting what Allah subhana wa ta'ala or his Messenger sallallahu 'alaihi wasallam is saying and therefore you are changing the revelation as the Bani Israel did with the Torah and the Christians changed with the Injeel and so that person would be in the same category and that's made very dangerous for a person to work towards or to do something that would be changing the Quran.

Now, some people say, well if I speak Arabic, especially if I am a native Arabic speaker, if I read the Quran and it makes sense to me why can't I explain it? One person came to my teacher, Murabit al-Hajj and he asked him that same question. He said I am a native speaker of Arabic, I read the Quran, why can't I explain it? Murabit al-Hajj said I will give you a basic quiz. He mentioned to him an ayah from Surah Al-Rahman (55:6) and said 'Wa najmu wa shajaru yas judan' the najm and the shajr yas judan, they both make prostration. Now if you ask most people what is meant by this ayat, when they hear the word najm they're going to think the star, the star in the sky, because najm is a word for the star but if you look at Surah al-Rahman, the entire surah, or the majority of the surah, is talking about pairs. The salt water and the freshwater, the rising of the sun and the setting and the sun, the jinn creatures and the humans. And so now you come to this ayat and it mentions the star and the tree prostrates to Allah subhana wa ta'ala. What is the pair between them? Well the proper understanding is that the najm is a name, although it can also be used for a star, it's the name for a tree that has no trunk. In Arabic, what we call in English a vine, could be called a tree. Like what is called a grape vine is called shajaru al 'aynab, a grape tree. But, the difference between it and other trees is that if the grape tree is left alone it cannot stand up, it does not stand up on its own. It has to climb upon something. You have to stand up a lattice work or you have to build something for it to climb upon, for it to grow upon. So that's a tree that cannot stand up on its own and so the Arabs call that al-najm whereas the shajar is the tree that can stand up on its own. So the najm and shajar is the vine, the trunkless tree, and the tree that has a trunk, they are both in a state of prostration to Allah subhana wa ta ala. So of course, at that point, the person realised that a seemingly simple ayat had a deeper meaning that he did not have access to because of his lack of knowledge and so therefore he had to recognise that he did not have the authority to give tafsīr of the Quran.

THE ANGELS, BOOKS, AFTERLIFE, QADR & THE UNSEEN

The same goes for the Hadith. A person cannot give an explanation of a Hadith unless they have heard it from a sound source, a scholar, or they have read it in a reliable source and at that point they could relay the meaning. If they feel like they have some understanding of an ayat in the Quran or a hadith and they feel like this may be a correct understanding, they can check it with a scholar and then they can relay it as an explanation of the Quran because there are things, there are secrets in the Quran that are revealed to every generation. So, if a person feels that they have an understanding of the Quran, they should check it with reliable sources, and then they can relay it as an explanation of the Quran, but not until they have done that due diligence of checking with authorities.

✦ The following prophets were sent scriptures (suhuf): Ibrahim alayhis salam and Musa alayhis salam.

See if you can find this reference in the Quran and write it here: _____

✦ The Prophet Muhammad ﷺ was given the Quran, which is the Clear Guidance. Additionally, he was given other forms of revelation (*wahy*), which translate into his words (*hadith*), actions (*amal*), and tacit approval (*taqreer*). These three things are called the Sunnah.

It is very important to note that just as revelation can come in the form of the Word of God as in the Quran, revelation can also come in the form of the sunna of the Prophet Muhammad ﷺ. Allah says about His prophet in Surah Al-Najm:

(By the star when it goes down to set, your fellow (the Holy Prophet) has neither missed the way, nor did he deviate. He does not speak out of (his own) desire. It is but revelation revealed (to him).) (Quran 53:1-4)

Imam al Qurtubi mentions that this verse is a proof that the Sunna is like revelation. If a person asks the question, "Why didn't the Prophet Muhammad ﷺ ever make a tafsīr on the Quran?" The answer is that his life was the tafsīr. Aisha said, "His character was the Quran." So if we want to know the Quran, we have to study his sunna.

✦ Just as we follow the revelation of the Quran, we have to follow the Sunna.

We believe that just as we must follow the Quran, which is revelation, we must also follow the Sunna, which is another form of Revelation. Aisha, radiya Allahu anha, was asked about the character of the Prophet Muhammad ﷺ and she said, "His character was the Quran." So if we want to know about the Quran, we have to look to his character, actions and speech to get an explanation. If anyone says that we do not have to follow the Sunna and that the Quran is sufficient, ask them where does it tell you a Muslim must pray five times a day? It's in the Sunnah, not the Quran. The Quran just says to pray and gives three general parts of the day.

Ibn 'Abbas said that there are three "double orders" in the Quran. What this means is that for the order to be fulfilled, you have to fill both parts of the order:

- Obey Allah and His Messenger (Quran 4:59)
- Thank Allah and your parents (Quran 31:14)
- Establish the prayer and give zakat (Quran 31:4)

The importance of following the sunna is such a part of faith, that Ibn Abi Zayd included the following statement in his text the Risala, which was written over 1200 years ago: " Belief is not complete without action, no actions is considered without an intention, and no action or intention is considered unless it is in line with the Sunna."

THE ANGELS, BOOKS, AFTERLIFE, QADR & THE UNSEEN

The Final Hour

✦ We believe the final hour will come once the trumpet is blown by Israfeel alayhis salam. There are many signs before the End of Time, some are large and some small.

The coming of the Prophet Muhammad ﷺ is the first sign of the end of times. He is the Prophet of the End of Times. There are many signs of the end of times and usually each Hadith collection will include a chapter on the signs. Knowing the signs of the end of times is an important part of the deen of Islam. A proof for it's importance is that fact that it was one of the four things that were asked about in the Hadith Jibril. If you are interested in learning more about this topic, there are a number of good books about it. One of the most authentic is *Al-Tadhkira* by Al-Qurtubi. An abridged version of that book has been translated into English.

✦ Large signs include:

- The Mahdi
  - Muhammad al-Barzanji said, in his book al-Ishaa'ah li Ashraat al-Saa'ah: "The major signs and the signs that will be immediately followed by the Hour: these signs are many, of which the Mahdi will be the first. Know that the ahaadeeth that have been narrated about him in various reports are numerous." He also said: "You know that the ahaadeeth which speak of the Mahdi, his appearance at the end of time, and his lineage and descent from the Prophet (Peace & Blessings of Allah be upon Him) via Faatimah reach the level of tawaatur in meaning, so there is no point in denying them."
- The return of 'Isa alayhis salam who will kill the dajjal.
- Yajooj and Majooj
  - See Sura Kahf
- Dajjal and the Jassasah
- Rising of the sun from the West
- The closing of the door of repentance
- The coming of the Dabba (talking beast)

- **(When the word will come to fall upon them, We will bring forth for them a beast from the earth who will speak to them that the human beings (i.e the infidels) did not believe in Our signs.)** (Quran 27:82)
  - In the Tafsīr of Jalalayn it says: And when the word [of judgement] falls upon them, [when] they deserve that chastisement befalls them as well as all [other] disbelievers, We shall bring forth for them a beast from the earth which shall speak to them [saying], that is, which shall speak in Arabic to those who are alive at the time when it appears, among its other statements, it will say to them on Our behalf: 'Indeed mankind had no faith in Our signs', in other words, they did not believe in the Qur'ān and what it comprises [of the mention] of resurrection, reckoning and requital. With its [the beast's] appearance the enjoining of decency and forbidding of indecency will cease, and thereafter no disbeliever will believe — just as God revealed to Noah [when He said to him]: None of your people will believe except he who has already believed [Q. 11:36].
- The removal of the Quran and knowledge from the pages and from the hearts.
- The destruction of the Ka'bah

✦ **Small signs include:**

- Barefoot, unclothed shepherds competing to build tall buildings.
- Women being clothed and unclothed at the same time.
- Children disrespecting their parents.
- Murder becomes rampant.
- The embargo on Iraq and Sham.
- Increase of alcohol, silk clothing, music and adultery/fornication (zina)

THE ANGELS, BOOKS, AFTERLIFE, QADR & THE UNSEEN

Akhira

In the next few sections, I will discuss some of the stages of the afterlife, from death and beyond. We must believe in all stages of the afterlife that have been explained to us through the Quran or in Sound Hadiths. One of the pillars of faith mentioned in Hadith Jibril is believing in the "The Last Day" which also includes belief in all the things that happen after death. We cannot merely say that we believe in Allah, His messengers, His Angels, His books but say that we don't know what will happen in the afterlife.

To learn what are the stages of the afterlife, there are some very good books that cover the topic in detail. I mentioned the *Tadhkira* of Al-Qurtubi (and there is an English version of the abridged form of the text). There is also a book called "The Lives of Man" by Imam al-Haddad which I encourage you to get. It goes over all the stages of a person's life, from before conception to the life in Heaven or Hell. One of the things that both of these aforementioned books do is cite Quran and Hadith for the descriptions that they give. This is very important, in fact utterly crucial, and brings me to the next point about belief in the afterlife and other matters of the unseen (ghayb).

The matters of the afterlife (akhira) and unseen (ghayb) can only be verifiably transmitted if they have come through revelation (wahy) and the only ones who get revelation are prophets. Therefore, what we hear from saints and through dreams of people is not something that is incumbent to believe and it must always be checked against the Quran and Hadith. I have seen some people who speak about the unseen and the afterlife and speak from an Islamic viewpoint, but really they are just philosophizing and presenting their own theories. Speaking without knowledge of the unseen is very dangerous.

<u>Death</u>

The first stage of the afterlife is death and it is the "lesser Final Hour." One of the reasons that we should think about death is that it will motivate us to take our lives seriously.

'A'isha (may Allah be pleased with her) who said: "Some tough men among the Bedouin came to the Prophet ﷺ and asked him when the Hour would be. He would look at the youngest of them and say: **"If this one lives, old age will not catch up with him until your Hour begins."** Hishaam [one of the narrators of the hadeeth] said: This means their death. (Bukhaari, 6146 and Muslim, 2952).

Al-Qaadi said: What was meant by "your Hour" was their death; meaning that generation would die, or that those who were being addressed would die. (Quoted from *Sharh Muslim* by al-Nawawi.)

Al-Karmani said: This answer was very wise, *i.e.*, it was a wise way of telling them not to ask about the time of the greater Hour, for no one knows that except Allah; rather they should ask about the time when their generation would come to an end; it is more appropriate to know this because it will motivate you to keep doing righteous deeds before it is too late, because none of you knows who will die before the other.

Al-Raaghib al-Isfahaani said: The word saa'ah (hour) means a portion of time and is used to refer to the Resurrection, to indicate that the Reckoning will be very swift. Allah says, **(And He is the Swiftest in taking account)** (al-An'aam 6:62). Or it may indicate the meaning stated in the following verse, **(On the Day when they will see that (torment) with which they are promised (i.e. threatened, it will be) as if they had not stayed more than an hour in a single day.)** (al-Ahqaaf 46:35)

The word saa'ah is used to refer to three things: al-saa'ah al-kubra (the greater Hour), which is when the people will be resurrected to face the Reckoning; al-saa'ah al-wusta (the middle Hour) which is the death of a generation; and al-saa'ah al-sughra (the lesser hour) which is a person's death. So the Hour of each person is his death. (From *Fath al-Bari* by Ibn Hajar)

In terms of our belief about death, we affirm that no one dies except by the decree (qadr) of Allah. Even though the means in which people die might be many, all of them come from the decree of Allah. Everyone has an appointed length to their life (ajal) and when that time comes, there is no way around it. The following story of Sulayman alayhis salam who used to visit with the Angels of Death helps remind us of this fact:

It is narrated that one day, a man entered the court of Prophet Solomon (alayhis salam), looked around at all the people and went out again. When the court adjourned, one of the people present approached Prophet Sulaiman (alayhis salam) and asked him whether he knew this strange man. "The person you saw was the Angel of death (Izrael)" replied Prophet Solomon (alayhis salam). The man was taken aback and looked worried. "Why was he staring at me as though he wanted to take my soul?" he asked. "What do you want me to do?" enquired Prophet Sulaiman (alayhis salam). "O Solomon!" exclaimed the man. "You have power over the wind. Command it to transport me to the land of Hind (India)." As the man was a believer, Prophet Solomon (alayhis salam) agreed and granted his wish. A few days later, Prophet Solomon (alayhis salam) saw the Angel of death again. He asked him why he had been staring at the man so intently on that particular day. "O Solomon!" replied the Angel of death. "Allah (SWT) commanded me to take the soul of that man on the soil of Hind. When I saw him sitting in your court, I could not understand how I could carry out

THE ANGELS, BOOKS, AFTERLIFE, QADR & THE UNSEEN

Allah's order. Nevertheless, as it was a divine command, I left for Hind and fortunately found the man there. I took his soul as Allah (SWT) had commanded."

We believe that the souls are taken at the time of death by the Angel 'Izraeel, alayhis salam, who is responsible for taking the souls of all animate life. The souls are taken from the believers gently while they are severely ripped from the disbelievers.

(I swear by those [Angels] who pull out [the souls of the infidels] with extreme force, and by those [Angels] who untie the knot [of the souls of the believers] smoothly.) (Quran 79:1-2)

We do not delve into discussion about the soul (ruh) rather, we say **(The soul is a matter from my Lord)** and He knows where it is, what it is made of and where it resides (*i.e.*, all the details about it). (Al-Isra 17:85)[3]

The souls are everlasting and are either rewarded or punished forever. We do not say that the martyrs are dead, rather they are living and the Lord provides their sustenance (Al-Baqarah 2:154). Like the martyrs, and even more important than them, is that we believe that the Prophets are not dead, rather they are living in a way we cannot comprehend.[4] Refer to the story of the Isra where Musa alayhis salam was seen in the red hill praying, then in Jerusalem, then in the highest heaven. How could he be in all those places and yet be dead in his grave? This makes it clear that we do not comprehend the matters of the Afterlife and the Unseen.

After death, two Angels (Munkar and Nakeer) come and awake the dead person to ask him the Questions of the Grave. They are frightening and have voices like thunder. They ask three things, "Who is your Lord?" "Who is Your Prophet?" "What is your religion?" and "What is your book?" Those who believed during their lives will be given the strength and firmness to answer.

---

[3] This verse is sometimes translated as **(The soul is by the command of my Lord)** and while this translation is technically accurate, some people try to distort the meaning of this phrase to imply that the soul is uncreated or "part" of Allah. This is kufr. When you say "such-and-such min amri Rabbi" in Arabic, it is akin to saying "Go ask Allah about the soul, it is His business, not mine!" Meaning what Shaykh Rami says above: Allah is the One Who knows where it is located, what it is made of and how it functions. Those details are beyond our comprehension.

[4] Meaning that we do not deny that the prophets no longer live in this world, but they are in the Intermediate Realm (Barzakh) experiencing a type of existence that is similar to their life in this world and they are not necessarily confined to their graves in the same way that most other people are. This is clear from the several hadiths which described what the Prophet alayhi salam witnessed during Al-Isra wa al-Mi`raj where he actively interacted with the previous prophets in the Unseen realm. This is discussed in the next section.

For the believers who did good there will be a reward in the grave and it will hug him or her like a mother hugs their child. For the non-believers and the disobedient Muslims, there will be a punishment in the grave. The grave will squeeze them. We believe that sadaqa, dua and recitation of Quran reach and benefit the dead.

> Narrated by Abu-Huraira (may Allah be pleased with him): 'Allah's Messenger (May Allah exalt his mention and protect him from imperfection) said: "When the son of Adam dies no further reward is recorded for his actions, with three exceptions: charity whose benefit is continuous, knowledge from which benefit continues to be reaped, or the supplication of a righteous son (for him)." (Muslim)

This Hadith is an encouragement to establish sadaqa jariya for the dead Muslims. I remember when my father passed away in 2007, I visited Mauritania soon after. When I spoke to my shuyukh and told them of his passing, they each said that they would recite the Quran from memory once and give the reward to my late father. One of my shuyukh, Murabit Ahmed Fal, told me to do something for my father every morning and evening.

He told me to recite Sura Ikhlas 10 times in the morning and 10 times in the evening. He said before the recitation to make dua that the recitation I am about to make is intended for my father. Then, after finishing it, that I make dua that the recitation I just did was for my father. In this way, he said, the reward is sure to get to him because we know that it is the "supplication of the son" for the father. Since that time, I have been regular in doing this, and it has allowed me to maintain a relationship and connection with my father. You will learn more in the ADAB 101 course about what you can do for your parents once they pass away.

A final note about my father is that he loved teaching. His last student in this life was a brother who I initially met while visiting a state prison in California. Once the brother got out and got a job, he wanted to study Arabic and asked my father if he would teach him, which he did. On the day of the funeral, maybe because everything was happening so fast, I did not have tears to shed until I hugged Faruq. I told him, "You were my father's last student." My advice to those whose parents are still alive; spend as much time as you can with them. Serve them, watch them, learn from them. Ask for advice and stories from their life. May Allah have mercy on my father, Abu Faisal. Please make dua for him.

<u>NOTE</u>: While preparing this course material, Faruq sent me an email with salam and a dua. I shared with him the above section on this course to which we replied, ""I will do the same Shaykh Rami [i.e. Make dua]. For he was my first Shaykh....Ameen...Thank you for such

a beautiful jewel..." Then, during one of the last ten nights of Ramadan, he sent me this message:

Bismi Allahir Rahmaanir Raheem. Salaatu wa Sallam alay siyyadinaa Muhammad Ibn Abdullahi Khatimah Nabi'eenah Imaam Mursaleen Salay Allah alaihe wa sallam...Tonight I ask Allah to grant me success in riding the horse of the night for my niyyat is to gift all the reward and blessings out of it to my spiritual father and shaykh of the Arabic language Abu Faisal. May Allah strengthen him in the grave for the questions in regards to who is Lord , what's your Deen & who is Muhammad is a severe Affair.....Today we are brothers by mean of lineage to Abu Faisal yours zahir (outer) mine baton (inner). Next life brothers at the Basin....Inshallah.....maa salaam shaykh.

Then a follow-up dua of, " Oh Allah grant forgiveness and mercy to my shaykh Abu Faisal. And accept what was done giving all reward to him...By Your mercy and by means of the tasleemah upon your Beloved Salay Allah alaihe wa sallam...Amen. Ramadan 25th. 1437AH."

I mention this story to illustrate the connection that learning creates. You learned about this in the ADAB 100 course, and now you see a living example of how learning brings people together who previously did not have a connection. I also am mentioning it to show the loyalty of a student to his teacher. My father is in his grave and myself and my siblings make dua for him. But we are not alone, we have his students who also make dua for him. This story should encourage you to teach, so that you have people who will remember you once you pass on. Also, you should be encouraged to make dua for those who taught you.

Barzakh

This is the state where souls are after they die and before the Resurrection (Qiyama). During this time, the soul will either be getting a reward or a punishment, depending on it's state:

(It is the Fire before which *they are presented morning and evening*. And on the day when the Hour (of final judgment) will take place, (the order will be released,): "Admit the family of Pharaoh into the most severe punishment.) (Quran 40:46)

People in their graves can hear the voices of the living who come to visit them. They can even hear the sound of the sandals of the people as they walk away.

It was narrated from Anas (may Allah be pleased with him) that the Prophet (peace and blessings of Allah be upon him) said: "When a person is placed in his grave and his companions leave him, **and he can no longer hear the sound of their sandals (footsteps)**, two Angels come to him and make him sit up, and they ask him, 'What did you say about this man Muhammad (peace and blessings of Allah be upon him)?' He says, 'I bear witness that he is the slave of Allah and His Messenger.' It is said, 'Look at your place in Hell which Allah has replaced for you with a place in Paradise.'" The Prophet (peace and blessings of Allah be upon him) said, "And he sees them both. But as for the kaafir or hypocrite, he says, 'I do not know, I used to say what the people said.' It is said, 'You did not know and you did not follow those who knew.' Then he is struck a blow with an iron hammer between his ears and he screams a scream which everything around him can hear apart from the two races (of mankind and the jinn)." (Narrated by al-Bukhaari, 1222)

Anas ibn Malik narrated to us: he said:

Allah's Prophet (Allah bless him and grant him peace) said: **"Verily when the servant is put in his grave, and his companions turn away from him, he hears the noise of their sandals."** (Sahih Muslim)

Ibn 'Umar narrated that:

The Messenger of Allah spoke to the People (buried) in the Well saying: **"Have you found out that what your Lord had promised you is true?"** Then someone exclaimed: "Are you calling out to the dead!" The Prophet replied: **"You do not hear better than they do, except they do not respond."** (*Sahih Bukhari, Volume 2, Book 23, Number 452*)

This halfway life, where they can hear and yet not respond, is what we are referring to when we say the barzakh. This is the life they live until they are either given eternal life in the hellfire or in heaven. There is one exception to the path of punishment or reward, there are those who are in the 'Araf.

'Araf

This is a place that is not jannah or jahannam. Some people will reside in here for a time and then go to janna. It is mentioned in a Hadith that there is a group of people that did some good things but they disobeyed their parents in going out to do that good. So, they have good deeds and bad deeds and that's why they have to wait in this place before going into janna. Imam Al Qurtubi said:

The scholars discussed the people of the 'Araf and there are ten opinions about them. Abdullah ibn Masud, Hudhayfa ibn Al Yamani, Ibn Abbas, Al Shu'bi, Al Dahhak, and Ibn Jubayr all said, "They are people whose good deeds and evil deeds are equal." Ibn 'Atiya said, "In the Musnad of Khaythama bin Sulayman (in the end of the 15th volume) there is a Hadith on the authority of Jabir bin Abdullah who said, 'The Messenger of Allah (sal Allahu alayhi wa sallam) said, 'The scales will be set down on the Day of Resurrection and the good deeds and sins will be weighed. Whoevers good deeds outweigh the sins by the weight of the egg of a louse will enter Paradise. And whoevers sins outweigh their good deeds by the weight of a louse's egg will enter the Hellfire." It was said to him, "O Messenger of Allah, what about the people whose good deeds and sins are equal?" He said, "Those are the people of the 'Araf; they will not enter Paradise but will covet it."

The people of the 'Araf are discussed in the following tafsīr:

After Allah mentioned that the people of Paradise will address the people of the Fire, He stated that there is a barrier between Paradise and the Fire, which prevents the people of the Fire from reaching Paradise. Ibn Jarir said, "It is the wall that Allah described, (So a wall will be put up between them, with a gate therein. Inside it will be mercy, and outside it will be torment.) 57:13 It is also about Al-A'raf that Allah said,(and on Al-A'raf will be men)." Ibn Jarir recorded that As-Suddi said about Allah's statement, (And between them will be a screen) "It is the wall, it is Al-A'raf." Mujahid said, "Al-A'raf is a barrier between Paradise and the Fire, a wall that has a gate." Ibn Jarir said, "Al-A'raf is plural for 'Urf, where every elevated piece of land is known as 'Urf to the Arabs." As-Suddi said, "Al-A'raf is so named because its residents recognize (Ya'rifun) the people. Al-A'raf's residents are those whose good and bad deeds are equal, as Hudhayfah, Ibn 'Abbas, Ibn Mas'ud and several of the Salaf and later generations said." Ibn Jarir recorded that Hudhayfah was asked about the people of Al-A'raf and he said, "A people whose good and bad deeds are equal. Their evil deeds prevented them from qualifying to enter Paradise, and their good deeds qualified them to avoid the Fire. Therefore, they are stopped there on the wall until Allah judges them." (Tafsīr of Ibn Kathir)

Ba'th

The trumpet is blown by the Angel Israfeel whose only duty it to blow the horn. With the blowing of the trumpet, everything will die and everything will be destroyed. Nashr is the Arabic term for when all animate life (humans, jinn, animals, insects, etc.) will be resurrected from their graves and their bodies will come back to its original form. Hashr- All will be brought together on the plain of standing on the Day of Standing (Yaum al qiyamah). There are many frightening things that will occur on that day and these are called "hawl" (ahwal is the plural).

Everything will be turned to dust except for humans and jinn. This is what is being referred to at the end of Sura Naba' (Al-Naba 78:18-20).

It was narrated by 'Abd ar-Razzaaq in his *Musannaf*, by Ibn Jubayr, and by al-Bayhaqi in *al-Ba'th* from Abu Hurayrah, that he said concerning the verse (interpretation of the meaning), **(There is not a moving (living) creature on earth, nor a bird that flies with its two wings, but are communities like you. We have neglected nothing in the Book, then unto their Lord they (all) shall be gathered)** [al-An'aam 6:38]: All creatures will be gathered on the Day of Resurrection, animals, beasts, birds and everything. Then Allah's justice on that day will reach such an extent that Allah will settle the score for the hornless animal with the horned one. Then He will say, "Be dust," at which point the disbeliever will say: **(Would that I were dust!)** [an-Naba' 78:40].

The believers will gaze upon Allah during the Standing and in Jannah. We should not delve into how this "gaze" will occur but remember that Allah does not resemble creation so looking at Him will be in a way that is different than looking at creation. The people of the Hellfire will not gaze at Allah. Some will take their books in their right hands (the people who did good) while others will take it in their left hands or behind their backs (the people who did bad).

✦ The Scales (Mizan)

All humans and jinn will have their actions weighed on the scales. The actions are recorded in a person's book (kitab, suhuf). Every person and even animals, which are owed a right, will be given it on the Day of Judgment. If another harms a person, the victim will take from the perpetrator's good deeds. If there are not any good deeds to take from, then the victim will give him his bad deeds.

✦ The bridge (Sirat)

All humans and jinn will cross over a bridge that is finer than a hair and sharper than a sword. The bridge is set up across the Hellfire. Some will cross like lightening, some like the wind, some like a fast horse, some will run, and some will fall into the Hellfire.

THE ANGELS, BOOKS, AFTERLIFE, QADR & THE UNSEEN

✦ The Basin (Hawd)

The Prophet Muhammad ﷺ is given a Basin on the Day of Judgment to give his community (*ummah*) water to drink from. Whoever drinks from it will never be thirsty afterwards. The drink is sweeter than honey and whiter than milk. It's distance is that of Medina to Yemen and its cups are like the stars in number. Only those Muslims who did not innovate will be allowed to drink.

✦ The Intercession (Shafa'ah)

Some people, starting with the Prophet Muhammad ﷺ will be allowed to intercede on behalf of some believers that will headed to the Fire or in it. After the Prophet ﷺ, other prophets intercede. Others that will intercede include martyrs (shuhada'), teachers, and those who memorized the Quran. The Prophet ﷺ will intercede for the people of his ummah that did kaba'ir.

✦ Paradise (*Janna*)

It is a created place that is in existence now. It will remain forever as an everlasting reward for those who believed in Allah.

✦ Hellfire (Jahannam)

It is a created places that is in existence now. It will remain forever as an everlasting punishment for those who disbelieved in him.[5] Allah knew before He created anything, who would go into Heaven and who would go into Hell. We do not say that anyone is definitely going to Janna or Jahannam unless there is an Ayah or Hadith (like Abu Lahab or Firoun). We

---

[5] Imam Tahawi says "Paradise and Hell are two created things that will not perish and not come to an end." The opinion that the Hellfire shall come to an end eventually is an aberrant opinion and is impermissible to believe in, no matter who may have said it. The scholars are in agreement over this point and making taqlid to anyone in a matter of aqida is not permissible. We go into detail in IMAN 101 about how this false opinion is disproved by the Quran and Ahadith beyond any reasonable doubt. However, it should not really be necessary. Scholarly consensus has formed around this fact based on the implications of verses like: **(They will wish to leave from the Fire, but they will not leave from it; theirs will be a lasting punishment.)** (Al-Ma'idah 5:37) **(Whoever joins other gods with Allah, then surely Allah has forbidden him the Garden and the Fire will be his abode.)** (Al-Ma'idah 5:72) We can have a discussion about the Arabic, but **(They *will not leave* from it)** and **(Then *surely* Allah *has forbidden* him the Garden)** are perfectly clear and unambiguous declarations. If someone claims that the Hellfire will eventually come to an end, even after a very long time, then they are in fact saying that people will exit from it and thus, these two verses are lies, no matter how hard someone may try to distort the meaning of verses such as these that are perfectly clear.

can say that we feel that a person was good or bad and that he may be rewarded or punished. Only Allah knows the final state of people and whom He will forgive and who He will not forgive.

Some people will live their whole lives as a Muslim then leave Islam at the end of their life. Some people will live their life as a non-believer and then accept Islam in their final moments. But we may not know that this occurred. We should regularly ask Allah to give us the best seal (khatimatan hasana) which is to die as a Muslim. The people who are believers and go to jahannam for bad actions they did will not stay there forever. (4:48) No believer will stay in jahannam forever, even if there faith (iman) was the weight of a speck. We should pray for the forgiveness for all Muslims and for guidance for all humanity.

Qadr (Divine Decree)

We must believe that everything happens because of the decree of Allah (qadr). We believe all things, whether sweet or bitter, good or bad, happen because of the decree of Allah. This is something referred to explicitly in the Hadith of Jibril when the Prophet ﷺ said, "It's good and evil." Thus, we must refrain from making statements such as "Only good comes from Allah." We believe that everything is by the decree of Allah. Although we also refrain from attributing certain things to Allah out of adab, or respect.

I will give you an example from something that I learned during my first year of studies in Mauritania when I was studying Arabic grammar (nahw). In the section on the "mabni lil majhul" (verb where the doer/subject is not mentioned). For the sentence "Zayd was hit" you would say "duriba zayd." There are a number of reasons that a person would use this form, such as not knowing the doer or not wanting to mention his name. One of the reasons they list for not wanting to mention the name of the doer is when having respect for the Name of Allah. So, for example, if we are talking about the animals that were created, then when we come to the pig, we should say, "The pig was created." In this way, we do not mention the name of Allah in the same sentence. In the same way, when we are talking about the Qadr, just because we believe that everything happens by the decree of Allah, we should not mention His Name along with it.

We do not say that Allah decrees only good and that bad is from us. This insinuates that we can create our own actions, which is false. Allah creates all actions. Surah al-Safat states, **(He created you and that which you do)** which includes both the good and the bad.[6]

A term that you should be familiar with is sa'eed and shaqi. These terms are mentioned in a Hadith mentioned as Hadith #4 in the 40 Hadith of Imam Nawawi. They are basically terms that mean believer and non-believer:

Verily the human's body is brought together in the womb of his mother for 40 days as a drop. Then it becomes a clot of blood for the same amount of time and then like a morsel for the same amount of time. Then an Angel is sent to blow a spirit into him and that Angel is given four orders; to write his sustenance, lifespan, actions and whether he will be wretched (*shaqi*) or blissful (*sa'eed*).

---

[6] That being said, we must keep in mind that "good" and "bad" are relative terms that apply only to human beings and jinn. It does not apply to other orders of creation that have no moral responsibility, let alone the Creator of everything in existence. "Good" and "bad" are designations that Allah characterizes our actions with, they do not apply to Him. And our doing "good" and "bad" deeds is a consequence of freewill and is intimately connected to it. So the idea of "good" and "bad" must be seen in its proper context.

Some people are believers (sa'eed) because that is what was decreed for them and others are decreed as non-believers (shaqi). Allah makes whoever He wants to be a sa'eed or shaqi. However, each is judged according to what they choose for themselves.

Free Will and Determinism/Decree (Qadr)

One of the most difficult concepts in the study of aqida is how to join between the understanding that Allah is in control of everything (qadr) and that we have free will. The first and most important thing to note in this discussion is that we can never fully understand how the two fit in with each other. This is what Imam Tahawi points out in his text (which you will study in IMAN 101):

The exact nature of the decree is Allah's secret in His creation, and no Angel near the Throne, nor Prophet sent with a message, has been given knowledge of it. Delving into it and reflecting too much about it only leads to destruction and loss, and results in rebelliousness. So be extremely careful about thinking and reflecting on this matter or letting doubts about it assail you, because Allah has kept knowledge of the decree away from human beings, and forbidden them to enquire about it, saying in His Book, "He is not asked about what He does but they are asked." (al-Anbiya' 21:23)

There is another verse in the Quran which speaks about how our actions are in reality not our actions, but rather everything is the action of Allah. This is describing the victory at the Battle of Badr:

(So, it is not you who killed them, but in fact Allah killed them. And you did not throw when you threw but Allah did throw, so that He might bless the believers with a good favour. Surely, Allah is All-Hearing, All-Knowing.) (Quran 8:17)

So even though the Muslims fought and killed the enemies, it was not them who were really making the victory occur. It was Allah who was making the victory occur. To further clarify that we can never fully comprehend the joining between the two, I turn to the example given by Imam Ali:

Once a nomad came to Imam Ali ibn abi Talib (karram Allahu wajhahu), inquiring about freewill and determinism.[7] Imam Ali ibn abi Talib (karram Allahu wajhahu) asked him to stand up then asked him to lift one leg, which he did, then asked him to lift the other one, which obviously he couldn't do. At this juncture Imam Ali Ibn abi Talib (karram Allahu wajhahu) told him that this is how much free will there is and this is how much determinism there is.

In other words, we have a partial role in what is happening, and that partial role is what we are accountable for. Some of the scholars have called this partial role "kasb," which means "to acquire" as there are many verses in the Quran which say that we will be taken to account for "what we acquire." We have the free will (kasab) to either choose to do good or evil.

The question which arises all the time when this discussion occurs is "If Allah is in control of everything, then why should we work to do good things? If He knows whether or not I will go into the fire anyway, what's the point?" To begin an answer to this I turn to when the Sahaba asked a similar question to the Prophet ﷺ:

The Prophet (sal Allahu alayhi wa sallam) said: **"No one of you will enter Paradise by his deeds alone."** They asked, "Not even you, O Messenger of Allah?" He said, **"Not even me, unless Allah covers me with His Grace and Mercy"** (Bukhari, Riqaq, 18; Muslim, Munafiq, 71-73).

Our good deeds are not what get us into Paradise, it is the Mercy of Allah which allows us to enter. One way that it has been explained is that our good deeds are a sabab (cause) that Allah has made for His Decree. So just like we believe that Allah is the one who quenches our thirst, and it is not water that quenches our thirst (since we believe that nothing has power except Allah), but He has made water a sabab (cause) for His quenching of thirst to reach the person. In the same way, Allah is the One who takes us into jannah, but He has made our good actions a sabab (cause) for us to enter jannah.

Another question that comes up, and one that I personally had and asked my teachers, is "If Allah has decreed everything, then what is the point of dua (supplication)?" The answer I was told, and later read in the books of the scholars, is that certain things written in the Lawh (Preserved Tablet) are written as contingent items. So, for example, it may say something like, "This person will live until he is 70 years old, unless he makes dua to live longer, then he will live to 80." But ultimately, this is a matter of the unseen, and we can't comprehend the Qadr of Allah, and thus we should just submit, which is what Islam is all about.

---

[7] Some people make a big deal out of the du`a "karram Allahu wajhahu" (Allah ennoble his face) as if it is some excessive singling out of Ali ibn Abi Talib from the rest of the Companions for no reason. That is not the case. During the time of Yazid, people were ordered to curse Imam Ali on the mimbar. So the scholars responded by making this du`a instead and it thereafter became the custom of the Muslims.

I will end this section with mentioning what two deviant groups historically have affirmed about Qadr. While both of them no longer exist, there may be people who hold onto those beliefs. The first is the Jabariya, which were a group that believed we have absolutely no free will and that we are like robots. This is false, as the Quran shows that we have a part in the action. The other group is the Qadariya, who believe that we create our actions and in this way have given people an aspect of being able to create, whereas we know that only Allah creates. So imagine that they are on separate ends of the spectrum in this discussion. The truth lies in the middle, and only Allah knows that truth. We can try to attempt to reach that truth with the discussions the scholars have and the proofs they bring, but the reality is, only Allah knows the secret of the Qadr.

Decrees of Allah

Nobody is ever in a state where they do not need Allah. Examples are:

- That we need Him for nourishment and we don't get our nourishment from food or water. Rather it is from Allah but it happens through food or water.
- We need Allah to keep us warm and to give us a way to cook and He does it through fire. It is not the fire that burns, rather Allah burns but through the fire. This is why when He told the fire not to burn, it did not burn Ibrahim alayhis salam.
- Allah cuts and it is not the knife. This is why when He told the knife not to cut, it did not cut Ismael alayhis salam.

Everything and all decrees are written on the Preserved Tablet (lawh al mahfudh) in the 7th heaven. Everything is written on the lawh (tablet) with the pen (qalam). Allah created the pen and told it to write everything that will be. The pen has been lifted and the ink has dried thus there is no one who can change the decree of Allah. Allah knew everything that was going to happen and does not need the Lawh to preserve the orders.

Everything has a defined lifespan (ajal) and when that ajal comes, there is no delaying it or expediting it. Living and inanimate things all have a pre-ordained limit and once that comes, there is no changing it. Reflect on the story of the minister of Sulayman alayhis salam.

We should not be angry when something ends. All our actions, good or bad, have been decreed. Good actions (*sing.* hasana; *pl.* hasanat) are rewarded at a rate of 10 times the original deeds and even up to 700 times or more. Bad actions (*sing.* Sayyi'ah; *pl.* sayyi'aat) are counted as one action.

THE ANGELS, BOOKS, AFTERLIFE, QADR & THE UNSEEN

Al-Ghayb (The Unseen)

One of the tenets of our faith is that we believe in the unseen. Allah says, describing those who are conscious of Allah as the ones who "Believe in the Unseen." (Al-Baqarah 2:2). The Unseen includes many things, including many of the points that have been discussed so far. There are many things that we do not know their ultimately reality, but we believe in them. We do not need to delve into discussions about what is the exact nature of those things to believe in them.

We do not need to know what the Throne looks like or what it is made of. We do not need to know what the Angels look like and how exactly they are created. These and other matters are things of the Unseen that we can only know through revelation. The source of revelation has ended with the passing of the Prophet (sal Allahu alayi wa sallam).

One of the matters of the unseen which we believe in are the Jinn. There is even a Sura named after them. We believe in the Jinn who are created from fire. There are good jinn and there are bad jinn. The bad jinn are called "shayateen" (*sing.* shaytan) after their leader Iblis alayhi la`ana. Dhikr will protect us from the bad jinn.

Other Tenets of Our Belief

✦ We believe in, love and respect the Sahaba who are the Companions of the Prophet ﷺ.

- Masculine singular is 'sahabi' and plural is 'sahaba'. For a female companion singular is 'sahabiyyah' and plural is 'sahabiyyaat.' When there are males and females, the masculine plural is used.
- The definition of a sahabi (companion) is someone who:
    - Was in the presence of the Prophet ﷺ even if only an instant. Even if a person was in his presence, but did not see him due to blindness (as some sahaba were blind) they are still considered a Sahabi. There were people who were alive at his time, believed in him but never were in his presence thus they are not a sahabi, such as Uways al Qarani.
    - The presence was while both were alive. Thus, if a person saw the Prophet ﷺ after he passed, then that would not make him a sahabi.
    - Believed in him. There were some people who were alive at his time, were in his presence but did not believe in him, thus they are not a sahabi. There were some who believed in him after his death, they too are not from the sahaba.
    - Then past away maintaining that belief. There were some people who became Muslim, met the Prophet ﷺ, but later left Islam. Thus, they are not from the sahaba.
- Allah chose them above all other humans to be the companions of the best of Creation ﷺ.
- They are the link between the ummah and the Prophet ﷺ.
    - Refer to charts of the sanad from us to them.
- Love of the Sahaba is from Iman.
- Hate for any of the Sahaba is a sign of nifaaq (hypocrisy) i.e. insincerity in the deen.
- We believe and love the "The Blessed Ten" who were specifically promised Paradise:
    - Abu Bakr
    - Umar
    - Uthman
    - Ali
    - Abdur Rahman ibn Awf
    - Talha ibn Ubayd Allah

OTHER TENETS OF OUR BELIEF

- - Zubayr ibn al Awwam
  - Sa'd ibn Abi Waqqas
  - Sa'eed ibn Zayd
  - Abu 'Ubaydah ibn Al Jarrah
- All the sahaba will be in Jannah and will never even touch the fire (Quran 21:101-102).
- All of the sahaba are just/upright (*pl.* 'udool and sing. *'adl*).
- The lowest in rank amongst the sahaba is better than the highest wali of the later generations. Ibn Hajr, in his book *Al-Sawa'iq al-Muhriqa*:

As for what the Sahaba (may Allah be pleased with them) were given specifically, and what they were successful in achieving from looking at his honorable and noble person, that is all a matter that is beyond our intellect. It is not conceivable for anyone to do actions, even if they were great, that would come close to those actions, and forget matching the actions. It is in this light that Abdullah ibn Al Mubarak (and it should be sufficient for you his grandness and knowledge) was asked, "Who is better, Mu'awiya or 'Umar ibn Abdul Aziz?" He said, "The dust which entered the nostril of the horse of Muawiyya when he was with the Messenger of Allah is better than Umar bin Abdul Aziz such and such times." He indicated by this the fact that the virtue of his companionship and his seeing [the Messenger of Allah sal Allahu alayhi wa sallam] cannot be compared to anything."

- We only mention the sahaba in a good manner and with utmost respect (adab).

Umar ibn Abdul Aziz was once asked about the disputes of the Sahaba and he said, "That is blood Allah purified us from, and I don't want to stick my tongue in it."

- We also love the Ahlul Bayt along with our love for the Sahaba.[1]

---

[1] The primary meaning of "Ahl al-Bayt" in Arabic and by the text of the Qur'an are the wives of the Prophet, the Mothers of the Believers. The term "Ahl al-Bayt" is therefore not exclusive to Ali, Fatima, and their descendants karram Allahu wajhahum, even though it most certainly includes them. Allah says (**And stay quietly in your houses, and make not a dazzling display, like that of the former Times of Ignorance; and establish regular prayer, and give regular zakat; and obey Allah and His Messenger. Allah only wishes to remove all abomination from you, O Ahl al-Bayt, and to make you pure and spotless.**) (Al-Ahzab 33:33) The previous verses are addressed directly to the Prophet's wives, who are the cause of the revelation of this verse, without any ambiguity, as is the subsequent verses. And so the phrase "Ahl al-Bayt" is being used as a synonym for "Nisa'a al-Nabi". Thus, this verse is primarily addressing the wives of the Prophet ﷺ by the title "Ahl al-Bayt" and so they are included in the meaning of phrase by Allah's own declaration. But it is not exclusively addressing them in this last statement, so we affirm, as the scholars affirmed based on the implications of the Arabic that "Ahl al-Bayt" refers to both the wives and descendants of the Prophet ﷺ.

OTHER TENETS OF OUR BELIEF

A wonderful reference on this, pointed out to me by a dear friend and dedicated seeker of knowledge, is that Shaykh Yusuf an-Nabhani (d. 1350 AH) said, "Know that the source of the virtue of the Ahlul Bayt—Prophet's Family—and the Companions is the Messenger of Allah (ﷺ). They are branches of this one source." What he says next is profound. It shows the reality of those who, either love Companions but hate Ahlul Bayt, or hate Companions but love Ahlul Bayt, or who hate companions and hate Ahlul Bayt (and they all exist). He says:

> The curse of Allah is upon those who separate between them—one who is pro one group and anti the next — because if you show enmity to one group then you shall not benefit from the other. The enemies of Allah and His Messenger ﷺ are those who fall into this category. (Yusuf an-Nabhani, *Sharaf al-Muabad li Aali Muhammad* (ﷺ). Translated by AS Al-Bukhari)

✦ We believe that the first three generations are the best of all people after the prophets.

- Sahaba: Any Muslim who met the Prophet ﷺ, even briefly, and then stayed a Muslim until death.
- Tabi'een: Any Muslim who spent time with a sahabi.
- Tabi' at tabi'een: Any Muslim who spent time with a tabi'ee.

It is fard to only say good things about the sahaba, the first generations (salaf) and the scholars in a good manner. We follow the way of the salaf and make dua for them, to be in accordance with the ayah (Quran 59:10). We need to do this at least once in our lifetime, like making dua for our parents. The reason for this is when there is an order given in the Quran for us to do something, the bare minimum we would have to do it is once, unless it is clear that the order is calling for a repeated action, like in the case of the prayer. As a note, this discussion about orders is covered in USUL 101, which you will cover in this program.

✦ We believe that our deen has been codified and preserved by the early imams.

Of these early imams, there are only four which there is agreement in terms of us being able to follow them and their methodology. The reason for this, is that they are the only ones who had their schools of thought preserved and codified. The schools of the other imams were lost.

OTHER TENETS OF OUR BELIEF

The four schools remaining until present day are:

- Imam Abu Hanifa
- Imam Malik
- Imam Ash-Shafi'i
- Imam Ahmed ibn Hanbal

✦ We should not speak ill of the dead.

- Sayyidina Mughira bin Shabiah radiallahu anhu has quoted the Messenger of Allah salalahu alayhi wa salam as saying, **"Do not call those who have died as bad people because to speak ill of the dead will hurt the living."**
- Also, Sayyidina Abdullah ibn Umar radiallahu anhu has said that the Messenger of Allah salalahu alayhi wa salam said, **"Speak of the good things of those of you who have died and refrain from speaking ill of them."**
- Bukhari reported from 'Aishah that the Prophet, peace be upon him, said: **"Do not speak ill of the dead; they have seen the result of (the deeds) that they forwarded before them."** Abu Da'wud and Tirmidhi have transmitted, but with a weak chain of narrators, from Ibn 'Umar a similar hadith that the Prophet, peace be upon him, said, **"Mention the good deeds of your dead and cover their evil deeds."**
- As for those Muslims who openly do evil or indulge in illicit innovation, it is permissible to mention their evil deeds if some public good so requires and as a warning to others in order to discourage anyone who might otherwise follow their bad example. If no such benefit is to be gained, then it is not permissible to mention anything evil about the deceased. Bukhari and Muslim reported that Anas said: "A funeral procession passed by and the people praised the deceased. The Prophet, peace be upon him, exclaimed, **'It is decided.'** Then another funeral procession passed by and the people said some bad things about the deceased. The Prophet, peace be upon him, remarked, **'It is decided.'** 'Umar asked: 'What is decided?' The Prophet, peace be upon him, answered, **'The one whom you praised is entitled to Paradise, and the one whom you described as bad is entitled to the Hell Fire. You are Allah's witnesses on earth'."**

OTHER TENETS OF OUR BELIEF

✦ We do not go to psychics.

There is a Hadith which states: **"Whoever goes to a fortuneteller and believes what he says has disbelieved in that which was revealed to Muhammad ﷺ."** The scholars have clarified that what is meant here is a form of rebuking the person, but not that the person would actually leave Islam. The proof for this is in another Hadith which states:

"Whoever goes to a fortune-teller and asks him about something, his prayer will not be accepted for forty nights." Narrated by Muslim (2230).

How could the person not be a Muslim and the Prophet ﷺ be discussing his prayers? If he is praying and his prayers are only accepted for 40 days, then after that his prayers would be accepted and thus he is a Muslim. The process of looking at multiple Hadith and joining between them is covered in our HDTH 101 and USUL 101, which you will cover in sha Allah.

✦ We believe that du'a will benefit and Allah will answer all dua

✦ We believe in magic and that it can affect people. Dua, Quran recitation, prayer, etc can protect us from magic.

- To perform magic takes a person out of Islam due to the need of reciting formulas with statements of kufr.

✦ We believe in the Mithaq (The Covenant)

Allah spoke to all of humanity and asked, **"Am I not your Lord?"** and we all responded saying, **"Yes."** Thus, those who are believers are fulfilling that covenant and those who are not have broken the covenant. (Quran 7:172). One of my teachers, Shaykh Muhammad Zain, said that he met a woman in Mauritania who actually remembered the covenant. At first, she did not mention this to people because she thought that everyone remembered answering. Later, when she found that people don't remember, she mentioned that she remembered. O Allah, make us from amongst the people who fulfill the covenant that we made with you!

OTHER TENETS OF OUR BELIEF

✦ We believe in Al-'Arsh wa-l-Kursi (The Throne and The Footstool)

- They are creations of Allah in the Heavens and they are enormous in size.
- Allah does not need The Throne or The Footstool.[2]
- Allah controls His 'Arsh and Kursi.
- They are over the 7 heavens and the earth.
- We only can know what Allah wants us to know.

✦ We believe in the Sidrat al-Muntaha (The Furthest Lote Tree), which is the last point in creation.

✦ We accept all those who are from the people of the Qibla (ahlul qibla) as being Muslim.

Whoever faces the direction of Mecca (Qibla) and eats the slaughter of Muslims, we consider him to be a Muslim. This is a term referring to anyone who even accepts these positions of Islam, even if they do not follow them. If a person says, "Yes, I know that I should face the Qibla for prayer and eat halal, but I do not do either." That person is still a Muslim and we treat him or her as such. Once a person says they are Muslim, we treat them as such. We do not have a negative opinion about a person who claims to be Muslims or acts Muslim and we have no reason to believe otherwise.[3]

There are two brothers I know, both with similar backgrounds and who shared a similar experience, although they were separated by about 13 years. The first brother was a man who spent over 10 years in prison (for a crime he admitted to) and became Muslim while in prison. Upon release, one of the first things that he did was go to a local masjid to pray dhuhr. When he entered, he saw an older man with a long white beard and a turban and said salam to him. The man responded by saying, "Wa alaykum." We know what that means and to whom that

---

[2] Imam Tahawi states "The Throne and the Footstool are real. He is independent of the Throne and what is below it. He encompasses every single thing and is above it." Imam Tahawi does not make a distinction between Allah's being "above" the Throne and His being "above" everything else in creation because of what Shaykh Rami said in the previous chapter.

[3] Which means that we don't use phrases like "so-called Muslims" which is casting doubt upon the validity of someone else's Iman due to their sins. This is as long as we know they do not hold beliefs which take them outside of the fold of Islam, such as Allah being a man or anyone being a Prophet or Messenger after Muhammad ibn Abdullah.

response is given.[4] The brother complained to the imam of the masjid after praying and the imam reprimanded the old man (with adab) and told him that he has to give his Muslim brother his right.

In the other case, there was a brother who spent over 25 years in prison, and was released through the Innocence Project. He went into a masjid wearing a kufi and said salam to someone inside who responded by saying, "Wa alaykum." He was so hurt that he teared up when relating the story, and you know brothers who have been in the penn don't cry easily. In both of these stories are examples of people rejecting a Muslim. We should never be like those people. If someone comes to us acting like a Muslim, we treat them as such.

✦ We also never say that any Muslim is a kafir (non-believer) or a munafiq (hypocrite).

- Ibn Umar related that the Holy Prophet said: **"If a Muslim calls another kafir, then if he is a kafir let it be so; otherwise, he [the caller] is himself a kafir.'"** (Abu Dawud).
- Abu Zarr reported that the Holy Prophet said: **"No man accuses another man of being a sinner, or of being a kafir, but it reflects back on him if the other is not as he called him."** (Bukhari, Book of Ethics; Book 78, ch. 44)

The Shafi'i scholars explained that the first hadith is referring to it as being a type of ridda (apostasy) to call another Muslim a kafir. Their reasoning is that it is either one of two scenarios. Either the person you are calling a kafir is actually such and so that is clear. If he is not a kafir, and is really a Muslim, then you are calling his Islam kufr, which is thus a form of kufr. To call Islam kufr is kufr. So let's not get caught in the web of calling others kafir, unless there is something clearly done or said which causes a person to leave Islam.

---

[4] "Wa alaykum" is technically an appropriate response to the salams since you are saying "Likewise to you" and the Prophet said we can say this instead of returning the full salam. But the Prophet also told 'A'isha radi Allahu anha to say this to some Jews in Madina who used to twist the salam and turn it into a curse. So many people unfortunately use it with this second meaning as a way of avoiding giving people their proper salams when they don't think think are "really" Muslim and so it is always better to say the full salams, especially if saying "Wa alaykum" will lead to someone thinking you are disrespecting them.

OTHER TENETS OF OUR BELIEF

◆ **We stick to the congregation of the Muslims by praying with the Muslims and obeying those in charge (ulil amr). We make dua for the ulil amr. Ulil amr are the leaders in charge of the land we reside in (bay'ah/allegiance to ruler) and the scholars.**

Sticking to the congregation of the Muslims here means that we do not rebel against our leaders. It is forbidden to rebel against established leaders, even if they are oppressive. The harm that comes from rebellion is worse than oppression. Just look at the states of Iraq, Syria and Libya. In those countries, the destabilization of the governments has led to mass anarchy, destruction, murder, rape, mayhem, etc that far out shadows the oppression of the dictators who ran those countries. This is why Imam Malik said, "70 years of an oppressive ruler is better than the ummah being without a leader for one hour of the day."

Abu Bakr al-Turtushi (may Allah have mercy on him) said, "Al-Fudayl (may Allah have mercy on him) said, 'The oppression of 60 years is better than anarchy for one hour. And so only an ignorant fool or a sinner wanting to do all sin will wish for the removal of a leader.'" Just a note about Imam Al-Turtushi, this is what other scholars have said about him: Al-Hafidh al-Dhahabi said about him, "The very knowledgeable imam, the role model who gave up the world, the Shaykh of the Malikis...the Alim of Alexandria and Turtusha." Abu Bakr ibn Al Arabi described him as having knowledge, virtue, renunciation of the world, and focusing on that which concerns him.

In the tafsir of Imam al-Qurtubi, it states:

> The oppression of a sultan for one year is less harmful than the people being in anarchy for one instant. It is for this reason that Allah created leaders so that things will go according to his opinion and to prevent the oppression coming from the masses.

So, we should not make dua for the removal of the ruler, rather we should ask for him or her to become righteous. This is why Imam Tahawi said in his book:

> We do not recognize rebellion against our Imam or those in charge of our affairs even if they are unjust, nor do we wish evil on them, nor do we withdraw from following them. We hold that obedience to them is part of obedience to Allah, The Glorified, and therefore obligatory as long as they do not order to commit sins. We pray for their right guidance and pardon from their wrongs.

Now, the next question is, "Who are the leaders?" The simple answer is that the government of any land are the leaders of that land. If you are in a Muslim land, then the president, king, prime minister, dictator, etc is the ruler. The same goes for the non-Muslim land a Muslim may visit or live in. Once you enter the land of a non-Muslim under a treaty, you are bound to follow all the laws of that land.

Recognizing that the leader, amir, ulil amri are the established governments of the land, I would like to make it as plain and clear as possible that no other person is to be considered an amir with all the privileges and rights of the amir as mentioned in the ayah about ulil amri. Therefore, if a group, community or masjid elect an "amir," that does not afford that person the rights which we are talking about here. The only thing that person shares is the word "amir" and that is it. It does not make it haram or prohibited to then leave that congregation. The only other person who is included in the ayah of ulil amri are the scholars.

When it comes to why the scholars are considered to be among ulil amri, Imam Shafi'i used the following verse to prove that scholars can derive rulings in matters where there is not a clear indication from the Quran or Sunna:

(When news concerning peace or fear comes to them, they go about spreading it. Had they referred it to the Messenger and to those having authority among them, the truth of the matter would have come to the knowledge of those of them who are able to investigate. But for Allah's grace upon you, and mercy, you would have followed the Satan, save a few.) (Quran 4:83)

So the scholars are considered like ulil amri in the sense that we go to their authority for scholarly answers. But it does not mean that they have any political capacity just by the mere fact of their scholarship. Nor does it mean that an individual has to obey their orders. The only ruler you have to obey the orders of are those of the established government. For the scholars, you just have the duty to go back to them to clarify matters of the deen. For community leaders, group leaders, masjid leaders and other "amirs," there is absolutely no obligation to follow their orders.

✦ We believe in the Awliya (Protected Friends of Allah).

Awliya is the plural of wali. Wali can be translated as "protected friend." While at one level, all believers are the "awliya" of Allah, there is another more specific type of wali. The verses which prove that all believers are considered to be from the awliya is the following:

OTHER TENETS OF OUR BELIEF

(Behold, the friends of Allah shall have no fear, nor shall they grieve. Those who have believed and have been fearful of Allah.) (Quran 10:62-63)

(Allah is the Protector of those who believe. He brings them out of the depths of darkness into the light. As for those who disbelieve, their friends are the Rebels. They bring them out from the light into the depths of darkness. Those are people of the Fire. There they will remain forever.) (Quran 2:257)

Note that here in the verse Allah describes Himself as the wali of the believers. In Arabic, there are certain words that can be used in two ways, and "wali" is one of them. It can be used for both the protecting friend and the protected friend. So we have seen in the above Ayah that the believers are from the awliya. But now let's move onto the more specific type of wali. For this, let us read a few Hadith:

Abu Hurairah, radiyallahu 'anhu, reported that the Messenger of Allah, sallallahu 'alayhi wasallam, said, "Allah the Almighty has said: 'Whosoever acts with enmity towards a closer servant of Mine (wali), I will indeed declare war against him. Nothing endears My servant to Me more than doing of what I have made obligatory upon him to do. And My servant continues to draw nearer to Me with supererogatory (nawafil) prayers so that I shall love him. When I love him, I shall be his hearing with which he shall hear, his sight with which he shall see, his hands with which he shall hold, and his feet with which he shall walk. And if he asks (something) of Me, I shall surely give it to him, and if he takes refuge in Me, I shall certainly grant him it.'" (Al-Bukhari)

Now, someone can say that this is talking to the non-Muslim and him acting with enmity to the Muslim, but the Hadith in Arabic says "مَنْ" meaning "whoever" which would also include that he is talking to the Muslim ummah. So yes, if a non-Muslim acts with enmity to the Muslim, he is doing something to a wali of Allah. But what about the Muslim who does something to the Muslim wali? And a further proof, and clearer in my opinion, is that the Hadith goes on to talking about how the person becomes a wali, by increasing in extra acts. That shows that there are different levels of believers. And this is something that we all can recognize, not all believers are at the same level of righteousness.

Allah gives some awliya miracles which are called a karama. This could be in the form of something out of the ordinary. But if a person has this, the key to making sure it is a wali and not a deluded one (mustadraj) is their adherence to the Quran and Sunnah. Imam Al-Akhdari, in his poem *Al-Qudsiyya*, says: "If you see a man fly, and walk on water, but he does not adhere to the boundaries of the Sharia, then know that he is a mustadraj and an innovator (bid'i)." What we learn from this is that merely having a miracle is not the sign of the wali. The person has to be following the shariah. But the greatest miracle of all, is to follow the sunna exactly. This is not a simple task. The sunna has to permeate all aspects of a person's life.

✦ We do not draw weapons on any person, especially a Muslim, someone under the protection of Muslims (dhimmi), or someone in a covenant with the Muslims (mu'ahid).

We believe that it is not permissible to draw weapons on others. This is whether the person is a Muslim or otherwise, if that person is under a treaty of dhimma or mu'ahada.[5] The dhimmi is the non-Muslim living under Muslim rule. The mu'ahid is the non-Muslim whom the Muslim lives in their land under the treaty of a citizenship, visa, residency, or otherwise. The Prophet said about this:

None of you must point a weapon at his brother for he does not know whether the devil may draw it out while it is in his hand as a result of which he will fall into a pit of Hell. (Bukhari, Muslim).[6]

✦ We love the people of obedience and we hate the actions of the disobedient. We pray for the guidance and forgiveness of those who are doing wrong.

We believe that we must have love and hate for the sake of Allah. For those who are not following the deen, we should make dua for their guidance.

---

[5] Even though Shaykh Rami is referring to literally drawing a weapon on someone, "drawing a weapon" in religious literature is a synonym for unprovoked violence of any kind.

[6] Even though the hadith says "his brother", the Prophet ﷺ on numerous occasions uses the term "akhi" to refer to humanity in general. For example, in commentary of the famous hadith **"None of you believes until he loves for his brother what he loves for himself"** Imam Nawawi comments "It is better to interpret this as brotherhood in general, such that it includes the disbeleiver and the Muslim. So he should love for his brother, the disbeleiver, what he loves for himself, which is his entering Islam, just as he should love for his brother Muslim that he remains in Islam." (Nawawi, 40 Hadith) And likewise, the above hadith should be taken to apply to humanity and so we should not point weapons at our fellow Muslims or our non-Muslims brothers in humanity unless we have a justifiable reason to do so. This applies even more to non-Muslim citizens of Muslim countries and non-Muslims who have granted Muslims citizenship in their lands. Both of these groups of people are afforded the same rights that Muslims are given to each other in a Muslim country.

OTHER TENETS OF OUR BELIEF

✦ We believe in tawbah.

Tawbah is seeking repentance from Allah. Allah will accept repentance (tawbah) for anything. Allah can forgive any sin (even if there was no tawba) other than shirk (associating partners with Allah/disbelieving in Allah/refusing Islam). Allah will accept all tawbah until:

- The sun rises from the West (which marks the end of time).
- A person's soul is being drawn out of his body (yughar-ghir).
  - Firoun's tawbah was too late. He was already dying and at that point, the chance for tawbah is lost.

We should never be in despair (ya's) from the Mercy and Forgiveness of Allah. There is mercy for believers in the Afterlife, even if their faith is the weight of a mustard seed. The conditions of tawbah are:

- Remorse over what was done.
- An intention never to do that again.
- Stop the action if involved in it.
- Redress any wrongs.

You will learn more about Tawbah in the FIQH 101/111/121, but here is a little about it from that course:

A person must have remorse for what has transpired. If a person stops doing wrong actions his stopping must be because he has remorse for doing that action. Whereas if a person stops it for other reasons, then he has not fulfilled this condition of repentance. For example, if a person is drinking alcohol and he stops because it's bad for his health, then he is not remorseful for what he has done. He must feel remorse. His heart must be broken (enkissarul al qalb) he must feel hurt because of his actions

And then there must be an intention never to return to the wrong action as long as he lives. He must have the intention that he stops it now and he will never go back to it again. Whereas if a person is remorseful for this wrong action that he did today, but he knows that he's going back to it tomorrow, then he has not fulfilled this condition of repentance so it is not a correct tawba (repentance).

Also, about the second condition, if the person for whatever reason has remorse and has an intention never to return to this, and then for whatever reason becomes weakened and goes back to the same sin that does not negate the original repentance. He must now make repentance for this new action and his first repentance is still valid.

He must also leave the disobedient action immediately if engaged in it at the time of repentance. It is not permissible for him to delay it. So, if a person is in the midst of committing a wrong action, and he feels remorse and he knows he doesn't want to go back to it again in the future, but right now he's going to complete it, then he's not doing tawba. Even though he's feeling remorseful, this is not considered tawba.

If a person has not made tawbah, they are a "faasiq" (disobedient Muslim) but they are still Muslim. If they pass away before doing tawbah, then we consider them Muslim and we say that it is up to Allah to forgive them or not.

Major sins (kabaa'ir) can only be wiped out through tawbah. Minor sins (sagha'ir) can be wiped out through specific tawbah or even just merely by doing good deeds, such as walking to the masjid, doing wudu or staying away from the major sins. Allah can also turn bad deeds into good deeds.

✦ We do not debate unless absolutely necessary and we do so in the best of manners.

Some of the things that mark the end of times are lack of knowledge, speaking without knowledge and being impressed with one's opinion. These converge in the form of debate that characterizes so many of our discourses in the modern times, especially in the realm of the deen. The rules of debating in accordance with the Sunna will be covered for you in detail in the courses of ADAB 100, ADAB 102 and USUL 101. But here are some general notes about the idea of debate. Allah says:

OTHER TENETS OF OUR BELIEF

(Do not debate with the people of the Book unless it is in the best manner, except with those of them who commit injustice. And say, "We believe in what is sent down to us and sent down to you, and our God and your God is One, and to Him we submit (ourselves).") (Quran 29:46)

Abu Umamah reported:

The Messenger of Allah, peace and blessings be upon him, said: **"No people go astray after being guided except that they indulge in arguments."** Then the Prophet recited the verse: **(They strike an example for you only to argue. Rather, they are a quarrelsome people.)** (Al-Zukhruf 43:58) (Tirmidhi)

Abu Umamah reported also reported: The Messenger of Allah ﷺ said: **"I guarantee a house on the outskirts of Paradise for one who abandons arguments even if he is right."** (Sunan Abu Dawud)

And Malik ibn Anas said: "Disputation and arguments about sacred knowledge cause the light of knowledge to extinguish in a man's heart." He also said: "Disputation about sacred knowledge causes the heart to harden and breeds hatred." Haytam ibn Jamil reported: "I said to Malik, 'O servant of Allah, if a man has knowledge of the prophetic tradition (sunnah), should he argue to defend it?' Malik replied: 'No, rather he should convey the Sunnah if they might accept it from him, otherwise he should remain silent.'"[7]

With these above quotes in mind, take a moment to think about how you have seen people debate about the deen of Islam. Has it been in the "best of fashions" as is the direction of the ayah above? If Allah is telling us to debate with the People of the Book in the "best of fashions," then what about our Muslim brothers that we share the same faith with (even though we may hold different views or practices)? How was Musa alayhis salam commanded by Allah to speak with the Pharaoh? And then compare how Musa was told to speak to a murderous tyrant with how we often speak with one another.

---

[7] Some may ask "Why Imam Malik would say this? Should you not defend the truth, period!?" There are two issues here: (a) argumentation and (b) enjoining the good/forbidding the wrong. Argumentation is haram as a general rule, while enjoining the good/forbidding the wrong is only obligatory if you *know* you will be listened to. If you think you may not be listened to, then it becomes recommended, permissible, disliked or unlawful depending on the response you are expecting. So Malik is saying here that if you have to choose between arguing and remaining silent, then you should remain silent since avoiding the haram is paramount and argumentation only becomes permissible if you think you will be listened to. We discuss the appropriateness of argumentation/debate in ADAB 100.

OTHER TENETS OF OUR BELIEF

✦ We believe in the fitna (trial) of life. This could be in the form of disbelief or not remembering Allah.

There are various trials that a person could face in this life. This could be as simple as the prick of a thorn in your foot all the way to the loss of health and wealth. It could also be a trial of faith in the form of not practicing Islam or to the point of leaving Islam. We ask Allah to save us from the trials of this life and the next.

✦ If someone is disobeying Allah outwardly (fasiq), we have to judge according to that and we leave the inwards to Allah.

If someone is outwardly sinful, then we treat them as such.[8] However we never say that a person is not Muslim because they are not following the rules. To call a person a kafir or munafiq is called takfeer and is not allowed. We also have to make sure that we see the good side of every person even if they are doing something bad. This is the aqida of ahlul sunna.

One of the best examples of this is that of the warrior who stole a horse. The scholars mention that if a person were to steal a horse and then goes to defend Islam and the Muslims and then is killed, the question becomes; "Is he a thief (sariq) or a martyr (shahid)?" The scholars have mentioned that it is the position of Ahlul Sunna wal Jama'ah that this person can still be considered a martyr even though he had stolen something. They use this as an example to show that a person can have two aspects of their state. This was stated as there were people in the past who used to say that a sin will negate the status of the goodness, and thus the person would not be a martyr.

The way we should relate this to our lives is that no matter what a person is engaged in, we have to look for the good that person is doing as well. That is not to say that we overlook the bad, but it is to say that we should also not overlook the good. We need to be fair and just, and look at both aspects.

---

[8] Meaning that they should not be making decisions on behalf of the community, they are not put in positions of leadership, they should not be leading the prayer, *etc*. Likewise, if they have a gambling or addiction problem, we don't entrust them with our wealth. However, we also do not completely ostracize or ex-communicate them either. So we do not refuse to let them pray in congregation, attend ta'leem or actively participate in the community as long as they are not actively causing fitna. Why would anyone want to prevent their fellow Muslims from the very things that may inspire them to make tawba?

OTHER TENETS OF OUR BELIEF

✦ We must accept all things that are readily known about the religion (ma'lum min al din bi darura).

Examples of this are the five pillars, well known prohibitions such as drinking alcohol, gambling, backbiting, adultery, and eating pork. If a person rejects one of these matters, they leave the fold of Islam (Apostate/murtad, apostasy/riddah).[9] Earlier in the text we discussed how we believe that we should not make takfir of another Muslim and consider them outside the fold of Islam without a valid cause. One of the valid causes would be if a person were to reject an aspect of Islam that is well known to him or her and the community in general. So, for example, most people (even non-Muslims) know that Muslims must pray five times a day, can't eat pork and can't drink alcohol. Therefore, if a person were to say that praying is not an obligation, or that wine is permissible, that would mean that they have left the fold of Islam.

The reason for this is that they rejecting an aspect of Islam that is taken from the Quran or the very strong Hadith and so it is like they are saying that Allah and His Messenger are wrong. When a person says that the five prayers are not an obligation, for example, they are rejecting all the verses and Hadith about prayer and so many of them have reached us that we have no doubt that the obligation of the five prayers comes from the Prophet salallahu alayhi wa salam.

✦ If a person adds something to the deen, that was not a part of it or not a method to maintain the deen, that is called a bid'ah (innovation).

We must maintain the religion as it has been passed down to us. There are only certain areas that a person may add things to the deen as a means. For more on this, I will use an excerpt from Imam Nawawi's commentary on the 40 Hadith, which is something you will study as part of the HDTH 101 course at Tayba:

Hadith 5: The Mother of the Believers, 'Aisha (radiya Allahu anha), narrated that the Messenger of Allah ﷺ said, **"If one adds something to this matter of ours and it is not from it, then it will be rejected."** Narrated by Bukhari and Muslim. In a narration of Muslim it says: **"If one does an action that is not in accordance with our matter, then it will be rejected."** This is

---

[9] And remember that "rejects" here means to reject these things as obligatory or impermissible. If someone claims that gambling is permissible, this is kufr, but if they refuse to stop gambling, they are merely sinful.

proof that if actions of worship such ghusl, wudu, prayer and fasting are not done in accordance with the Sharia, then they will be returned to the one who does them.

There are many different types of innovation, some of which are forbidden and some of which can be accepted. Some innovations can be in the matters of belief while others can be in the matters of practice. If the matter of innovation in belief becomes too severe, then it would lead to leaving Islam. Other innovations can even be in the matters of the permissible. You will learn more about these in the USUL 101 course here at Tayba. Here are some examples of the various types as mentioned by Shaykh Muhammad Jurdani, who said:

"Beware of matters newly begun", distance yourselves and be wary of matters newly innovated that did not previously exist", *i.e.*, things invented in Islam that contravene the Sacred Law, **"for every innovation is misguidance"** meaning that every innovation is the opposite of the truth, *i.e.*, falsehood, a hadith that has been related elsewhere as: **"for every newly begun matter is innovation, every innovation is misguidance, and every misguidance is in hell"** meaning that everyone who is misguided, whether through himself or by following another, is in hell, the hadith referring to matters that are not good innovations with a basis in Sacred Law. It has been stated [by Izz ibn Abd al-Salam] that innovations (bida) fall under the five headings of the Sacred Law (n: *i.e.*, the obligatory, unlawful, recommended, offensive, and permissible):

(1) The first category comprises innovations that are obligatory, such as recording the Qur'an and the laws of Islam in writing when it was feared that something might be lost from them; the study of the disciplines of Arabic that are necessary to understand the Qur'an and sunna such as grammar, word declension, and lexicography; hadith classification to distinguish between genuine and spurious prophetic traditions; and the philosophical refutations of arguments advanced by the Mu'tazilites and the like.

(2) The second category is that of unlawful innovations such as non- Islamic taxes and levies, giving positions of authority in Sacred Law to those unfit for them, and devoting ones time to learning the beliefs of heretical sects that contravene the tenets of faith of Ahl al-Sunna.

(3) The third category consists of recommended innovations such as building hostels and schools of Sacred Law, recording the research of Islamic schools of legal thought, writing books on beneficial subjects, extensive research into fundamentals and particular applications of Sacred Law, in-depth studies of Arabic linguistics, the reciting of wirds by those with a Sufi path, and commemorating the birth (mawlid), of the Prophet Muhammad (Allah bless him and give him peace) and wearing ones best and rejoicing at it.

OTHER TENETS OF OUR BELIEF

(4) The fourth category includes innovations that are offensive, such as embellishing mosques, decorating the Qur'an and having a backup man (muballigh) loudly repeat the spoken Allahu Akbar of the imam when the latter's voice is already clearly audible to those who are praying behind him.

(5) The fifth category is that of innovations that are permissible, such as sifting flour, using spoons and having more enjoyable food, drink and housing. (*al-Jawahir al-luluiyya fi sharh al-Arbain al-nawawiyya*, 220-21). [*Reliance of the Traveler*, 915-916]

[This section disturbs some people because many of us have been primed to believe that religious innovations can be anything but evil. A simple reflection on the examples above is enough to satisfy most, but some people are under the impression that what has just been said is clear misguidance and cannot get past this section. Since the footnote we had in previous editions did not seem to be enough, we have decided to give the issue a fuller treatment as a separate appendix in order to not disrupt the flow. So anyone who has an issue with what has been said here, please see "Appendix I: Religious Innovations" for a fuller discussion of the issue.]

✦ We believe in the Night Journey and Heavenly Ascent (al isra wal miraj).

This is mentioned in the books of aqida because the event is mentioned in the Quran and thus to reject it would be to reject the Quran. It is also mentioned in the Hadith collections and for that reason it must be accepted as well. The Prophet ﷺ went with his body and spirit to Jerusalem and then into the Heavens. It was not merely by spirit or in a dream.

Among the things we take from his Night Journey and Heavenly Ascent are that he saw Musa alayhis salam in the red hill praying in his grave, then saw Musa again in Bayt al-Maqdis when our Prophet led the rest of the prophets in prayer, and then he saw Musa again in the highest of the heavens. Thus, the prophets are alive in their graves.

Also, we affirm that he was taken to the highest heaven to receive orders, not because that would make him closer to Allah physically, but as an honor to the Prophet ﷺ. Allah

OTHER TENETS OF OUR BELIEF

does not have a direction, time or place.[10] Allah can give a message to Jonah (Yunus) alayhis salam in the belly of the whale at the bottom of the ocean.

About the Night Journey occurring in body and spirit, we have the following narration: Ibn 'Abbas said regarding the Statement of Allah: **(And We granted the vision (Ascension to the heavens) which We made you see (as an actual eye witness) was only made as a trial for the people.)** (Al-Isra 17:60) "The sights which Allah's Apostle was shown on the Night Journey when he was taken to Bait al-Maqdis (*i.e.*, Jerusalem) were actual sights [not dreams or visions]. And the Cursed Tree [mentioned] in the Quran is the [actual] tree of Zaqqum [that is in the Hellfire]. (*Sahih Bukhari*, Vol 5, Book 58, Hadith #228)

Imam Ibn Hajr writes in his commentary of *Sahih al-Bukhari* (1/460) that "No one should dispute the fact that al-Isra took place while the Prophet was awake. This is what the Qur'an clearly said about it, and also because the people of Quraysh disbelieved in it." Had Isra wal-Miraj been only a dream, the Quraysh would not have found it necessary to reject it, for people can dream anything. However, since the Messenger of Allah ﷺ claimed to have physically visited Jerusalem in a single night, (which in those days generally took almost three months of traveling) they denied and refused to believe his visit to Jerusalem, let alone the issue of visiting the Heavens and meeting with Allah. Even some who claimed to be Muslims rejected this great physical miracle of Isra and Miraj.

Likewise, Imaam an-Nawawi (rahimahullah) writes in his commentary of *Sahih Muslim* (2/209) that: "The truth cherished by the majority of people in general, and the Salaf (pious predecessors) in particular, the scholars of Fiqh, and scholars of Hadith is that the Prophet ﷺ went in the journey of Isra physically, *i.e.*, with his body."[11]

---

[10] While we affirm the Furthest Lote Tree is an actual tree in the heavens (as Shaykh Rami declared previously in the chapter), this represents the furthermost limits of the created universe. So when the Prophet ﷺ went past the Sidrat al-Muntaha into the Divine Presence, which the hadith confirm that Jibril didn't realize was even possible, this meant that the Prophet ﷺ crossed over into where time, space and place no longer had any relevance. The Quran describes this as **(Then he approached and descended, at a distance of two bow lengths or nearer. And He revealed to His servant what He revealed.)** The significance of "two bow lengths" is that this is the closest any visitor was allowed to approach a king in the world. But our Prophet came ever nearer in intimacy than that. However, he ﷺ was not any physically closer to Allah at that point than any of us are at any other time since **(He is closer to you than your jugular vein)** in a way that transcends time, space, and place. This is what Imam Tahawi means when he says "And exalted is Allah beyond limits, parameters, supports, parts, or instruments. The six directions do not contain Him as they do created things."

[11] And so we affirm that the Night Journey and Heavenly Ascension occurred in both body and spirit and it is the greatest proof of the Prophet's ﷺ supremacy over the rest of the prophets alayhim salam ajma'in given that our Prophet was allowed to experience in this world what all other prophets were only allowed to experience in the Afterlife.

OTHER TENETS OF OUR BELIEF

Outline Summary for "Beliefs of a Muslim"

Shahada

1) Once belief (iman) has entered the heart and the person accepts being Muslim, that person is a Muslim. The shahada is an outward expression for others to know that one is Muslim.
   a) The Prophet ﷺ said, **"I was ordered to judge based on the outward state of people."**
   b) In the *Mukhtasar of Khalil*, it says, "The ghusl is correct once a person has firmly resolved to accept Islam."
   c) If a person dies before stating the shahada, they are still a Muslim but the community will not bury them as a Muslim nor inherit their wealth.
   d) Remember the Hadith of the man being a hand span from the Hellfire.
2) We have to know what the shahada means and not just say it without knowing what it means.
   a) We cannot say, "I heard people saying it and so I said it."
   b) There are signs of oneness all around us.
   c) Signs will be different from person to person.
3) It may be said in English but it is more complete to be stated in Arabic.
   a) Remember the story of Khalid ibn Al Walid (may Allah be pleased with him) and those who said, "Saba'na."
   b) It should be said with proper tajwid (rules of recitation).
4) We believe that the only religion that that is true and that Allah will accept is Islam (Quran 3:19 and 3:38).
   a) Thus, if a person says the shahada, but has beliefs that contradict Islam, then the shahada is not valid.
   b) The Wars of Apostasy
5) Hadith of Jibreel alayhis salam shows us that the deen is Islam, Iman and Ihsan.
   a) Iman is belief with the heart, speech on the tongue and actions with the limbs.
   b) Belief is not complete without action, no action is considered without an intention, and no action or intention is considered unless it is in line with the Sunna.
6) The best action after faith (iman) is the prayer.
   a) One does not leave Islam for leaving the prayer.
7) Allah does not place a burden on a soul more than what it can bear.
   a) Those whom the Message has not reached are not responsible.

b) It is incumbent upon every person who is a responsible adult (mukallaf) to have made sure his or her beliefs (iman) are correct.

c) The age of responsibility (taklif) is contingent upon three things:
   i) Physical maturity (bulugh) which is indicated by:
      (1) Wet dream
      (2) Menstruation
      (3) Coarse pubic hair

d) Intellect ('aql) that is indicated by the ability of a person to give a reasonable response to a logical question.

e) That the message of Islam reached them (bulugh al risala).

8) The testimony of faith (shahada) contains all the tents of faith that a Muslim must accept as being true. This is why it is the sign/mark of faith.

9) It must never be suggested to another person to delay taking their shahada. According to Imam Nawawi, encouraging another person to delay the shahada is a form of apostasy.

Allah

10) Allah is One
11) Allah exists pre-eternally even before creation was in existence.
12) Allah is perfect in all ways.
13) Any imperfection is not attributed to Allah.
14) Allah exists without need
15) Allah exists without need for time, place or direction.
16) One without father, son, friend, spouse, or partner
17) First without beginning
18) Last without End
19) Totally independent and not in need of anything
20) Totally different than his creation
    a) Creation is everything from the arsh to the farsh (throne to the earth).
21) He speaks, but His Speech is different than that of creation.
    a) His speech is not created.
    b) He spoke to Musa alayhis salam.
22) He hears everything, but His Hearing is different than creation. He sees everything, but His Sight is different than his creation.
    a) The story of Al Junayd and his student.

23) He knows everything and nothing can escape his knowledge.
    a) Allah made people, their thoughts, and knows everything that enters their hearts.
    b) He knows all dry things and wet, all leaves and grains.
    c) He knows everything before it happened.
24) He has absolute power (Qudra)
25) He does whatever He wants (Irada)
26) He can create or leave things uncreated based on His choice.
27) No one can force Him to do anything
28) He is Living and never dies
    a) He was never born nor does He have children
29) We deny the opposites of the above mentioned matters, in that we reject that Allah:
    a) Is more than one.
    b) Has a beginning or an end.
    c) Needs anything from us.
    d) Has similarity to creation in speech, sight, knowledge, or any attribute.
    e) Is forced to do something.
    f) Can cease to exist or die.
30) Our mind and thoughts cannot imagine His true essence
    a) Everything that you can imagine, Allah is other than that
        i) Kullu ma yakhturu fi balik, fa Llahu bi khilafi dhalik
    b) We should think about His creation and not think about Him.
    c) We can only know what Allah lets us know.
31) Allah does not have a body nor an attribute of a body.
32) Only Allah creates and He is Al Khaliq.
    a) When we make things we are just manipulating the creation.
    b) But only He can bring something out of nothing (Al Fatir)
    c) He can sustain it (Al Qayyum) and only He can annihilate it.

The Prophets & Messengers

33) The following are the four necessary qualities of all prophets
    a) Sidq- Truthful is all that they speak
        i) Discuss the story of why the Quraysh called the Prophet ﷺ Al-Amin. Discuss the story of calling the family on Safa.

- b) Amanah- Trustworthy in all that is entrusted to them from Allah, angels or the people.
- c) Tabligh- They convey all that was given to them from Allah.
- d) Fatana- They are very smart and can debate with their people.
    - i) Ibrahim alayhis salam and his debates with his people and Nimrod.

34) The following attributes are impossible for all prophets:
   - a) Kadhib- Lying
     - i) The story of Ibrahim alayhis salam and the "three lies"
   - b) Khiyana- Abuse of trust
     - i) Discuss the trusts that the Prophet ﷺ had and took three days to distribute. Also the story of the caravan of Khdaija radiya Allahu anhu.
   - c) Kitman- Hiding the revelation, or a portion, they were ordered to convey
   - d) Being feeble minded

35) The following are possible for a prophet:
   - a) Light sickness. A wisdom (hikma) of this is that it makes us feel better when we experience similar situations by saying, "Well, so and so prophet experienced such and such." This is called tasalli.
   - b) Eating and drinking
   - c) Marriage
   - d) Human emotions such as sadness.

36) The following are impossible for a prophet:
   - a) To have disbelief. They all believed in Allah both before and after their prophethood.
     - i) The story of Ibrahim alayhis salam has to be clarified. The story of him saying that "The moon is my Lord..." is a tactic of debate that he employed. It was as if he was saying, "What if I were to say, 'the moon is my Lord..'" but he just dropped the supposition of "what if."
   - b) Severe sickness which is anything that would cause people to detract from their status. An example is something that would repulse people. Such as:
     - i) Leprosy: The sickness that Ayub (Job) alayhis salam experienced is not as the Torah mentions. We believe he got sick but not to where his skin was peeling off or that there were worms coming out of his skin.
     - ii) Blindness: The event that occurred to Yaqub (Jacob) alayhis salam was that a whiteness covered his eyes but he could still see.
   - c) To do the haram, or even think about it.
     - i) The prophets cannot do the minor (saghira) or major (kabira) sins both before their prophethood and afterward.

ii) Adam's alayhis salam eating from the tree. He did not do anything haram. there are explanations about what he did:
  (1) He forgot the order.
  (2) He thought the order was one of mandub.
  (3) He was tricked by the Shaytan and couldn't imagine someone could swear by Allah and be lying. His innocence was like a child in this respect.
  (4) He was always meant to go into the earth (ref ayah). Allah always knew that Adam and his children would inhabit the earth.
iii) The story of Yusuf (Joseph) alayhis salam must be clarified in that he never once even thought about doing anything haram with the kings's wife.
iv) We reject the stories mentioned in the Old Testament about the prophets doing haram (like the story about Nuh alayhis salam).

37) Allah sent us the prophets from His Generosity (fadlihi).
   a) Allah does not have to do anything for us.
   b) This rejects the notion that it is an obligation for Allah to send us prophets.
38) Allah has given the prophets all human perfection and prevented them from having any human defect.
39) Allah gave them protection ('isma) from all things that are not befitting of their status.
   a) They do not commit sin, either major (kabira) or minor (saghira) sins.
   b) They do not sin before or after their prophethood.
      i) Explain the story of Musa was something done unintentionally
      ii) Yusuf never did anything wrong or even thought about doing something wrong.
      iii) thinking
   c) No prophet ever experienced disbelief in Allah, even for the blink of an eye.
      i) Explain the story of Ibrahim alayhis salam
40) A prophet is a someone who was given revelation (wahy)
41) A person cannot become a prophet through any means other than Allah choosing them and sending them revelation. Thus a person cannot think that if they are very good and do a lot of reflection that they can attain the station of prophethood (maqaam an nabuwwwah).
   a) What a person can attain through work and self-reflection is the station of sainthood (maqaam al wilaya).
42) A messenger is a prophet who was given a specific message.
43) A prophet continues the message of a previous prophet
44) All messengers are prophets, but not all prophets are messengers.
45) All prophets were free men. Thus, the prophets were never slaves, women, or jinn.
46) There are 124,000 prophets.

47) There are 314 messengers.
48) The first prophet is Adam alayhis salam and the last is the prophet Muhammad ﷺ.
49) We know the names of 25 prophets in the Quran
   a) Adam
   b) Idris (Enoch)
   c) Nuh (Noah)
   d) Hud
   e) Salih
   f) Ibrahim (Abraham)
   g) Ismael (Ishmael)
   h) Ishaq (Isaac)
   i) Lut (Lot)
   j) Yaqub (Jacob)
   k) Yusuf (Joseph)
   l) Musa (Moses)
   m) Harun (Aaron)
   n) Shuayb
   o) Ayyub (Job)
   p) Yunus (Jonah)
   q) Ilyas (Elias)
   r) Al-Yasa'
   s) Dhul Kifl
   t) Dawud (David)
   u) Sulayman (Soloman)
   v) Zakariyya (Zackariah)
   w) Yahya (John)
   x) Isa (Jesus)
   y) Muhammad ﷺ
50) Luqman the Wise (Quran Chapter 31) and Iskandar Dhul Qarnayn (Quran 18:83-101) are not prophets but rather they are from the awliyaa.
51) There is a difference of opinion about Al-Khadir alayhis salam (Quran 18:65-82). We should not say affirmatively one way or the other.
52) We affirm that the best and greatest of all the prophets and messengers is our Messenger Muhammad ﷺ.
   a) Because of his high station, Allah honoured him with special gifts that He gave no other person such as:

i) Al Liwa (the banner) on the day of Judgement.

ii) Al Hawd (the basin) on the day of judgement.

iii) Al Wasila

iv) The Greatest Shafa'a

v) Al Fadila

vi) Isra wal miraj

vii) Ref chapter of khasa'is from Khalil and Minhaj

53) The Seal of the Messengers (the last prophet sent) is the Prophet Muhammad ﷺ.

   a) No new messenger or prophet will ever be sent after him.

   b) Isa alayhis salam will return and be from the ummah of the Prophet ﷺ

54) We do not distinguish (ref ayah) between any of the prophets in that we do not reject some and accept others.

   a) The Jews accept Musa alayhis salam and reject Isa alayhis salam and the Prophet Muhammad ﷺ.

   b) The Christians accept Musa and Isa alayhimus salam but reject the Prophet Muhammad ﷺ. We accept them all, upon them and upon our prophet be the peace and blessings of Allah.

   c) Ref hadith about Yunus ibn Matta as well as story of the Prophet ﷺ telling them that Musa will be first to be revived.

55) We do recognize that some prophets are higher in rank than others (ref ayah____)

56) There are five who are the Resolute Messengers (ulil 'azim –ref ayah_____). Their ranking also indicates their level:

   a) Muhammad ﷺ and he is Habib Allah (The Beloved one of Allah)

   b) Ibrahim (Abraham) alahis salam and he is Khalil Allah (The Friend of Allah)

   c) Musa (Moses) alayhis sala and he is Kaleem Allah (The one Allah spoke to) because Allah spoke to him with speech that does not resemble created speech.

   d) Isa (Jesus) alayhis salam and he is Ruh Allah (The Spirit of Allah)

   e) Nuh (Noah) alayhis salam and he is Naji Allah (The one Allah saved)

57) After the five greatest messengers then comes in rank:

   a) The remaining messengers.

   b) The remaining prophets

   c) The specific angels (like Jibreel alayhis salam)

   d) The sahaba

      i) The ten

      ii) The people of Badr

      iii) The people of Uhud

iv) The people of the Pledge of Ridwan
   e) Tabi'een
   f) Tabi' at tab'een
   g) The remaining people of the ummah
58) From amongst the women of the world, the best are:
   i) Khadija
   ii) Maryam
   iii) A'isha
   iv) Fatima
   v) Asia
59) Isa alayhis salam:
   a) Was born from Mayram the Pure and he did not have a father.
   b) Is not God nor is he the "son of God" as the Christians say.
   c) Was sent as a prophet and a messenger and given a book (Injeel).
   d) Was not crucified as the Christians believe. Rather, Allah made another person appear to the people as if he was Isa and they crucified that other man.
   e) Was saved by Allah ﷻ and then raised into the sky where he dwells now, alive, never having died.
   f) Will return to slay the Dajjal at the end of time.
   g) Will live with the Muslim ummah, marry, then pass away and be buried next to the Prophet Muhammad ﷺ.
   h) His pure mother, Maryam, will be a wife of the Prophet Muhammad ﷺ, in jannah.
60) We cannot claim someone is a prophet unless there is proof from the Quran or a Hadith. To claim that someone is a prophet who is not is kufr. To deny any prophet is kufr. If there is a person that could or could not be a prophet, we should just say "Allah knows best."
61) We believe the prophets were given miracles (mu'jizat) for them to prove to their people that what they were saying was truly from Allah.
62) "Their miracles are as if Allah said, "This servant has spoken the truth in all that he says." -Ibn 'Ashir
63) These miracles would sometimes come in the form similar to, but greater than, something that was common to their people at their time.
   a) At the time of Musa alayhis salam, magic was at a height. So, his miracle resembled some of the magic that was perfected at that time but was clearly not magic as was attested to by the experts of magic.

b) At the time of Isa alayhis salam, medicine was at a height and at the forefront of people's respect. He came with miracles of healing the sick and bringing the dead to life when no other medicine could do the same.

c) At the time of Salih, alahis salam, his people had perfected carving homes from the stone mountain. The miracle that he was given was bringing a live animal from the stone mountain.

d) At the time of the Prophet Muhammad ﷺ, Arabic poetry and language was at its height. His greatest miracle was the Quran which overshadowed anything that the people had at that time.

The Angels

64) Angels are a creation of Allah that were created to worship Allah.
65) They are made of light.
66) They are neither male nor female.
67) They do not have a mother or father.
68) They do not marry nor do they have children.
69) They do not eat food or drink water.
70) They obey all the commands of Allah and never disobey Him (reference Ayah).
71) They cannot even think about wanting to do sin.
   a) Iblis is not a "fallen angel" but rather he is a jinn that used to be righteous and then fell into a low state due to his arrogance/jealousy that caused him to refuse to bow to Adam.
72) We do not know how many angels there are in total.
73) Some angels only worship.
74) Some angels have specific duties.
   a) Jibreel alayhis salam (Angel that brings revelation)
   b) Mika'eel alayhis salam (angel that brings rain and sustenance)
      i) Sustenance is anything that you can get benefit from.
   c) Israfeel alayhis salam (angel that blows the trumpet)
   d) Izra'eel alayhis salam (angel that takes the souls at death).
   e) Munkar and Nakeer alayhimus salam (the angels that ask the questions in the grave).
   f) Malik alayhis salam (keeper of the Hellfire)
   g) Ridwan alayhis salam (keeper of jannah).

h) Raqeeb and Ateed (the general name for the angels that record our deeds on our right and left side).
   i) The angel who writes good deeds down writes them down immediately and the deed is multiplied 10-700 times or more.
   ii) The angel who writes the bad deeds is told by the other angel to not write down a bad deed once it happens. The person is given 6 hours to repent (tawbah) and then if that is not done the deed is written down.
i) We have guardian angels that protect us (hafadha). This could be as few as two (our Noble recorders) or even 400 or more according to the Hadith.
   i) Allah does not need the angels to protect us.
   ii) If we were to lose our angelic protection even for an instant we would be crushed by unseen forces that are trying to harm us.

75) To increase angelic protection we have to increase the things angels like:
   a) Good actions
   b) Dhikr
   c) Being properly covered with clothing
   d) Good smells
   e) Clean mouth (both in smell and not saying bad words
   f) Staying away from things they don't like such as:
      i) Sins
      ii) Bad smells
      iii) Dogs
      iv) Images
      v) Music
      vi) Nakedness

The Books

76) Allah sent books to His messengers.
77) It is revelation (wahy) that is sent to the Messengers.
78) There is no revelation to anyone after the Prophet Muhammad ﷺ.
79) The book or scripture was written down, it could be read and recited but it is the Speech of Allah (kalamul Allah) and does not resemble the speech of humans or jinn.
80) The following books were sent:
   a) Torah (torah) was given to Musa

b) Psalms (zabur) was sent to Da'wud (David)

c) Gospel (injil) was sent to Isa alayhis salam.

d) Quran

81) All the books have been changed or lost except the Quran as Allah has promised to preserve it (ref ayah_____)

a) Some changed their books intentionally

b) Some changed by mistake

c) We have the Quran preserved by isnad

d) Isnad is a khasiyya (special trait) only given to this ummah.

e) Memorization of the Quran is a khasiyya of this ummah.

f) The ummah of Muhammad ﷺ is described in the books of the previous people as "anajeeluhum fi sudurihim" (their injeel is in their hearts)

g) Allah also preserved the sciences needed to unlock the Quran such as Hadith, Arabic, Fiqh, Seera, Tafsir, etc.

82) We believe in everything mentioned in the Quran.

a) There are some ayahs that are ambiguous (mutashabih) and we do not try to explain these.

b) The other ayahs are clear (muhkamat) and we can understand and explain these.

c) Only the people of knowledge are allowed to give explanation to the Quran and Hadith. We go to the living scholars or the books of the scholars.

83) The following prophets were sent scriptures (suhuf).

a) Ibrahim alayhis salam.

b) Musa alayhis salam.

84) The Prophet Muhammad was given the Quran, which is the Clear Guidance.

a) Additionally, he was given other forms of revelation (wahy), which translate into his words (hadith), actions (amal), and approval (taqreer).

　i) These three things are called the Sunnah.

　ii) Ref ayah from sura najm

　iii) Aisha said, "His character was the Quran."

　iv) The answer to the question, "Why didn't he ever make a tafsir on the Quran?" His life was the tafisr.

b) Just as we follow the revelation of the Quran, we have to follow the Sunna.

　i) Ref ayah about obeying Allah and His Messenger.

　ii) Three "double orders" in the Quran

　　(1) Obey Allah and His Messenger

　　(2) Thank Allah and your parents

(3) Establish the prayer and give zakat

c) Belief is not complete without action, no action is considered without an intention, and no action or intention is considered unless it is in line with the Sunna.

The Final Hour

85) We believe the final hour will come once the trumpet is blown by Israfeel alayhis salam.
86) There are many signs before the End of Time, some are large and some small.
87) Large signs include:
    a) The Mahdi
    b) The return of 'Isa alayhis salam who will kill the dajjal.
    c) Yajooj and Majooj
    d) Dajjal and the Jassasah
    e) Rising of the sun from the West
    f) The closing of the door of repentance
    g) The coming of the Dabba (talking beast)
    h) The removal of the Quran and knowledge from the pages and from the hearts.
    i) The destruction of the Ka'bah
88) Small signs include:
    a) Barefoot, unclothed shepherds competing to build tall buildings.
    b) Women being clothed and unclothed at the same time.
    c) Children disrespecting their parents.
    d) Murder becomes rampant.
    e) The embargo on Iraq and Sham.

Akhira

89) We must believe in all stages of the afterlife that have been explained to us through he Quran or in Sound Hadiths.
90) The matters of the afterlife can only be verifiably transmitted if they have come through revelation (wahy) and the only ones who get revelation are prophets. Therefore, what we hear from saints and through dreams of people is not something that is incumbent to believe and it must always be checked against the Quran and Hadith.

Death

91) No one dies except by the decree (qadr) of Allah.
92) Everyone has an appointed length to their life (ajal) and when that time comes, there is no way around it.
   a) Mention the story of Sulayman's (alayhis salam) minister.
93) The souls are taken at the time of death by the angel 'Izraeel, alayhis salam, who is responsible for taking the souls of all animate life.
94) The souls are taken from the believers gently while they are severely ripped from the disbelievers. (ref ayah from Nazi'at_____)
95) We do not delve into discussion about the soul (ruh) rather, we "say the soul is a matter from my Lord" and he know where it is, what it is made of and where it resides (ie all the details about it).
96) The souls are everlasting and are either rewarded or punished forever.
97) We do not say about the martyrs that they are dead, rather they are living and the Lord provides their sustenance (ref ayah_____).
98) Like the martyrs, and even more importantly, is that we believe that the Prophets are not dead, rather they are living in a way we cannot comprehend.
   a) Refer to the story of the Isra where Musa Alayhis salam was seen in the red hill praying, then in Jerusalem, then in the highest heaven. How could he be in all those places and yet be dead in his grave? This makes it clear that we do not comprehend the matters of the afterlife and the unseen.
99) After death, two angels (Munkar and Nakeer) come and awake the dead person to ask him the Questions of the Grave. They are frightening and have voices like thunder. They ask three things, "Who is your Lord?", "Who is Your Prophet?", "What is your religion?" and "What is your book?" Those who believed during their lives will be given the strength and firmness to answer.
100) For the believers who did good there will be a reward in the grave and it will hug him or her like a mother hugs their child.
101) For the non-believers and the disobedient Muslims, there will be a punishment in the grave. The grave will squeeze them.
102) Sadaqa, dua and recitation of Quran reach and benefit the dead.
   a) Establish sadaqa jariya for the dead.

Barzakh

103) This is the state where souls are after they die and before the Qiyama.
104) People in their graves can hear the voices of the living who come to visit them. They can even hear the sound of the sandals of the people as they walk away.

'Araaf

105) This is a place that is not jannah or jahannam.
106) Some people will reside in here for a time and then go to jannah.
107) It is mentioned in a Hadith that there is a group of people that did some good things but they disobeyed their parents in going out to do that good. So, they have good deeds and bad deeds and that's why they have to wait in this place before going into jannah.

Ba'th

108) The trumpet is blown by the Angel Israfeel whose only duty is to blow the horn.
109) With the blowing of the trumpet, everything will die and everything will be destroyed.
110) Nashr- All animate life (humans, jinn, animals, insects, etc.) will be resurrected from their graves and their bodies will come back to its original form.
111) Hashr- All will be brought together on the plain of standing on the Day of Standing (Yaum al qiyamah).
112) There are many frightening things that will occur on that day (hawl).
113) Everything will be turned to dust except for humans and jinn.
114) The believers will gaze upon Allah during the Standing and in jannah. We should not delve into how this "gaze" will occur but remember that Allah does not resemble creation so looking at Him will be in a way that is different than looking at creation.
   a) The people of the Hellfire will not gaze at Allah.
115) Some will take their books in their right hands (the people who did good) while others will take it in their left hands or behind their backs (the people who did bad).
116) Scales (mizan): All humans and jinn will have their actions weighed on the scales. The actions are recorded in a person's books (kitab, suhuf)
117) Every person and even animals, which are owed a right, will be given it on the Day of Judgment.

118) If another harms a person, the victim will take from the perpetrator's good deeds. If there are not any good deeds to take from, then the victim will give him his bad deeds.

119) The bridge (sirat): All humans and jinn will cross over a bridge that is finer than a hair and sharper than a sword. The bridge is set up across the Hellfire. Some will cross like lightening, some like the wind, some like a fast horse, some will run, and some will fall into the Hellfire.

120) The Basin (hawd): The Prophet Muhammad is given a Basin on the Day of Judgment to give his community (ummah) water to drink from.
   a) Whoever drinks from it will never be thirsty afterwards. The drink is sweeter than honey and whiter than milk.
   b) Its distance is that of Medina to Yemen and its cups are like the stars in number.
   c) Only those Muslims who did not innovate will be allowed to drink.

121) Intercession (shafa'ah): Some people, starting with the Prophet Muhammad ﷺ, will be allowed to intercede on behalf of some believers that will be headed to the Fire or in it. After the Prophet ﷺ, other prophets intercede. Others that will intercede include martyrs (shuhada'), teachers, and those who memorized the Quran.
   a) The Prophet ﷺ will intercede for the people of his ummah that did kaba'ir.

122) Paradise (jannah): It is a created place that is in existence now. It will remain forever as an everlasting reward for those who believed in Allah.

123) Hellfire (Jahannam): It is a created places that is in existence now. It will remain forever as an everlasting punishment for those who disbelieved in him.

124) Allah knew before He created anything, who would go into Heaven and who would go into Hell.
   a) We do not say that anyone is definitely going to jannah or Jahannam unless there is an Ayah or Hadith (like Abu Lahab or Firoun)
   b) We can say that we feel that a person was good or bad and that he may be rewarded or punished.
   c) Only Allah knows the final state of people and whom He will forgive and who He will not forgive.
   d) Some people will live their whole loves as a Muslim then leave Islam at the end of their life. Some people will live their life as a non-believer and then accept Islam in their final moments. But we may not know that this occurred.
   e) We should regularly ask Allah to give us the best seal (khatimatan hasana) which is to die as a Muslim.

125) The people who are believers and go to jahannam for bad actions they did will not stay there forever. (4:48)

126) No believer will stay in jahannam forever, even if there faith (iman) was the weight of a speck.
127) We should pray for the forgiveness of all Muslims and for guidance for all humanity.

Qadr (Divine Decree)

128) We must believe that everything happens because of the decree of Allah.
129) We believe all things, whether sweet or bitter, good or bad, happen because of the decree of Allah.
130) We do not say that Allah decrees only good and that bad is from us. This insinuates that we can create our own actions, which is false. Allah creates all actions. (ref Ayah "He created you and that which you do").
131) Some people are believers (sa'eed) because that is what was decreed for them and others are decreed as non-believers (shaqi).
   a) Allah makes whoever He wants to be a sa'eed or shaqi.
132) We have the free will (kasab) to either choose to do good or evil.
133) Nobody is ever in a state where they do not need Allah. Examples are:
   a) That we need Him for nourishment and we don't get our nourishment from food or water. Rather it is from Allah but it happens through food or water.
   b) We need Allah to keep us warm and to give us a way to cook and He does it through fire. It is not the fire that burns, rather Allah burns but through the fire. This is why when He told the fire not to burn, it did not burn Ibrahim alayhis salam.
   c) Allah cuts and it is not the knife. This is why when He told the knife not to cut, it did not cut Ismael alayhis salam.
134) Everything and all decrees are written on the Preserved Tablet (lawh al mahfudh) in the 7th heaven.
135) Everything is written on the lawh (tablet) with the pen (qalam).
   a) Allah created the pen and told it to write everything that will be.
   b) The pen has been lifted and the ink has dried thus there is no one who can change the decree of Allah.
136) Allah knew everything that was going to happen and does not need the lawh to preserve the orders.
137) Everything has a defined lifespan (ajal) and when that ajal comes, there is no delaying it or expediting it.

a) Living and inanimate things all have a pre-ordained limit and once that comes, there is no changing it.
b) The story of the minister of Sulayman alayhis salam.
c) We should not be angry when something ends.

138) All our actions, good or bad, have been decreed.
139) Good actions (sing hasana; pl. hasanat) are rewarded at a rate of 10 times the original deeds and even up to 700 times or more.
140) Bad actions (sing. Sayyi'ah; pl. sayyi'aat) are counted as one action.
141) Ref ayah whoever does an atom's weight...
   a) Discuss what is a dharra

Ghayb

142) We believe in the jinn who are created from fire.
   a) There are good jinn (ref sura al jinn)
   b) Bad jinn are called shayateen (sing shaytan)
   c) Dhikr will protect us from the bad jinn.

Other Tenets of Our Belief

143) Sahaba: The Companions of the Prophet ﷺ.
   a) Masculine singular is 'sahabi' and plural is 'sahaba'. For a female companion singlular is 'sahabiyyah' and plural is 'sahabiyyaat.' When there are males and females, the masculine plural is used.
   b) The definition of a sahabi (companion) is someone who:
      i) Was in the presence of the Prophet ﷺ even if only an instant. This is even if they did not see him as some sahaba were blind. There were people who were alive at his time, believed in him but never were in his presence thus they are not a sahabi, such as Uways al Qarani.
      ii) The presence was while both were alive. Thus, if a person saw the Prophet ﷺ after he passed, then that would not make him a sahabi.
      iii) Believed in him. There were some people who were alive at his time, were in his presence but did not believe in him, thus they are not a sahabi. There were some who believed in him after his death, they too are not from the sahaba.

iv) Then passed away maintaining that belief. There were some people who became Muslim, met the Prophet ﷺ, but later left Islam. Thus, they are not from the sahaba.
c) Allah chose them above all other humans to be the companions of the best of Creation ﷺ.
d) They are the link between the Ummah and the Prophet ﷺ
  i) Refere to charts of the sanad from us to them.
e) Love of the Sahaba is from Iman.
f) Hate for any of the Sahaba is a sign of nifaaq (hypocriscy) i.e. insincerity in the deen.
g) We believe and love the "The Blessed Ten" who were specifically promised Paradise:
  i) Abu Bakr
  ii) Umar
  iii) Uthman
  iv) Ali
  v) Abdur Rahman ibn Awf
  vi) Talha ibn Ubayd Allah
  vii) Zubayr ibn al Awwam
  viii) Sa'd ibn Abi Waqqas
  ix) Sa'eed ibn Zayd
  x) Abu 'Ubaydah ibn Al Jarrah
h) All the sahaba will be in jannah and will never even touch the fire (ref ayah).
i) All of the sahaba are just (pl. 'udool and sing. 'adl).
j) The lowest in rank amongst the sahaba is better than the highest wali of the later generations.
  i) Mention the story of the dust that entered Mu'awiyas horse's nose.
k) We only mention the sahaba in a good manner and with utmost respect (adab).

144) We believe that the first three generations are the best of all people after the prophets.
  a) Sahaba: Any Muslim who met the Prophet ﷺ, even briefly, and then stayed a Muslim until death.
  b) Tabi'een: Any Muslim who spent time with a sahabi.
  c) Tabi' at tabi'een: Any Muslim who spent time with a tabi'ee

145) It is fard to only say good things about the sahaba, the first generations (salaf) and the scholars in a good manner.

146) We follow the way of the salaf and make dua for them
  a) Ref ayah and mention that we need to do this at least once in our lifetime, like making dua for our parents.

147) We believe that our deen has been codified and preserved by the early imams:
   a) Imam Abu Hanifa
   b) Imam Malik
   c) Imam Ash-Shafi'i
   d) Imam Ahmed ibn Hanbal
148) We should not speak ill of the dead.
149) We do not go to psychics.
150) We believe that du'a will benefit and Allah will answer all dua ref Ayah
151) We believe in magic and that it can affect people. Dua, Quran recitation, prayer, etc can protect us from magic.
   a) To perform magic takes a person out of Islam due to the need of reciting formulas with statements of kufr.
152) Al-Mithaq (The Covenant): Allah spoke to all of humanity and asked, "Am I not your Lord?" and we all responded saying, "Yes." Thus, those who are believers are fulfilling that covenant and those who are not have broken the covenant. (7:172).
153) Al-'arsh wal kursi (the throne and the footstool) ref ayah
   a) They are creations of Allah in the heavens and they are enormous in size.
   b) Allah does not need the throne or the footstool.
   c) Allah controls his arsh and kursi.
   d) They are over the 7 heavens and the earth.
   e) We only can know what Allah wants us to know.
154) Sidratul muntaha (The furthest Lote Tree), which is the last point in creation.
155) We accept all those who are from the people of the Qibla (ahlul qibla) as being Muslim.
   a) Whoever faces the direction of Mecca (Qibla) and eats the slaughter of Muslims, we consider him to be a Muslim.
   b) We never say that any Muslim is a kaafir (non believer) or a munafiq (hypocrite). Ref Hadith
156) We stick to the congregation of the Muslims by praying with the Muslims and obeying those in charge (ulil amr).
157) We make dua for the ulil amr.
158) Ulil amr are:
   a) The leaders in charge of the land we reside in. (bay'ah/allegiance to ruler).
   b) The scholars.
159) Awliya (Protected Friends of Allah).
   a) We believe that Allah protected some people more than others.
   b) There are different levels of protection.

OUTLINE SUMMARY OF IMAN 100

    c) Allah gives some awliya miracles.
160) We do not draw weapons on any person, especially a Muslim, someone under the protection of Muslims (dhimmi), or someone in a covenant with the Muslims (mu'ahid).
161) We love the people of obedience and we hate the actions of the disobedient.
162) We pray for the guidance and forgiveness of those who are doing wrong.
163) Tawbah
    a) Allah will accept repentance (tawbah) for anything.
    b) Allah can forgive any sin (even if there was no tawba) other than shirk (associating partners with Allah/disbelieving in Allah/refusing Islam).
    c) Allah will accept all tawbah until:
        i) The sun rises from the West
        ii) A person's soul is being drawn out of his body (yughar-ghir)
            (1) Firoun's tawbah was too late.
    d) We should never be in despair (ya's) from the Mercy and Forgiveness of Allah.
    e) There is mercy for believers in the afterlife, even if their faith is the weight of a mustard seed.
    f) The conditions of tawbah are:
        i) Remorse over what was done.
        ii) An intention never to do that again.
        iii) Stop the action if involved in it.
        iv) Redress any wrongs.
    g) If a person has not made tawbah, they are a "faasiq" (disobedient Muslim) but they are still Muslim.
        i) If they pass away before doing tawbah, then we consider them Muslim and we say that it is up to Allah to forgive them or not.
    h) Major sins (kabaa'ir) can only be wiped out through tawbah
    i) Minor sins (sagha'ir) can be wiped out through specific tawbah or even just merely by doing good deeds, such as walking to the masjid, doing wudu or staying away from the major sins.
    j) Allah can also turn bad deeds into good deeds.
164) We do not debate unless absolutely necessary and we do so in the best of manners.
    a) Ref ayah about "best of ways"
    b) Story of Musa with firoun
    c) It is not from the sunna to debate about the sunna
165) We believe in the fitna (trial) of life. This could be in the form of disbelief or not remembering Allah.

166) If someone is disobeying Allah outwardly (faasiq), we have to judge according to that and we leave the inwards to Allah. (ref Hadith)
   a) However we never say that a person is not Muslim because they are not following the rules.
   b) To call a person a kaafir or munafiq is called takfeer and is not allowed. Ref hadith about takfeer
   c) As long as a person faces our Qibla and eats our slaughtered meat, then we consider them Muslim.
   d) We also have to make sure that we see the good side of every person even if they are doing something bad. This is the aqida of ahlul sunna.
      i) Example of a warrior who stole a horse.
167) We must accept all things that are readily known about the religion (ma'lum min al din bi darura). Examples of this are the five pillars, well known prohibitions such as drinking alcohol, gambling, backbiting, adultery, and eating pork. If a person rejects one of these matters, they leave the fold of Islam (Apostate/murtad, apostasy/riddah).
168) If a person adds something to the deen, that was not a part of it or not a method to maintain the deen, that is called a bid'ah (innovation).
169) The Night Journey and Heavenly Ascent (al isra wal miraj)
   a) The Prophet ﷺ went with his body and spirit. It was not merely by spirit or in a dream.
   b) He saw Musa alayhis salam in the red hill praying in his grave, then saw him again in Bayt al-Maqdis when he led the prophets in prayer, then in the highest of the heavens.
   c) Thus, the prophets are alive in their graves.
   d) He was taken to the highest heaven to receive orders not because that would make him closer to Allah physically, but as an honor to the Prophet ﷺ.
      i) Allah does not have a direction, time or place.
      ii) Allah can give a message to Jonah (Yunus) alayhis salam in the belly of the whale at the bottom of the ocean.

Who are the Angels and Why do We Believe in Them?[1]

Allāh says:

(Righteousness is not that you turn your faces to the East and the West; but righteousness is that one believes in Allāh, and the Last Day, and the Angels, and the Book, and the Prophets) (Qur'an 2:177)

And He also says:

(The Messenger has believed in what has been revealed to him from his Lord, and the believers as well. All have believed in Allāh and His Angels and His Books and His Messengers. "We make no division between any of His Messengers!") (Qur'an 2:285)

And:

(Whoever disbelieves in Allāh, and His Angels, and His Books, and His Messengers, and the Last Day has indeed gone far astray.) (Qur'an 4:136)

The understanding of why we are obligated to believe in the Angels can be gathered from these few verses of the Qur'an. We can also see that if we reject this belief then we are not recognized as being Muslims. In fact, Allāh says,

(Whoever disbelieves in Allāh, and His Angels......has indeed gone far astray) (Qur'an 4:136)

But how are we supposed to put this belief in the Angels into perspective? Is it sufficient to just say that we believe in the Angels and that's it? The scholars of Qur'anic tafsīr say that this is not the case. One of the reasons that they give for this understanding is found in the Āya that we just cited and the additional fact that merely claiming to believe in something does not qualify as Iman, as Allāh says in the Qur'an,

(The Desert Arabs say, "We believe." You have no faith, but you [should] say, "We have submitted our wills to Allāh," for not yet has faith entered your hearts. But if

---

[1] This and the concluding chapter are summaries that have been written by Ustadh Abdul Muhaymin based upon the books *The World of the Angels* by Shaykh 'Abdu'l-Hamid Kishk (*trans*. Aisha Bewley) and *The Lives of the Prophets* by Leila Azzam to which a few points were added in accordance with our overall objective of writing IMAN 100 as a text on the fundamentals of aqida.

you obey Allāh and His Messenger, He will not belittle anything from your deeds: for Allāh is Often-Forgiving, Most Merciful.) (Qur'an 49:14)

It is clear from this Āya that Allāh ﷻ does not accept the mere lip-service of a person saying something without it being a reality in their heart. It also shows that our actions are not the qualifiers of His acceptance. Along with everything else that Allāh has told us to believe in, the Angels (may Allāh's peace cover them all) are real and not metaphorical. The reality of the Angels has been attested to throughout history, but the truth of who they are and how they interact with the creation has been a source of confusion for a lot of people.

We read in the Qur'an where Allāh ﷻ informs us of how the pagan Arabs would consider the Angels to be akin to women and the "daughters of Allāh"—we seek refuge from falsely ascribing things to our Lord. Some people are of the opinion that Angels are capable of disobeying our Lord ﷻ, but this is false as Allāh ﷻ tells us in the Qur'an,

(The Messiah does not refuse to be a worshipper of Allāh neither the Angels who are nearest to Allāh....) (Qur'an 4:172)

He ﷻ also says,

(O you who believe, save yourself and your families from a fire whose fuel is men and stones, over which are Angels stern and severe who do not disobey Allāh, but do exactly what they are commanded.) (Qur'an 66:6)

These two Ayāt clearly demonstrate that the Angels are Allāh's faithful and obedient servants and it is incumbent upon us to believe in them as has been revealed. Anyone who has doubts about this or rejects the truth of it has unfortunately forfieted their Islam.

The Creation of the Angels

There is a blessed Ḥadith in Ṣaḥīh Muslim that informs us about the creation of the blessed Angels (peace be upon them) where in it is reported

'Aishah (May Allah be pleased with her) reported: The Messenger of Allah ﷺ said, **"Angels were created from light, jinns were created from a smokeless flame of fire, and Adam was created from what has been described to you [meaning from clay]."** (Muslim)

UNDERSTANDING THE ANGELS

Imam Ibn Ḥajar al-Asqalani reported in his peerless commentary on *Ṣaḥīḥ Al-Bukhari* that Imam Sa'id ibn Al-Musayyab (may Allah be pleased with them both) said, "The Angels are neither male nor female. They do not eat or drink. And they do not marry nor have children." These are beings that have been created solely to carry out the command of Allah ﷻ and have no hesitation in carrying out His commands. Allah also addresses the false belief that people have about the Angels having either a gender or familial relationship with Allah,

(And they have made the angels, who are servants of the Most Merciful, females. Did they witness their creation? Their testimony will be recorded, and they will be questioned.) (Qur'an 43:19)

Allāh ﷻ also says,

(And they attribute to Allah daughters - exalted is He - and for them is what they desire.)

(And when one of them is informed of [the birth of] a female, his face becomes dark, and he suppresses grief.)

(He hides himself from the people because of the ill of which he has been informed. Should he keep it in humiliation or bury it in the ground? Unquestionably, evil is what they decide.)

(And they attribute to Allah that which they dislike, and their tongues assert the lie that they will have the best [from Him]. Assuredly, they will have the Fire, and they will be [therein] neglected.") (Qur'an 16:57-59, 62)

Here Allah us informs about the Pagan Arabs who would say that Allah ﷻ had daughters from among the Angels, but when they themselves would have daughters would be so ashamed that they took up the foul and murderous practice of burying them alive. So not only would they ascribe to Allah something that they did not wish for themselves, they took to killing their innocent infant girls because they viewed them as something shameful, burdensome and unworthy of love and care. This shows you how false beliefs can cause us to do very despicable things in the name of "honor" or "righteousness". This should also serve as a reminder that we have to be conscious of how our beliefs affect our actions. Do not be led to believe that adopting or promoting attitudes and behaviors that cause us to be foul, abusive, destructive, or dismissive of people (Muslim or otherwise) is from the Religion because this is far from it and a clear indication of misguidance.

UNDERSTANDING THE ANGELS

The Form of the Angels and Their Beauty

The Angels (peace be upon them) have a size that is difficult for us to fathom. The Angel Jibrīl (peace be upon him) once revealed his true form to Prophet Muhammad ﷺ and when the Prophet saw Jibrīl, he ﷺ fainted at the sight of him. Jibrīl (peace be upon him) has 600 wings and each one covers the horizon. And there are narrations which suggest that some Angels (peace be upon them all) are bigger than Jibrīl.

Allāh ﷻ says:

(All the praises belongs to Allah, the Creator of the heavens and the earth, who made the Angels messengers having wings, two or three or four. He increases in creation what He wills. Indeed, Allah has control over all things.) (Qur'an 35:1)

The different tafsirs of this Āya say that **(He increases in creation what He wills)** is referring to the wings of the Angels, among other things, and Allah knows best. Other accounts from the Hadith relate to us the size of other Angels. The Messenger of Allah is reported to have said,

Jabir b. 'Abd Allah reported the Prophet ﷺ as saying: **I have been permitted to tell about one of Allah's angels who bears the throne that the distance between the lobe of his ear and his shoulder is a journey of seven hundred years.**

In another hadith, the Messenger of Allah ﷺ said:

"I have been granted permission to speak of an Angel, one of the bearers of the Throne. His feet are in the lowest earth and the Throne is resting on his horn. The distance from his earlobe to his shoulder is like that of a bird flying for seven hundred years. That Angel says, 'Glory be to You, wherever You are.'" (Tabarani in *Al-Mujam al-Awsat*)

As we have learned from the Qur'an and Hadith, the Angels vary in size and form. They have bodies and wings that are as large and as numerous as Allah wants them to be. This last Hadith is also one of numerous proofs against the claim that Allah ﷻ physically resides on the Throne. If He was on the Throne, why would this Angel make such a statement?[2] Allah is Exalted above the false things ascribed to Him, Most High and Majestic.

---

[2] I.e., if Allah was literally on the Throne, then why would one of the bearers of the Throne praise Allah by saying "Glory be to You, wherever You are"?

UNDERSTANDING THE ANGELS

The Angels are also beautiful as Ibn ʿAbbas (may Allah be pleased with him and his father) said that the word used in Sura Najm, verse 6 (*i.e.*, "dhu marra") means to have a beautiful appearance. It is also understood from Sura Yusuf (peace be upon him) where it is said,

(She said to Joseph, "Come out and show yourself to them!" and when the women saw him, they were stunned by his beauty, and cut their hands, exclaiming, "Great God! He cannot be mortal! He must be a precious angel!") (Qur'an 12:31)

The commentators on the Qur'an mention that this was because of his tremendous beauty.[3] So we see that the comparison of Prophet Yusuf, peace be upon him, to the Angels in beauty is fitting.

How Many Angels are There?

Allāh says:

(*...and none can know the forces of thy Lord*, **except He and this is no other than a warning to mankind.**) (Qur'an 74:31)

As shown here in this Aya, the number of Angels is unknown. Anyone who claims to have an exact number is deluded and should not be listened to as this knowledge is something only Allah knows and is one of the matters of the Unseen Realm (Ghayb).

There are Angels assigned to every corner of the universe and for everything that Allah has created. There are 70,000 Angels, that have been reported in the Hadith, that go into Bayt al-Maʿmur daily. It has been mentioned in the ahadith that the Bayt al-Maʿmur is an often frequented house in the upper levels of Paradise that is directly above and like the Kaʿba in the Unseen realm. These Angels go into it to worship Allah each day and never to return to it after they emerge from it, this has been going on since they were created.

It has also reached us through the Hadith,

From Jabir (may Allah be pleased with him) that the Messenger of Allah said: **"There is no space in the seven heavens a foot's length or a hand span or a palm's width which does not have an angel standing, bowing, or prostrating on it."** (Tabarani)

---

[3] And our Prophet also told us that he was given half of all beauty and so we affirm that he was even more beautiful that Prophet Yusuf (peace be upon him).

UNDERSTANDING THE ANGELS

Different Types of Angels

The Chiefs of the Angels

Among the Angels there are ranks that each of them occupy in terms of honor and importance. There are several that we should know of as they have been mentioned throughout the Qur'an and the Hadith. They are:

- **Jibrīl/Jibra'il** (peace be upon him): He is the greatest in terms of honor and rank among the Angels. He is the one who carries the revelation to the Prophets and Messengers and he is also responsible for carrying out Allah's command regarding punishment among the disobedient among the people of the creation in this life. He (peace be upon him) is also called the "Trustworthy Spirit" and "Holy Spirit" as stated in the following Aya,
    - **(The Trustworthy Spirit brought it down)** (Qur'an 26:193)
    - Allah also says, **(Say that the Holy Spirit has brought the Revelation with the Truth step by step from your Lord, to strengthen the believers and as a guidance and good news to the devout.)** (Qur'an 16:102)

- **Mika'il** (peace be upon him): He is in charge of the plants and the rain. He also was said to have taught Prophet Muhammad ﷺ during the first two years of him receiving Nabuwwa. He is also called the Angel of Mercy, as he prays for Allah to show mercy to His creation and he is consistent in doing this.
    - There is a Hadith in Imam Tabarani's book of narrations that says "Ibn 'Abbas (may Allah be pleased with him and his Father) reported that the Prophet ﷺ asked Jibrīl (peace be upon him) **'What is Mika'il in charge of?** He replied **'The plants and the rain.'**"

- **Israf'il/Israfil** (peace be upon him): He is the Angel of the Horn/Trumpet. It is said about him that his feet are at the bottom of the creation and his head reaches the apex of creation. He stares at the 'Arsh/Throne of Allah with his mouth on the Horn awaiting the manifestation of the Divine Decree for the Day of Judgement to begin when he will blow his Horn.
    - Prophet Muhammad ﷺ said, **How can I enjoy myself when the one with the Trumpet has raised the Trumpet to his mouth, knitted his brow and is waiting to blow."** They said: "What should we say, Messenger of Allah?" He said: "Say, **Allah is enough for us and the best Guardian. We have put our trust in Allah."** (Ahmad)

These Three (3) Angels, peace be upon them all, are the Chiefs among the Angels. They are the mightiest and among those who are in the "Highest Assembly" of the Angels. There are also other Angels who have important duties and we interact with them daily, or we will at least once in the life of this World or the Barzakh.

The Angel of Death

His name is Azra'il, peace be upon him. He is the Chief among the Angels who are responsible for taking the souls of all living creatures. Allah ﷻ says,

(Say, "The Angel of Death put in charge of you will reclaim you, and then you will be brought back to your Lord.") (Qur'an 32:11)

Each soul is taken in accordance with their state at the time of their death, the sinful soul will experience torment and the righteous soul will experience pain. Allah ﷻ also says about the righteous at the time of death,

(Those whose lives the angels take in a state of goodness. They will say to them, 'Peace be upon you. Enter the Garden as a reward for what you have done.') (Qur'an 16:32)

And He say about the arrogant Disbelievers,

(Who could be more wicked than someone who invents a lie against God, or claims, "A revelation has come to me," when no revelation has been sent to him, or says, "I too can reveal something equal to God's revelation"? If you could only see the wicked in their death agonies, as the angels stretch out their hands [to them], saying, "Give up your souls. Today you will be repaid with a humiliating punishment for saying false things about God and for arrogantly rejecting His revelations.") (Qur'an 6:93)

(Those who turn on their heels after being shown guidance are duped and tempted by Satan; they say to those who hate what Allah has sent down, "We will obey you in some matters"—Allah knows their secret schemes. How will they feel when the angels take them in death and beat their faces and their backs) (Qur'an 47:25-27)

It is also found in the Hadith how the Angels take the souls of those who were in either state at death,

Sayyiduna Bara ibn Aazib narrated that they went with the Prophet to the funeral of an Ansar man. They came to the grave but it had not been dug. So, Allah's Messenger ﷺ sat down and they sat down around him as though birds were perched on their heads. He had a stick in his hand and he etched lines with it on the ground. Then, raising his head, he said, **"Seek refuge in Allah from the punishment in the grave."** Twice or thrice. He then said, **"As a believer is on the point of departing from this world and entering the next, Angels with faces as white as the sun come down from heaven to him with a shroud of paradise and some of its perfume. They sit as far away from him as a sight can behold. The angel of death comes and sits at his head and says, ' 'O pious soul, emerge to forgiveness and pleasure of Allah' So, it emerges as through a drop of water flows from a water-skim. He takes it but the other angels do not let him hold it for an instant. They take it quickly and put it in that shroud and that perfume. So that it emits a fragrance similar to the sweetest musk found on the surface of the earth. Then, they carry it up and whichever group of angels they pass, enquire, 'who is this pious soul?' They identify it by name and parentage with the best of its names by which the earthlings had called him. They come with it to the lowest heaven and call for the gate to be opened for it. The gate is opened and (from then on) at every heaven, its chief angels lead it to the next heaven and so to the seventh.**

Allah, Mighty and Glorious, says, 'place the record of my slave in 'Illiyun, Take it back to earth, since I have created mankind from it and I shall return them to it and I shall raise them again from it.' His soul is restored to his body and two Angels come to him, make him sit up, and ask him, 'who is your Lord?' He says, 'My Lord is Allah.' They ask, 'what is your religion?' He says, 'Islam is my religion. They ask 'who is this man who was sent to you?' He says, 'Allah's Messenger!' They ask, 'How do you know? He says, 'I read Allah's Book, believed in it, and confirmed it as true.' A crier from heaven calls, 'My slave has spoken the truth. Spread out for him carpets from Paradise, clothe him from paradise and open a gate for him into paradise.' Its breeze and sweet smell come to him. His grave is widened for him as far as the eye can see.

Then a man with a beautiful face, beautiful dress, and sweet smell comes to him and says, 'Be happy as you wish for this is your day that has been promised to you.' He asks, 'who are you with such a beautiful face and good tidings?' He says, 'I am your good deeds.' He then prays, 'My Lord, let the Last Hour come! My Lord, let the Last Hour come that I may return to my people and my property.'

He then said, **"As a disbeliever is about to depart from this world and enter the next world, black-faced angels come down to him from heaven with hairy cloth and sit as far away from him as the sight can perceive. The Angel of Death comes and sits at his head and calls, 'O evil soul emerge to Allah's wrath. It scatters in his body unwilling to emerge, but he extracts it as spit is drawn out from moistened wool. He seizes it but the other Angels do not let him hold it for an instant. They snatch it quickly and place it in the hairy cloth from which it gives a nasty stench similar to the most unbearable stench of a corpse found on the surface of the earth. Then, they carry it up and whichever group of angels they pass, enquire, 'who is this evil soul' they identify it by name and parentage with the ugliest of its names by which the earthlings had called him. They come with it to the lowest heaven and ask for the gate to be opened for it, but it is not opened."** Then Allah's Messenger recited:

(The gates of heaven shall not be opened for them, nor shall they enter the garden until the camel passes through the eye of the needle.) (Qur'an 7:40)

And he ﷺ then said, "Allah Mighty and Glorious, will say 'Place his record in sijjin in the lowest earth,' His' soul is thrown down." Then he ﷺ recited:

(And whosoever associates anything with Allah, it is as though he had fallen from heaven and the birds snatch him away. Or the wind sweeps him to a remote place.) (Qur'an 22:31)

His soul is restored to his body and two Angels come to him and make him sit up. They ask him, "Who is your Lord?" but he is unable to answer. They ask him about his religion, but he cannot answer. They ask him about the man sent to them, but he cannot say anything. So, a crier calls from heaven, "He lies. Stretch a carpet from hell for him and open for him a gate to hell." So the heat of hell and hot air come to him and his grave is narrowed over him till his ribs are pressed on one another. A man of an ugly appearance and ugly dress with a repulsive odor appears before him and says, "Grieve with that which hurts you! This is the day of yours that was promised to you." He asks, "Who are you? Your face is the ugliest and brings evil." He says, "I am your evil deeds." He prays, "My Lord, put off the Last Hour."

According to another version that is very much like it and adds the following:

When a believer's soul comes out (of his body), every Angel between heaven and earth and every Angel in heaven prays for mercy on him. The gates of heaven are opened for him and the keeper of every gate prays to Allah that his soul may be taken up from the front of them. The soul of the disbeliever is extracted with his reins. All the Angels between heaven and earth and all the Angels in heaven curse him. The gates of heaven are locked on him and all the keepers of the gates pray to Allah that his soul should not be taken up past them.   (Ahmad)

Our Guardian Angels

Allah ﷻ has assigned each of us Angels to guard over us as we sleep and move around the creation from the day we are born. The number of these Angels have varied according to the numerous reports about them, the understanding being there are a lot of Angels that we have protecting us. Some Hadith have reported more than 400.

Allah ﷻ says in the Qur'an

(He is the Supreme Master over His subjects. He sends out guardians to watch over you until, when death overtakes any of you, those sent by Us take his soul—they never fail in their duty.) (Qur'an 6:61)

He also says

> ([E]ach person has Guardian Angels before him and behind, watching over him by Allah's command. Allah does not change the condition of a people unless they change what is in themselves, but if He wills harm on a people, no one can ward it off apart from Him, they have no protector.) (Qur'an 13:11)

Ibn `Abbas (may Allah be pleased with him) said about this last Aya that "[E]ach has a succession of Angels in front and behind him keeping him safe by Allah's command." Likewise, Mujahid (may Allah be pleased with him) who is from the Tabi'in and was a student of Ibn `Abbas said that

> There is no one who does not have an Angel who is entrusted with protecting them, both when sleeping and awake, from Jinn, Men, and reptiles. None of them comes to him (or her) without finding an Angel blocking its path except for something that Allah has given permission to reach them.

A good lesson from this is to be mindful that our Lord has complete control of His creation and all things happen by His Permission, Subhanahu wa Ta`Ala. We do not believe in Fatalism, but we do believe that Allah is in control of everything, and He Guards and Watches over His entire creation.

Raqib and Ateed (Our Recording Angels): The Kiraman Katibin

Allah says about these two Noble Angels,

> (We created man. We know what his soul whispers to him: We are closer to him than his jugular vein with two receptors set to record, one on his right side and one on his left. He does not utter a single word without an ever-present watcher.) (Qur'an 50:16-17)

The Angel on the right is in charge and he is responsible for writing out your goods deeds. While the Angel on the left is responsible for writing out your bad deeds. Whenever we do a good deed the Angel on the right writes it down immediately but when we do a bad deed, the Angel on the left is instructed by the Angel on the right to wait for Six (6) hours. If you do not repent then he is instructed to write the bad deed but if you repent then you do not have a bad deed against you but you have a good deed in its place. A Hadith in Sahih Muslim says,

> Abu Huraira reported that Muhammad, the Messenger of Allah said: "**When it occurs to my servant that he should do a good deed but he actually does not do it,**

record one good act for him, but if he puts it into practice, I make an entry of ten good acts in his favour. When it occurs to him to do evil, but he does not commit it, I forgive that. But if he commits it, I record one evil deed against his name. The Messenger of Allah ﷺ said, The angels said: 'That slave of Yours intends to commit evil.' Though His Lord is More Observant than he. So then He ﷻ said: Watch him; if he commits (evil), write it against his name but if he refrains from doing it, write one good deed for him, for he desisted from doing it for My sake. The Messenger of Allah said: He who amongst you is good of faith, all his good acts are multiplied from ten to seven hundred times and all the evils that he commits are recorded as such until he meets Allah." (Muslim)

These two Noble Angels are with us at all times and they only leave us when we are in a state of janaba (major ritual impurity) or when we are using the restroom and relieving ourselves. We also know that they go a distance from us when we lie or do an evil act because of the stench we emit because of our foul state.

Munkar and Nakir (The Questioners of the Grave)

These Noble Angels are the ones who will question us in our grave right after we are buried. They will ask us three questions, or four depending on the tradition, and depending on how we lived in this life and our answer at that time. Our time in our grave will be one of blessings or torment. Anas narrated that:

The Prophet ﷺ said, "When a human being is laid in his grave and his companions return and he even hears their footsteps, two angels come to him and make him sit and ask him: What did you use to say about this man, Muhammad ? He will say: I testify that he is Allah's slave and His Messenger. Then it will be said to him, 'Look at your place in the Hell-Fire. Allah has given you a place in Paradise instead of it.'" The Prophet ﷺ said, "The dead person will see both his places. But a non-believer or a hypocrite will say to the Angels, 'I do not know, but I used to say what the people used to say! It will be said to him, 'Neither did you know nor did you take the guidance.' Then he will be hit with an iron hammer between his two ears, and he will cry and that cry will be heard by whatever approaches him except human beings and jinns." (Muslim)

He ﷺ also said, on the authority of Abu Hurayrah, that

When the deceased or one of you is buried, there come to him two black and blue angels, one of whom is called al-Munkar and the other al-Nakir. They say: "What did you say about this man?" and he says what he used to say: "He is the slave of Allah and His Messenger. I bear witness that there is no god but Allah and that Muhammad is His slave and Messenger." They say: "We knew that you would say that." Then his grave is made spacious for him, seventy cubits by seventy, and it is illuminated for him. Then it is said to him: "Sleep," and he says: "May I go back to my family and tell them?" They say: "Sleep like the bridegroom who will be woken by none but the dearest of his family to him," until Allah raises him from that resting-place of his. But if he is a hypocrite, he says: "I heard the people saying something so I said something like what they said. I do not know." They say: "We knew that you would say that." Then it is said to the earth: "Squeeze him." So it squeezes him until his ribs interlock, and he will continue to be tormented therein until Allah raises him from that resting-place of his.

Ridwan and Malik: The Guardians of The Gates of Heaven and Hell

These two Noble Angels (may Allah be pleased with them both) are the Guardians of Jannah and Jahannam respectively. Ridwan is the Chief of the Angels who stands guard at the Gates of Jannah and he will greet those of us who are fortunate to enter that Blessed Place. Allah says,

(Those who were mindful of their Lord will be led in throngs to the Garden. When they arrive, they will find its gates wide open, and its keepers will say to them, 'Peace be upon you. You have been good. Come in, you are here to stay,' and they will say, 'Praise be to Allah who has kept His promise to us and given us this land as our own. Now we may live wherever we please in the Garden.' How excellent is the reward of those who labor!) (Qur'an 39:73)

Ibn Kathir commented, "The Custodian of the Garden is an Angel called Ridwan. This is explicitly stated in the Hadith." Allah also said,

(But the evildoers will remain in Hell's punishment, from which there is no relief: they will remain in utter despair. We never wronged them; they were the ones who did wrong. They will cry, "Malik, if only your Lord would finish us off," but he will answer, "No! You are here to stay." We have brought you the Truth but most of you despise it.) (Qur'an 43:74-78)

Malik is also the Chief Angel among the nineteen Angels who are guardians over Jahannam as Allah says in the Qur'an,

(And what will explain to thee what Hellfire is? It spares nothing and leaves nothing; it scorches the flesh of humans; there are nineteen in charge of it, none other than angels appointed by Us to guard Hellfire and We have made their number a test for the disbelievers. So those who have been given the Scripture will be certain and those who believe will have their faith increased: neither those who have been given the Scripture nor the believers will have any doubts, but the sick at heart and the disbelievers will say, 'What could Allah mean by this description?' Allah leaves whoever He will to stray and guides whoever He Wills. No one knows your Lord's forces except Him, this is a warning to mortals.) (Qur'an 74:27-31)

Some of The Benefit That We Gain From The Angels

There are a number of things that the Angels do so that we can reap the benefit from their kindness to us. The most beneficial of these things is that they make du`a for us. The Angels are intelligent beings who cannot disobey Allah, but they also have the ability to think and reason to the degree that does not negate that unquestioning obedience to our Lord ﷻ. They also have a deep care and concern for the creation that Allah has revealed in the Qur'an:

(Those (Angels) who carry the Throne and those who surround it celebrate the praises of their Lord and have faith in Him. They beg forgiveness for the believers: 'Our Lord, You embrace all things in mercy and knowledge, so forgive those who turn to You and follow Your path. Save them from the pains of Hell and admit them, Lord, to the lasting Gardens You have promised to them, together with their righteous ancestors, spouses, and offspring: You alone are the Almighty, the All Wise.) (Qur'an 40:7-8)

And it has come in the Hadith

Abu Darda reported the Messenger of Allah ﷺ said, "**No Muslim servant supplicates for his brother behind his back but the Angel says: And for you the same.**" (Muslim) Likewise, Anas (may Allah be pleased with him) said that the Messenger of Allah ﷺ said "**No people sit to remember Allah but that a caller from heaven calls out to them, 'Arise forgiven.**" (Ahmad & Tabarani)

Allah also says in the Qur'an

(Believers, remember God often and glorify Him morning and evening it is He who sends blessings on you, as do His angels, in order to lead you out of the depths of darkness into the light. He is ever merciful towards the believers) (Qur'an 33:41-43)

Abu Darda (may Allah be pleased with him) also reported that the Messenger of Allah ﷺ said,

Whoever travels a path in search of knowledge, Allah will make easy for him the path to Paradise. Verily, the angels lower their wings for the seeker of knowledge. The inhabitants of the heavens and earth, even the fish in the depths of the water, seek forgiveness for the scholar. The virtue of the scholar over the worshiper is like the superiority of the moon over the stars. The scholars are the inheritors of the Prophets. They do not leave behind gold or silver coins, but rather they leave behind knowledge. Whoever has taken hold of it has been given an abundant share. (Abī Dāwūd)

So we see that good deeds allow us to gather a great deal of favor with our Lord thanks to the Du`a of the Angels. May Allah allow us to increase in good deeds and the gain the Baraka of the du`a of His most noble Angels.

Reasons for The Angels Cursing Us

There are also reasons for the Angels to curse us, may Allah preserve us from their cursing. While they are our guardians, they are first and foremost Allah's creation and His obedient servants who support us in our obedience and upright states.

Allah says,

(If anyone seeks a religion other than Islam (complete submission) to Allah, it will not be accepted from him, he will be one of the losers in the Hereafter. Why would Allah guide people who deny the truth, after they have believed and acknowledged that the Messenger is true, and after they have been shown clear proof? Allah does not guide evildoers, such people will be rewarded with being cursed by Allah, by the Angels, by all people and so they will remain, with no relief or respite for their suffering.) (Qur'an 3:85-88)

And so among the reasons for the Angels cursing us are the following:

- Trying to keep the Laws of Allah and His Rasul from being implemented when there is a lawful sentence to be carried out.
    - Abdullah ibn Abbas narrated: The Prophet said: **"If anyone is killed blindly or, when people are throwing stones, by a stone or a whip, his bloodwit is the bloodwit for an accidental murder. But if anyone is killed intentionally, retaliation is due. If anyone tries to prevent it, the curse of Allah, of Angels, and of all the people will rest on him."** (Abu Dawud)
- Being a leader of unlawful innovation (the one who originates the idea or promotes it strongly) or someone who gives shelter/support to them.
    - Qays ibn Abbad narrated: **I and Ashtar went to Ali and said to him: "Did the Messenger of Allah give you any instruction about anything for which he did not give any instruction to the people in general?" He said: "No, except what is contained in this document of mine." Musaddad then said: "He then took out a document." Ahmad added: "A document from the sheath of his sword." It contained [the following words]: The lives of all Muslims are equal; they are one hand against others; the lowliest of them can guarantee their protection. Beware, a Muslim must not be killed for an infidel, nor must one who has been given a covenant be killed while his covenant holds. If anyone introduces an innovation,**

he will be responsible for it. If anyone introduces an innovation or gives shelter to a man who introduces an innovation (in religion), he is cursed by Allah, by His angels, and by all the people. (Abu Dawud)

- Women who do not respond to their husbands call for intimacy and who leave the house without their husbands consent (*i.e.*, against their wishes when there is no valid reason to do so).
  - Abu Huraira: Allah's Messenger ﷺ said, **"If a husband calls his wife to his bed (i.e. to have sexual relation) and she refuses and causes him to sleep in anger, the angels will curse her till morning."** (Bukhari)

<u>NOTE</u>: We are briefly breaking from our discussion on the Angels to mention a few Hadith that give context and clarity to these issues. These two reasons for the Angels cursing women should not be viewed in a manner that would cause you to believe that our Lord ﷻ or His Messenger ﷺ have given an oppressive ruling on this matter as this tends to be viewed in the context of Western thought and sensibilities. Neither should you think that this gives men the right to abuse, malign or oppress women. Our women should and must be honored and respected and anyone who does differently should be dealt with accordingly![4]

'Umara ibn Ghurab reported that an aunt of his told him that:

> She asked 'A'isha, Umm al-Mu'minin, may Allah be pleased with her: "If a woman's husband desires her and she refuses to give herself to him either because she is angry or not eager, is there anything wrong with that?" "Yes," she replied. "Part of his right over you is that if he desires you when you are on a saddle, you must not refuse him." She said, "I also asked her, 'If one of us is menstruating and she and her husband only have a single cover, what should she do?' She replied, 'She should wrap her wrapper around her and sleep with him. He can have what is above it. I will tell you what the Prophet ﷺ did on one of his nights with me. I had cooked some barley and made loaf for him. He came in, stopped at the door, and then went into the mosque. When he wanted to sleep, he closed the door, tied up the waterskin, turned the cup over and put out the light. I waited for him and he ate the loaf. He did not go until I fell asleep. Later he felt the cold and came and got me up.

---

[4] This does not mean that we take matters into our own hands and act as if we have the legal authority to physically punish or force another person to do anything against their will. We come to the assistance of our fellow human beings, while not overstepping the bounds into oppression. So if they will not change their behavior after talking peacefully to them, the next step would be to call the police, assist the wife and/or children taking refuge in a women's shelter, or any other legal means for the situation to be redressed if such drastic measures need to be taken. And if it comes to that, no one should think that calling non-Muslim authorities to stop a fellow Muslim's sin is tantamount to "allying with the Kuffar over the Believers" when he has already refused to heed the admonition of the Muslims.

"**Warm me! Warm me!**" he said. I said, "I am menstruating." He said, "**Then uncover your thighs,**" so I uncovered my thighs and he put his cheek and head on my thighs until he was warm. Then a pet sheep belonging to our neighbor came in. I went and took the loaf away. I disturbed the Prophet ﷺ and he woke up, so I chased the sheep to the door. The Prophet ﷺ said, "**Take what you got of your loaf and do not injure your neighbor's sheep.**"

There are a lot of benefits (fawa'id) to be taken from this hadith, but for our purposes, it shows the extent to which physical touching is allowed between husband and wife while she is on her menses.

Regarding leaving the home without the husband's permission, Ibn 'Umar (may Allah be pleased with both him and his father), said:

I saw a woman who came to the Prophet ﷺ and said, "Messenger of Allah, what rights do a husband have over his wife?" He said, "**His right over her is that she does not leave his house without his permission. If she does that, the Angels of mercy and Angels of anger curse her until she repents or returns.**" (Abu Dawud)

The scholars clarify that a wife has a general permission to move about in her local area in order to fulfill the needs of her household, including things like: buying groceries, taking the children back-and-forth to school, or visiting her parents. But if he forbids her to leave the house in general, then she should oblige. So things like this should be discussed before a couple gets married, especially if the husband is from a culture in which women typically only leave the house for necessities.

The final major reason why the Angels curse us is:

- Someone pointing a weapon at another Muslim.
    - Abu Hurairah (may Allah be pleased with him) said: "The Messenger of Allah ﷺ said, "**None of you should point at his brother with a weapon because he does not know that Satan may make it lose from his hand and, as a result, he may fall into a pit of Hell-fire (by accidentally killing him).**" (Bukhari)
    - Abul-Qasim (*i.e.*, the Messenger of Allah) ﷺ said, "**He who points at his (Muslim) brother with a weapon is cursed by the angels even if the other person should be his real brother.**" (Muslim)

These are some of the more essential things that we should know and believe about the Noble Angels of Allah (Subahaanahu wa Ta`Ala). Strive to do more of the things that we know will increase their love and their du`a for you as well. We ask Allah to make it easy for you to learn and understand all of these matters of the Din so that your Day of Standing will be easy for you and all of the Believers. We also ask that our families will accept the message of Islam and that we can all meet in Jannah, Ameen. *Al Hamdulillahi Rabbil `Alameen.*

Our Beloved Prophets عليهم السلام

It has been related in the Prophetic Hadith that there were over 124,000 Prophets and 314 Messengers (peace be upon them all). There is another Hadith that is not as well known to the average Muslim which states that there were over 224,000 Prophets (peace upon them). Either way, humanity has a storied history with regard to the reality of who Allah is and what was brought to us by these blessed and noble men of Allah. The greatest of all these men, by the attestation of Allah Himself (Glorified & Exalted) is Prophet Muhammad ibn Abdullah. He is the one that they all called, preached and guided their people to in preparation for his coming ﷺ. Allah says,

(Allah took a pledge from the prophets, saying, "If, after I have bestowed Scripture and wisdom upon you, a messenger comes confirming what you have been given, you must believe in him and support him. Do you affirm this and accept My pledge as binding on you?" They said, "We do." He said, "Then bear witness and I too will bear witness.") (Qur'an 3:81)

He ﷻ also says,

(We took a solemn pledge from the prophets and from you [Muhammad], from Noah, from Abraham, from Moses, from Jesus, son of Mary, and We took a solemn pledge from all of them.) (Qur'an 33:7)

In this final chapter we will talk about the particular Prophets that Allah ﷻ has mentioned in His final Divine Revelation. There are 25 Prophets in total that Allah has named in the Qur'an and we will mention some of them here as well as a few of the most important things about them here, bi idhnillah (with Allah's Permission).

Our Father Adam عليه السلام

Unlike the Jews and Christians who consider our Father Adam to be merely our genetic origin, we consider him to be one of the greatest of Prophets. Because of their failure to recognize his position with Allah ﷻ, he has been made a scapegoat for our own personal failings. One of the most egregious things ever said of our Father Prophet Adam (peace be upon him) in regards to his story is that he was disobedient to Allah ﷻ and the reason we are all not in Jannah today. This is a great lie and a sign of people's ignorance of what Allah ﷻ

OUR BELOVED PROPHETS

Himself has said in the Qur'an about His beloved creation. It is also likely a sign of their wretchedness on the Day of Judgement—may Allah preserve us from misguidance and wrong understandings.[1] The fact is that Allah clearly stated in the Qur'an what He was doing and why. The reality of our Father Adam going through what he went through set in motion what our Lord had Decreed since before Adam was even created.

Allah says

(Behold, your Lord said to the Angels: "I will create a vicegerent on earth." "How can You put someone there who will cause damage and bloodshed, when we celebrate Your Praise and proclaim Your Holiness?" but He said, "I know things you do not.") (Qur'an 2:30)

In this Blessed Āya Allah is clearly informing us of His intention to place a **(Vicegerent on Earth.)** He did not say that he made our Father to be a vicegerent in the Heavens. There was also the fact that Allah says,

(I know things you do not.) (Qur'an 2:30)

This was said to the Angels, and to us by extension, so we should be mindful of questioning our Lord because of how we think something "should" be.

As we mentioned about the Noble Angels in the previous chapters, there are some things that we should also know about each of our Prophets/Messengers. The specific beliefs regarding Prophets/Messengers in general has already been discussed, so here we will look at a few important points about some of the 25 Prophets mentioned in the Qur'an.

To continue with our Father Adam (peace be upon him) these are some of the things that we know about him specifically.

✦ Allah created him from clay and blew the Ruh into him.

Many people believe that Allah physically interacted with His creation and this is false. Because far too many of us take everything that Allah and His Messenger ﷺ describe literally, many of us have imagined very foul and inappropriate things about Allah.[2]

---

[1] Since slandering a Prophet is unquestionably a deplorable sin. And in the case of this particular slander, an entire false ideology has been built around this lie which laid down the philosophical foundation for the shirk the Christians would eventually concoct.

[2] Some of this may be a problem of language. What many people mean by taking the Qur'an and Hadith "literally" is merely affirming that it actually happened. This, on its own, is not a problem. But the term

If we read into the Āya of Allah that says,

(Then He moulded him and He breathed from His Spirit into him.) (Qur'an 32:9)

And then we understand it literally, we will come to some very disturbing things in regards to Allah. What do I mean? A literal meaning, following the principles of the people of Excessive Literalism, would demand that we believe that Allah ﷻ breathed "a piece" of His Divine Essence into His creation. This would make us share in the Divine Essence and to believe this is clear Kufr (disbelief). Historically speaking, not even the Excessive Literalists have went so far as to claim this as a possible interpretation of this verse, but this is the logical consequence of their principles.

However, the clear problems with taking certain phrases literally has not stopped them from believing that Allah made physical contact with His creation. For example, Allah says:

(Allah said, "Iblis, what prevents you from bowing down to the man I have made with My own hands? Are you too high and mighty?") (Qur'an 38:75)

People with excessively literal interpretive tendencies take the saying of Allah **([The one whom] I have made with My own hands)** to mean that Allah physically created Adam with physical hands in a similar way we would make a pot of clay. They even go so far as to condemn those who refuse to affirm this as a possible interpretation of this verse. *And surely our Lord is exalted above these false notions that people have of Him (Glorified & Majestic)!* We all should know and understand that Allah ﷻ cannot be understood through our rational minds. So any Āyāt or Ahadith which appear to make a comparison between Allah and His creation we affirm while negating any and all similarities based on the verse **(There is nothing whatsoever like unto Him.)** (Qur'an 42:11) So we believe what Allah (and His Messenger) has said about Himself, while at the same time upholding His Divinity and absolute distinction from creation. We also have to remember that we are understanding the Qur'an and Hadith through the words of a translator. So we do not try to interpret what may come across in translation as being what Allah Most High necessarily intended since a translation, by definition, is an interpretation. So we say "We believe in what Allah and His Messenger said as they had intended" and do not overstep our bounds. May Allah ﷻ grant us sound understanding and shield us from believing something that is not appropriate for Him.

"literally" in tafsir, aqida and logic has a very specific meaning. When we take something "literally" we are saying that the first meaning that comes to mind regarding that thing is what has been intended. This is what Ustadh Abdul Muhaymin is referring to in the discussion below.

✦ Allah gave our Father Adam two special gifts,

Unlike the Angels at the time, Allah gave Adam:

1) Intelligence to discern right from wrong; and
2) The will to do what is right and refrain from evil.

This by extension has been passed down to us as his children and so we also have the ability to know right from wrong and to choose to do one or the other. But we affirm that right and wrong ultimately come from Revelation, apply only to human beings and jinn, and cannot be independently discerned by the mind.

✦ Allah taught our Father Adam (peace be upon him) the names of all things in creation and by extension we have been blessed to be able to identify and name things with precision, Al Hamdulillah.

Allah ﷻ said

(And He taught Adam the names of all things; then He placed them before the Angels, and said: "Tell me the names of these if ye are right.) (Qur'an 2:31)

✦ Allah commanded all the inhabitants of Jannah to prostrate to our Father Adam.

This is what is known as a prostration of honoring and it was not an act of worship. Prostrations can done for two different reasons: veneration and worship. It was permissible to do prostrations of venerations to people worthy of respect in the past. But with our Prophet ﷺ it was made unlawful in order to remove that potential door to misguidance.

✦ Allah ﷻ blessed our Father Adam with our Mother Hawwa (Eve) [peace be upon them both] and gave us the blessed tradition of marriage and family, Al Hamdulillah.

Prophet Idris (Enoch) عليه السلام

This blessed Prophet of Allah was the grandson of our Father Adam through his son Seth, another Prophet of Allah (may Allah be pleased with them all). Prophet Enoch initiated a number of things that we all benefit from to this day. He was also the first of Prophet Seth's descendants to be a Prophet after a period of time when none of them held this distinction. Some of the things that we know Prophet Enoch initiated for us were the following:

- **He was the first person to use the pen and teach the art of writing.**
- **He was the first to set out the weights and measures.**
- **He was the first to record the movement of the stars.**
- **He was the first to sew and to wear weaved clothing, up until that time the people were accustomed to wearing animal skins.**

It is said that whenever he would sew a stitch he would praise Allah, and if he would forget to do so he would undo the stitch and redo it properly with the praise of Allah.

- **He was the first man to take up arms in the Path of Allah.**

This was against some people in his time who had started to worship fire and refused to heed his call as a Prophet for them to abandon their idol worship. When it comes to Prophets, belief in them is obligatory and so fighting against people who refused to heed their call was permissible since they came with clear, undeniable proofs (usually in the form of inimitable miracles) from their Lord. This is why the Hebrew Prophets waged war against their people and why our Prophet waged jihad against the Arabs of the Peninsula. In the case of the Jews with Moses or the Arabs with our Prophet, they had the capacity to truly understand what and who they were, and so belief in them was obligatory and disbelief or rejection was punished with the sword. However, as for non-Prophets go (*i.e.*, us), war is not waged against Disbelievers merely due to their disbelief, but only when they pose a threat to safety and security to Believers or other non-aggressive non-Believers.[3]

We believe that Prophet Enoch was taken up directly in the Heavens without dying a natural death and that he was blessed with this honorable station because of Allah's particular love for his righteous state. Allah says in the Qur'an about this blessed Prophet,

---

[3] Some people think that Muslims have an obligation to wage war against everyone who doesn't believe in Allah and His Messenger for that fact alone. But consider the verse (**And were it not for Allah checking some people by means of others, monasteries, churches, synagogues and masajid in which Allah's Name is often mentioned would have been destroyed.**) (Qur'an 22:40) The scholars of tafsir explain that this verse is speaking about human history as a whole, but it remains the case that our Prophet forbade killing monks, priests and rabbis who do not pose an active threat. But the larger point is that this verse establishes that the reason for jihad is the preservation of worship.

(Mention too, in the Book, the story of Idris. He was a man of truth, a Prophet. And We raised him to a lofty station.) (Qur'an 19:56-57)

Prophet Nuh (Noah) عليه السلام

This Blessed Messenger was the first of five with respect to order of arrival that bore the title "Ulil `Azim" (Possessors of Firm Resolve) but the last in the order of ranking, which in no way should diminish his rank in the eyes of people. The well-known story of how he called his people to focus on worshipping Allah in truth and sincerity has been discussed in several places in the Qur'an and has been shared in a number of stories and Hadith.

He was neither from a wealthy family nor was he a leader of his people, but Allah distinguished him with the noble station of Messengership (peace be upon him). He spent 950 years calling his people to Allah before Allah sent the flood that wiped out all of the sinful people from the face of the earth. His people began erecting statues in honor of some righteous people (Suwa`, Yaghuth, Ya`uq, and Nasir) who had passed on generations before, which was lawful in their Shari`a during that time. But as time passed the Shaytan convinced them to start worshipping them through stages.[4]

Allah eventually revealed to Prophet Nuh that he should begin to build a boat to prepare for the impending flood that was going to occur as a punishment for those who rejected Prophet Nuh and his message. People witnessed Prophet Nuh building the Boat/Ark and they would make fun of him (peace be upon him). Allah says,

(It was revealed to Nuh, "None of your people will believe, other than those who have already done so, so do not be distressed by what they do. Build the Ark under Our eyes and with Our inspiration. Do not plead with Me for those who have done evil, they will be drowned." So he began to build the Ark, and whenever leaders of his people passed by, they laughed at him. He said, "You may scorn us now, but we will come to scorn you, you will find out who will receive a humiliating punishment, and on whom a lasting suffering will descend!") (Qur'an 11:36-39)

Another thing that we come to learn from the story of Prophet Nuh is that just because someone may be closely connected to you does not guarantee that either you or they will be

---

[4] And we have to remember that this is how Shaytan works. He doesn't try to get you to abandon everything all at once, but slowly leads you along the path of deception until you are so thoroughly immersed in sin or misguidance that you often do not even realize what has happened to you. May Allah protect us from the fitna of the Shaytan.

spared from Allah's punishment. This is clear from what happened to the son of prophet Nuh (peace be upon him) as Allah describes,

(When Our command came, and water gushed up out of the earth, We said, "Place on board this Ark a pair of each species, and your own family except those against whom the sentence has already been passed and those who have believed," though only a few believed with him. He said, "Board the Ark. In the Name of Allah it shall sail and anchor. My Lord is Most Forgiving and Merciful." It sailed with them on waves like mountains, and Nuh called out to his son, who stayed behind, "Come aboard with us, my son, do not stay with the disbelievers." But he replied, "I will seek refuge on a mountain to save me from the water." Nuh said, "Today there is no refuge from Allah's Command, except for those on whom He has mercy." The waves cut them off from each other and he was among the drowned. Then it was said, "Earth, swallow up your water, and sky, hold back," and the water subsided, the command was fulfilled. The Ark settled on Mount Judi, and it was said, "Gone are those evildoing people!" Nuh called out to his Lord, saying, "My Lord, my son was one of my family, though Your promise is true, and You are the most just of all judges." Allah said, "Nuh, he was not one of your family. What he did was not right. Do not ask Me for things you know nothing about. I am warning you not to be from among the ignorant." He said, "My Lord, I take refuge with You from asking for things I know nothing about. If You do not forgive me, and have mercy on me, I shall be one of the losers!") (Qur'an 11:40-47)

As one last reminder before we close out: we do not believe the lies that were said against Prophet Nuh by the previous communities who received Revelation, the chief of them being that he became intoxicated and was tricked into doing unspeakable things with his own daughters. As Shaykh Rami mentioned in the chapter on prophethood, these sorts of things go against the noble and dignified station that Allah ﷻ has given his Prophets and Messengers (peace be upon them all). We believe that they are necessarily protected from committing foul acts, sins, and kufr as part of their role as ambassadors of the Divine.

Prophet Hud عليه السلام

The Prophet Hud (peace be upon him) was a grandson of Prophet Nuh through his son Shem. He was sent to the people of `Ad, a people who populated the southern area of the Arabian peninsula now known as Yemen. His people were the first after the flood to re-start worshipping idols and going against the command of Allah in general. They were also very prosperous and were well-known for living lives of luxury in lavishly built homes and gardens.

Prophet Hud's father was one of the people who were responsible for serving in the temple of the three idols that the people worshipped. Prophet Hud would constantly warn his people about transgressing the limits Allah had established. They would mock Allah, and they would chide and challenge Prophet Hud to call upon Allah to punish them if what he was saying was really true. After giving them ample opportunity to repent, Allah sent clouds with strong winds which raged until they were completely destroyed. Allah says

(Mention [Hud] of the tribe of Ad: he warned his people among the sand dunes - other warners have come and gone both before and after him- ' Worship no one but Allah, I fear for you, that you will be punished on a terrible Day,' but they said, 'Have you come to turn us away from our gods? If what you say is true, bring down that punishment you threaten us with!' He said, 'Only Allah knows when it will come: I simply convey to you the message I am sent with but I can see you are an insolent people.' When they saw a cloud approaching their valley, they said, 'This cloud will give us rain!' 'No indeed! It is what you wanted to hasten: a storm-wind bearing a painful punishment which will destroy everything by its Lord's command.' In the morning there was nothing to see except their [ruined] dwellings: this is how We repay the guilty. We had established them in a way we have not established you [people of Mecca]; We gave them hearing, sight, and hearts, yet their hearing, sight, and hearts were of no use to them, since they denied Allah's revelations. They were overwhelmed by the punishment they had mocked.) (Qur'an 46:21-26)

We should learn to be thankful to Allah (Glorified & Exalted), for His many blessings and not become deluded by our worldly possessions that we falsely believe is a sign of our virtue.

Prophet Salih عليه السلام

Prophet Salih (peace be upon him) was a Prophet that was sent the people of Thamud shortly after the flood as well. His people inhabited the area now known as Jordan. The surviving ruins of the cities of Petra and Mada'in Salih are considered to be among their former dwellings. Prophet Salih's Father was a righteous man who refused to be a part of his people's idol-worship and flagrant disobedience. After Prophet Salih started to call his people to purify their worship, they also began to mock him and were so bold as to demand he produce miracle after miracle until Allah granted their request ﷺ. This was the famous incident of the she-camel.

The people of Thamud asked Prophet Salih to ask his Lord to produce a she-camel of a specific description from the rock of a nearby mountain in order to prove that he was a true Prophet. Allah granted their request, but on the condition that if they do not do what they were commanded, His punishment would be severe. Despite the clear, mind-blowing miracle that appeared before their eyes, they did not take heed. They convinced a man named Quddur to hamstring the she-camel and this was the last straw. Allah says about this incident,

(To the Thamud, We sent their brother Salih. He said, "My people, worship Allah! You have no god other than Him. It was He who brought you into being from the earth and made you inhabit it, so ask forgiveness from Him, and turn back to Him: my Lord is near, and ready to answer." They said, "Salih, We used to have such great hope in you. Will you forbid us to worship what our fathers worshipped!? We are in grave doubt about what you are asking us to do." He said, "My people, just think: if I did have clear proof from my Lord, and if He had given me mercy of His own, who could protect me from Allah if I disobeyed Him? You would only make my loss greater. My people, this camel belongs to Allah, a sign for you, so leave it to pasture on Allah's earth and do not harm it, or you will soon be punished." But they hamstrung it, so he said, "Enjoy life for another three days, this warning will not prove false." And so, when Our command was fulfilled, by Our mercy We saved Salih and his fellow believers from the disgrace of that day. It is your Lord who is the Strong, the Mighty One. The blast struck the evildoers and they lay dead in their homes, as though they had never lived and flourished there. Yes, the Thamud denied their Lord, so away with the Thamud!) (Qur'an 11:61-68)

So Allah did away with the people of Thamud after they spent the three days plotting to murder their Prophet instead of seeking repentance as any reasonable person would under the circumstances. However, around 4,000 or so people did in fact repent after the miracle of the she-camel and were saved along with Prophet Salih (peace be upon him). This is an excellent lesson for people who choose to belittle the command of Allah and His threats of punishment to those who disobey Him (Mighty & Majestic).

Our Father Ibrahim (Abraham) عليه السلام
&
His Son Prophet Isma'il (Ishmael) عليه السلام

Prophet Ibrahim is the patriarch of all the Abrahamic Traditions—that of the Jews, the Christians, and the Muslims. He is the grandfather of our Prophet Muhammad, and the

OUR BELOVED PROPHETS

Intimate Friend (Khalil) of Allah ﷻ. And he is another of the "Ulil `Azim" (peace be upon him and his sons). He was a strongly devout and upright servant of Allah (Glorified & Exalted). History has attested to his uprightness and you will be hard-pressed to find anyone who dares to say anything bad against him who is not utterly devoid of any faith. He was the father of two righteous Prophets, Isma`il and Ishaq (peace be upon them all), who were born much later in life than is normal.⁵ There are many wonderful stories that have been relayed about him. We strongly suggest that you seek them out for all of the benefits that they provide to our hearts and our faith. We will only share a few points from a couple of them now, *InShaa'Allah*.

Ibrahim was from among a group of people who were completely consumed with the worship of idols. He lived with a man named Azar. Some of our scholars say he was his father, while others say that he was his uncle. We are of the latter opinion. Some of our students have had a hard time accepting the idea that Azar was his uncle because of how the Qur'an describes him. So we will take a few moments to explain why we have adopted the position that Azar was his uncle as an example of what we said above about the mistakes of excessive literalism, especially for people who are not native speakers of Arabic. The Qur'an does indeed call Azar "أبِيهِ" on a few occasions, which literally means "his father". However, the word "أب" in Arabic can refer to a father or an uncle, even a grandfather. This is easily proven in reference to Prophets Isma`il and Ya`qub (peace be upon them both). Prophet Ya`qub was the son of Prophet Isaac, yet when he asked his sons on his deathbed, **(What will you worship after me?)** they replied **(We will worship your God and the God of your fathers (ءَابَآئِكَ), Ibrahim, Isma`il and Ishaq.)** Some may understand why Ibrahim is referred to as a father since they are part of his progeny, but Isma`il is not part of their direct ancestry. Rather, he is the older brother of Ya`qub's father. Yet Prophet Ya`qub's sons describe Isma`il, his uncle, as his father.

Thus, the mere fact that the Qur'an uses the word "أب" for Azar isn't explicit proof that he was his biological father. It is part of the common knowledge of the Jewish scholars that

---

⁵ Men are able to have children well into their senior years and so Isma`il being born to Hajar wasn't too out of the norm. However, Ishaq's birth was a minor miracle. The oldest woman to give birth naturally without *modern* fertility treatments is a Chinese woman who was 65 when she gave birth in 2019. The next oldest woman to have a natural birth was a British woman; she was 58 in 1818. By comparison, the Hebrew Bible asserts that Sara was 90 years old when she gave birth to Ishaq. Allah knows best her actual age, but she was clearly post-menopausal. She describes herself as "عَجُوزٌ" in the Qur'an which comes from the root "عَجَزَ" meaning "to be weak, incapable or unable to do something" and is only used to describe extremely old women. By contrast, the oldest woman on record to give birth with modern fertility treatments was 72 years old, but she did so with donated eggs. So Sarah gave birth at an age that is well beyond what is possible even with modern medicine.

Ibrahim's (peace be upon him) father passed away when he was young and so Ibrahim was raised by his uncle. So he took the place of Ibrahim's father and so is referred to as such. And so historians and many of the scholars of tafsir say that Ibrahim's father was actually named Tarikh, while Azar was Tarikh's younger brother whom he tasked to raise Ibrahim as part of his last will and testament. There are many proofs besides the above that point towards Azar being Ibrahim's uncle, but among the strongest proofs of them is the Qur'an Itself. So Allah says,

(It is not for the Prophet and those who have believed to ask forgiveness for the polytheists, even if they were relatives, after it has become clear to them that they are companions of the Hellfire. Abraham asked forgiveness for his father because he had made a promise to him, but once he realized that his father was an enemy of God, he washed his hands of him. Abraham was tender-hearted and forbearing.) (Qur'an 9:113-114)

This occurred when Ibrahim was obviously a young man and Allah makes it clear that Prophets do not ask forgiveness for idol-worshippers, even their own relatives, once it is clear that they are destined for the Hellfire. But later in his life, the Qur'an states that Ibrahim supplicated,

(Praise be to God, who has granted me Ishmael and Isaac in my old age: my Lord hears all requests! Lord, grant that I and my offspring may keep up the prayer. Our Lord, accept my request. Our Lord, forgive me, my parents, and the Believers on the Day of Reckoning.) (Qur'an 14:41)

His parents had obviously passed away by then. So if Ibrahim already washed his hands of Azar and it was not fitting for him (or anyone who believes in Allah and the Last Day) to ask forgiveness for Disbelievers who have passed away, then Azar cannot be Ibrahims' father since he asked for forgiveness for both of his parents out of gratitude to Allah ﷻ for the blessing of being given sons.

Either way Azar was the man who sold idols to his community and was a central figure in the town as a result. One day, Ibrahim had enough and questioned how people could be caught up into worshipping things that they crafted with their own hands, believing that they could be of benefit to them to the extent that they offered them food and other things. He questioned his people, including Azar, at length and found them firmly committed to their false beliefs and practices. After debating with them, he decided to use the idols themselves to make people see the error of their ways. So he waited until the day they held a celebration for their idols to make his move. Allah ﷻ says,

⟨Mention too, in the Quran, the story of Abraham. He was a man of truth, a prophet. He said to his father, "Father, why do you worship something that can neither hear nor see nor benefit you in any way? Father, knowledge that has not reached you has come to me, so follow me: I will guide you to an even path. Father, do not worship Satan. Satan has rebelled against the Lord of Mercy. Father, I fear that a punishment from the Lord of Mercy may afflict you and that you may become Satan's companion!" His father answered, "Abraham, do you reject my gods? I will stone you if you do not stop this. Keep out of my way!" Abraham said, "Peace be with you: I will ask my Lord to forgive you. He is always gracious to me but for now I will leave you, and the idols you all pray to, and I will pray to my Lord and trust that my prayer will not be in vain."⟩ (Qur'an 19:41-48)

Allah ﷻ also says,

⟨Long ago We bestowed right judgement on Abraham and We knew him well. He said to his father and his people, "What are these images to which you are so devoted?" They replied, "We found our fathers worshipping them." He said, "You and your fathers have clearly gone astray." They asked, "Have you brought us the truth or are you just playing about?" He said, "Listen! Your true Lord is the Lord of the heavens and the earth, He who created them, and I am a witness to this. By Allah I shall certainly plot against your idols as soon as you have turned your backs!" He broke them all into pieces, but left the biggest one for them to return to. They said, "Who has done this to our gods? How wicked he must be!" Some said, "We heard a youth called Abraham talking about them." They said, "Bring him before the eyes of the people, so that they may be witnesses." They asked, "Was it you, Abraham, who did this to our gods?" He said, "No, it was done by the biggest of them. This one! Ask them, if they can talk." They turned to one another, saying, "It is

you who are in the wrong," then were they confounded with shame: (they said), "Thou know full well that these (idols) do not speak!" Abraham said, "How can you worship what can neither benefit nor harm you, instead of Allah? Shame on you and on the things you worship instead of God! Have you no sense?" They said, "Burn him and avenge your gods, if you are going to do the right thing!") (Qur'an 21:51-68)

Prophet Ibrahim's people resolved to burn him for what he did to their idols, but Allah will never allow the people of disbelief to have control over his Prophet, Messengers, and righteous servants in a way that opposes His will. This doesn't mean that the Prophets and Messengers (and the righteous by extension) do not suffer hardship. They most certainly do. But as Shaykh Rami said in the previous chapters, they do not suffer the type of hardships that undermine their mission. And because they see their hardships as coming from their Lord, it only increased them in their faith. In fact, the Prophets and Messengers are tested more than most.[6] But We know that Allah did not want the fire to harm Prophet Ibrahim (peace be upon him), so He commanded the fire to be a place of safety and security. Allah says,

(But We said, "Fire, be cool and safe for Abraham." They planned to harm him, but We made them suffer the greatest loss.) (Qur'an 21:69-70)

And so their own attempt to punish Prophet Ibrahim was turned into yet another proof against them.

There was another blessed event related to Prophet Ibrahim that mankind has benefitted from since it first occurred and will continue to benefit from until the Final Hour. As we alluded to already, Allah granted Prophet Ibrahim his first child, a righteous son named Isma'il that he had with his wife Hajar [Hagar] (peace be upon them all). After not having any children by his first wife Sara, she suggested that he marry Hagar—a young Ethopian slave that she had purchased and freed—in hopes that she could bear him a son. Sara was then given a child herself whom they named Ishaq.

As any woman naturally would, Sara became a bit jealous of Hagar and Isma'il and so Allah commanded Prophet Ibrahim to take Hagar and Isma'il to a place in the desert far from normal trading routes. Once they arrived at their destination, Prophet Ibrahim (peace be upon him) gave them the remaining food and water, as Allah had commanded him, and started to

---

[6] Our Prophet said "[The most severely tested] are the Prophets, then the next best [of humanity], then the next best [after them]. A man is tried according to his religion. If he is firm in his religion, then his trials will be more severe. If he is weak in his religion, then he is tried according to his strength in religion. The servant will continue to be tried until he is left walking upon the earth without any sin." (Tirmidhi)

depart. Realizing what he was about to do, Hagar asked him if he was going to leave them there, but he kept walking and did not respond. Hagar asker him again, but this time asked if Allah had commanded him to do this and Prophet Ibrahim responded that He had indeed did. So Hagar told him to do as his Lord commanded and trusted that she and her son were in His tender loving care.

Naturally, their water and food eventually ran out and Hagar became concerned when her son began crying out of the pains of hunger. Out of desperation, she began running back and forth between the hills of Safa and Marwa, hoping to come across someone who maybe passing by who may be able to offer something to keep her blessed child from starving to death. It is mentioned in the Hadith that once she reached Marwa for the final time and was about to give up, she heard a voice and followed it until she came upon an Angel digging the well of Zamzam. Once the water began flowing, she drank from it, which provided her with the water her body needed in order to produce milk so she could suckle her child (peace be upon them both). The Angel then told her that she no longer had anything to fear, Ibrahim would return and build a house of worship with Isma`il. Because of the newly created well, a group of travelers noticed a particular bird that was known to stay near water in the desert and while investigating, came upon Hajar and baby Isma`il.

When Prophet Isma`il had grown a bit, Prophet Ibrahim had his famous dream where he was commanded to sacrifice his son. Remember that at the time, this was Prophet Ibrahim's only son. Being commanded to kill your own son is hard enough, but the fact that he was his sole heir at the time made it even more difficult. But Prophet Ibrahim, not wanting to trick Isma`il, told him of his dream and asked his opinion. Isma`il was a righteous child and already a Prophet in Allah's eyes and so he told his father to do what his Lord had commanded him. Instead of fear and anger, he was patient and content with Allah's Decree. But before Ibrahim carried out the sacrifice, Allah informed him of His pleasure with his actions and permitted him to sacrifice a ram instead.

Allah said about this incident,

(And he said, "Indeed, I will go to my Lord; He will guide me. Lord, grant me a righteous son," so We gave him the good news that he would have a patient son. When the boy was old enough to work with his father, Abraham said, "My son, I have seen myself sacrificing you in a dream. What do you think?" He said, "Father, do as you are commanded and, God willing, you will find me steadfast." When they had both submitted to God, and he had laid his son down on the side of his face, We called out to him, "Abraham, you have fulfilled the dream." This is how We reward those who do good, it was indeed a clear test. We ransomed his son with a momentous sacrifice, and We let

him be praised by succeeding generations, "Peace be upon Abraham!" This is how We reward those who do good. For he was one of our believing Servants.) (Qur'an 37:99-111)

We should all familiarize ourselves with the rest of this blessed story, as this is the roots of our rites of Hajj and founding of the blessed city of Makka Mukarrama. However, since it is so important to our story, we will briefly mentioned rebuilding of the Ka'ba by Prophet Ibrahim and Prophet Isma'il (peace be upon them both) before moving on to the next Prophet.

The Ka'ba was originally built by our Father Prophet Adam (peace be upon him) and was destroyed during the Great Flood in Prophet Nuh's time. Once Hajar and Isma'il resettled the area, Allah instructed Prophets Ibrahim and Isma'il to rebuild the Ka'ba on its original foundations and make it a place of pilgrimage for all of mankind. During the time that the Ka'ba was being built, the Angels came down and gave them the Sacred Black Stone (which was originally from Paradise) in order to place it in the corner of the Ka'ba. Allah ﷻ says about this,

(The first House [of worship] to be established for people was the one at Mecca. It is a blessed place; a source of guidance for all people; there are clear signs in it; it is the place where Abraham stood to pray; whoever enters it is safe. Pilgrimage to the House is a duty owed to God by people who are able to undertake it. Those who reject this [should know that] God has no need of anyone.) (Qur'an 3:96-97)

He ﷻ also says

(When Abraham's Lord tested him with certain commandments, which he fulfilled, He said, "I will make you a leader of people." Abraham asked, "And will You make leaders from my descendants too?" God answered, "My pledge does not hold for those who do evil." We made the House a resort and a sanctuary for people, saying, "Take the spot where Abraham stood as your place of prayer." We commanded Abraham and Ishmael: "Purify My House for those who walk round it, those who stay there, and those who bow and prostrate themselves in worship." Abraham said, "My Lord, make this land secure and provide with produce those of its people who believe in God and the Last Day." God said, "As for those who Disbelieve, I will grant them enjoyment for a short while and then subject them to the torment of the Fire—an evil destination." As Abraham and Ishmael built up the foundations of the House [they prayed], *"Our Lord, accept [this] from us. You are the All Hearing, the All Knowing. Our Lord, make us devoted to You; make our descendants into a community devoted to You.*

Show us how to worship and accept our repentance, for You are the Ever Relenting, the Most Merciful. <u>***Our Lord, make a messenger of their own rise up from among them, to recite Your revelations to them, teach them the Scripture and wisdom, and purify them:***</u> ***You are the Mighty, the Wise." Who but a fool would forsake the religion of Abraham? We have chosen him in this world and he will rank among the righteous in the Hereafter.)*** (Qur'an 2:124-130)

The beauty of this powerful du'a uttered by two of Allah's Prophetic Messengers was that it was answered by the Prophethood of our Beloved Prophet Muhammad ﷺ. And so we each are indebted to these two blessed men of Allah (may Allah's Peace and Blessings cover them all) and the supplication they made which became a means for our individual guidance.

Prophet Yusuf (Joseph) عليه السلام

Prophet Yusuf was the great-grandson of the Prophet Ibrahim through Ishaq (Isaac). As we mentioned, Ishaq had a son named Ya`qub (Jacob) and Prophet Ya`qub eventually gave birth to Prophet Yusuf (peace be upon them all). Allah blessed Prophet Yusuf with both physical beauty and the ability to interpret dreams. Our Prophet ﷺ described him as being the most beautiful (*i.e.,* handsome) of all of humanity at the time. These favors, among other things, caused his brothers to hate him, both Yusuf and his younger brother. Yusuf and Benyamin (Benjamin) both had the same mother and their father paid close attention to them because of the special status that he knew Allah ﷻ was going to bestow upon them. He was also well aware of his half-brother's jealousy over them both. This was especially the case for Prophet Yusuf (peace be upon him). Like Ibrahim, his story is well-known to all of those who follow the Abrahamic tradition. We encourage you to read Sura Yusuf on your own in order to delve deeper into his story and appreciate all of the challenges that this blessed Prophet of Allah faced.

Allah ﷻ says

(Alif. Lam. Ra. These are the verses of the Scripture that makes things clear. We have sent it down as an Arabic Quran so that you may understand. We do relate to you the most beautiful of stories in revealing this Quran to you. Before this you were one of those who knew nothing about them. Joseph said to his father, 'Father, I dreamed of eleven stars and the sun and the moon: I saw them all bow down before me,' and he replied, 'My son, tell your brothers nothing of this dream, or they may plot to harm you, Satan is man's sworn enemy. This is about how your Lord will choose you, teach you to interpret dreams, and perfect His blessing on you and the House of Jacob, just as He perfected it earlier on your forefathers Abraham and Isaac: your Lord is All Knowing and Wise.' There are lessons in

the story of Joseph and his brothers for all who seek them.) (Qur'an 12:1-7)

May Allah allow us to be in the company of the upright people of the House of Ibrahim and his children. *Amin.*

Prophet Musa (Moses) عليه السلام

Prophet Musa (peace be upon him) was another of Allah's select group of Messengers—the "Ulil 'Azim". He was sent to the Children of Israel at a very critical time in their history. The story of Prophet Musa has been told in numerous places throughout the Qur'an and its overall themes should be well-known to us all. Prophet Musa was born at a time when the Children of Israel were being systematically persecuted by the Pharaoh of Egypt. He had put a policy in place which dictated that the first born male children would be killed every other year in order to try and thwart a prophecy that he feared would put him out of power. However, people plan, and Allah plans, and Allah is the best of Planners.

Allah says,

(We recount to you [Prophet] part of the story of Moses and Pharaoh, setting out the truth for people who believe. Pharaoh made himself high and mighty in the land and divided the people into different groups: one group he oppressed, slaughtering their sons and sparing their women, he was one of those who spread corruption but We wished to favour those who were oppressed in that land, to make them leaders, the ones to survive, to establish them in the land, and through them show Pharaoh, Haman, and their armies the very thing they feared. We inspired Moses' mother, saying, "Suckle him, and then, when you fear for his safety, put him in the river: do not be afraid, and do not grieve, for We shall return him to you and make him a messenger." Pharaoh's household picked him up later to become an enemy and a source of grief for them: Pharaoh, Haman, and their armies were wrongdoers.) (Qur'an 28:3-8)

Imagine thinking that you can try and thwart the Decree of Allah. Allah used Pharoah's own plans against him and made his downfall occur from within his own household. We all can gain a few lessons from this story about having confidence in the fact that Allah will never allow someone to completely overpower and destroy His believing servants.

After Prophet Musa (peace be upon him) brought the Children of Israel from out of bondage, they spent a number of years in wandering in the desert due to the disobedience of some of the people who were with them. There are a number of beautiful stories of Prophet

Musa throughout the Qur'an and told in detail in the Hadith and historical reports that we all should become familiar with. One particular thing that is known through information that has reached us through sound chains is that Musa was a very strong and powerful man. It is said that Allah sent the Angel of Death to Prophet Musa (peace be upon them both) and Prophet Musa fought him and won. After the Angel of Death was beaten, he returned and was questioned by Allah about what had happened (even though He knew better). Azra'il told his Lord what Musa did and so Allah instructed him to go back, tell him to find a cow or bull, place his hand on its back and he would be allowed an extension of one year for every strand of hair he was able to grab. When Prophet Musa heard this, he told the Angel of Death that he would rather be taken now and not wait. And this was the end of his blessed life here in this world. He was perhaps the only person who was allowed to choose his time of death.

Prophet Dawud (David) عليه السلام

This distinguished and noble Prophetic Messenger (peace be upon him) was the second King of Israel. He was also given a number of special gifts by Allah.

✦ **A beautiful voice.**

We have been informed that he would sing and the birds, the mountains and other creatures of the creation would sing with him:

(We made the mountains join him in glorifying Us at sunset and sunrise; and the birds, too, in flocks, all echoed his praise.) (Qur'an 38:18-19)

✦ **He was given the ability and knowledge of how to manipulate and shape iron with his bare hands and make weapons and chainmail to protect himself.**

(We graced David with Our favour. We said, "You mountains, echo Allah's praises together with him, and you birds, too." We softened iron for him, saying, "Make coats of chain mail and measure the links well." "Do good, all of you, for I see everything you do.") (Qur'an 34:10-11)

✦ **He was also given the Revelation from Allah called the Zabur (Psalms).**

He was a deeply devout man and spent the majority of his time worshipping Allah and attending to the affairs of the Children of Israel. It was during his time that the wise and righteous man named Luqman was alive and there are Hadith that speak of the interactions between them. He was also known to only eat from the work of his own hands.

One last thing that we should discuss before we close this section is the lies that were told against this noble Prophet (peace be upon him). Prophet Dawud *did not* send a soldier in his army to his death in order to have his wife to himself. According to the narrations that have reached us, which are more reliable than the Biblical accounts, one of two things happened. Prophet Dawud either: (a) asked the man to allow him to marry the woman and not pursue marriage with her or (b) asked the man to divorce her so that he could marry her. As you are reading this you may think that these two options are in line with what was said about Prophet Dawud (peace be upon him) in the Hebrew Bible, but that is not correct. Both of these acts were lawful in the Shari`a of the Children of Israel and the Prophet Dawud (peace be upon him) did not do anything wrong. The most that we can say is that it might not have been the best thing for him to have done, similar to how our Prophet ﷺ turned away from a blind man who believed in him in order to focus his attention on giving Da'wah to the Quraysh. Neither of these two things was sinful, but were minor mistakes of judgement with regard to what is most preferable. And among the things that people rarely mention about Prophet Dawud's choice and Allah's clear acceptance of it is that the Prophet Sulayman was born from the marriage of the Prophet Dawud and this righteous woman (peace be upon them all).

Prophet Sulayman (Solomon) عليه السلام

The stories of the greatness of Prophet Sulayman are another one of the well-known stories across faith traditions. However, there have been a number of lies told against this great Prophet of Allah as well that need to be clarified. The most egregious of the slanders against him is that Prophet Sulayman became an idol worshipper in order to appease one of his wives—and we seek refuge with Allah from saying such things about his Prophets and Messengers. As Shaykh Rami mentioned in the previous chapters, anything that we read or hear which detracts from the station of the Prophets or undermines their mission is logically impossible and necessarily false. And the most egregious thing that can be said about any of the men of Allah is that they committed shirk. We reject this wholeheartedly and do not even give ear to such lies.

Among the most well-known things about Prophet Sulayman was his ability to talk to and understanding the languages of all the animals on the earth. He also was a man of unmatched wisdom and wealth. And perhaps the most famous of all, Allah placed the Jinn and other creatures of the creation under his control (sometimes against their will) and they helped to make his kingdom the greatest to ever exist on the face of the earth. Allah says

> (We gave knowledge to David and Solomon, and they both said, "Praise be to Allah, who has favoured us over many of His believing servants." Solomon succeeded David. He said, "People, we have been taught the speech of birds, and we have been given a share of everything: this is clearly a great favour." Solomon's hosts of jinn, men, and birds were marshalled in ordered ranks before him, and when they came to the Valley of the Ants, one ant said, "Ants! Go into your homes, in case Solomon and his hosts unwittingly crush you." Solomon smiled broadly at her words and said, "Lord, inspire me to be thankful for the blessings You have granted me and my parents, and to do good deeds that please You; admit me by Your grace into the ranks of Your righteous servants.") (Qur'an 27:15-19)

Allah also says

> (And [We subjected] the wind for Solomon. Its outward journey took a month, and its return journey likewise. We made a fountain of molten brass flow for him, and some of the jinn worked under his control with his Lord's permission. If one of them deviated from Our command, We let him taste the suffering of the blazing flame. They made him whatever he wanted: palaces, statues, basins as large as water troughs, fixed cauldrons. We said, "Work thankfully, family of David, for few of my servants are truly thankful." Then, when We decreed Solomon's death, nothing showed the jinn he was dead, but a creature of the earth eating at his stick: when he fell down they realized—if they had known what was hidden they would not have continued their demeaning labour.) (Qur'an 34:12-14)

And He says

> (We gave David Solomon. He was an excellent servant who always turned to Allah. When well-bred light-footed horses were paraded before him near the close of day, he kept saying, "My love of fine things is part of my remembering my Lord!" until [the horses] disappeared from sight "Bring them back! [he said] and started to stroke their legs and necks. We certainly tested Solomon, reducing him to a mere skeleton on his throne. He turned to Us and prayed: 'Lord forgive me! Grant me such power as no one after me will have- You are the Most Generous Provider.' So We gave him power over the wind, which at his request ran gently wherever he willed, and the jinn—every kind of builder and diver and others chained in fetters. 'This is Our gift, so give or withhold as you wish without

account.' His reward will be nearness to Us, and a good place to return to.) (Qur'an 38:30-40)

Allah ﷻ has praised this blessed Prophet (peace be upon him) and we do not take the rumors and slander over the testimony of our Lord. So we should not believe any of the false things that have been said about any of Allah's Prophets and Messengers (peace be upon them all). Even mentioning them is a sin in most situations.

Prophet Ayyub (Job) عليه السلام

This blessed Prophet (peace be upon him) was very wealthy and well loved by his people. Allah tested him by taking away his wealth, his children, and giving him an illness that physically weakened him. We reject the notion that this illness was anything like what the people who lie against Allah and His prophets have said about him. He did not have leprosy nor was flesh rotting from his body. As Shaykh Rami stated, we consider illnesses impossible which undermine their Prophetic mission and which one of us would heed the call of a man who was afflicted with a highly contagious bacteria that caused his flesh to rot off his bones? Prophets did not spread disease and death. Any Muslim who believes otherwise needs to be corrected and taught what is appropriate and inappriopriate to believe about the Prophets and Messengers. The Christians and Jews claim that this illness came as a result of Allah removing his Divine protection from Ayyub and thereby giving Shaytan power over him in order to prove that Ayyub would be a grateful servant, despite his material or physical condition. To believe that Allah would allow one of his chosen Prophets to be under the whim of our immortal enemy for even a second is Kufr and we should not spread these stories as if they are even potentially true.

Allah ﷻ says about Prophet Ayyub,

(Remember Job, when he cried to his Lord, "Suffering has truly afflicted me, but you are the Most Merciful of the merciful." We answered him, removed his suffering, and restored his family to him, along with more like them, as an act of grace from Us and a reminder for all who serve Us.) (Qur'an 21:83-84)

He ﷻ also says

(Bring to mind Our servant Job who cried to his Lord, 'Satan has afflicted me with weariness and suffering.' Stamp your foot! Here is cool water for you to wash in and

drink,' and We restored his family to him, with many more like them: a sign of Our mercy and a lesson to all who understand. 'Take a small bunch of grass in your hand, and strike [her] with that so as not to break your oath.' We found him patient in adversity; an excellent servant! Indeed he always turned to Allah.) (Qur'an 38:41-44)

Even though Prophet Ayyub (peace be upon him) appears to attribute his condition to Shaytan, it is not a declaration that Shaytan has any power or control over Allah's creation. This is another place where an overly simplistic interpretation of the Āya can lead to misunderstanding. Shaytan does not have the power to create even a fly, let alone afflict a Prophet with illness and fatigue. Rather, Prophet Ayyub made this statement out of good adab with Allah ﷻ, not wishing to show any displeasure to His Lord for the decisions that He has made. Hence, Allah ﷻ said

(We found him patient in adversity; an excellent servant! Indeed he always turned to Allah.) (Qur'an 38:44)

Prophet Dhu Al-Nun *aka* Yunus (Jonah) عليه السلام

This Prophet of Allah (peace be upon him) was sent to the people of Nineveh to call them to Allah and away from their disobedience and corruption. He called them for a number of years, but after a period of time became frustrated with their stubborness and ridicule. Believing that he had failed in his mission and any further da'wah was hopeless, he fled the city without seeking Allah's approval. He soon found himself on a boat and in the middle of a storm. Due to the weight, the crew feared that the boat would capsize if the problem wasn't corrected and so they drew lots to decide who they would throw overboard. The lot fell on Prophet Yunus (peace be upon him) and so they threw him overboard. Almost immediately after being thrown overboard, Allah caused him to be swallowed by a large fish—some say it was a whale, but Allah knows best what it was—and he proceeded to make this beautiful du`a:

(And remember Dhu Al-Nun, when he went off angrily, thinking We could not restrict him, but then he cried out in the deep darkness, *"There is no God but You, glory be to You, I was wrong."* We answered him and saved him from distress: this is how We save the faithful.) (Qur'an 21:87-88)

Allah ﷻ also said

(Jonah too was one of the Messengers. He fled to the overloaded ship. They cast lots, he suffered defeat, and a great fish swallowed him, for he had committed blameworthy acts. If he had not been one of those who glorified Allah, he would have stayed in its belly until the Day when all are raised up, but We cast him out, sick, on to a barren shore, and made a gourd tree grow above him. We sent him to a hundred thousand people or more. They believed, so We let them live out their lives.) (Qur'an 37:139-148)

Again, we have another verse where knowledge of Arabic is important to properly understand what is being said. Someone may say "Allah calls his actions 'blameworthy' so how can you all say that the Prophets are sinless?" The Qur'an uses the word "مُلِيم" (from the root "لَام" which means to "blame, censure, rebuke, chide or scold") to describe Prophet Yunus' actions and is the same word as the verse **(And I swear by the reproaching soul (nafs al-lawwama))** (Qur'an 75:2) So the word "mulim" is not necessarily synonymous with sin or disobedience. Rather, as we explained above, Prophet Yunus made an error in judgment that caused him to be rebuked by his Lord. He most certainly did not refuse Allah's command. Rather, he simply failed to get permission before halting his mission. Once the Prophet Yunus repented from his mistake and returned to his mission, he was successful in calling the entire city of over 100,000 people to the Haqq.

There are a number of lessons that can be learned from the challenges and adversities that Prophet Yunus experienced, among them that we should look at our responsiblity to call people to Islam in the best possible way while trusting in Allah and not allowing what appears to be a lack of progress to deter us from our responsiblities. As long as we aren't turning people off by our behavior or lack of tact when delivering the message, it is rare for people to respond to the call immediately. Instead, what we usually do is plant seeds in the heart that someone else harvests long after we are gone when those seeds are ready to sprout. May Allah help us all to call to the Din of Islam in they way of His Rasul ﷺ according to what is best.

Prophet Zakariyya (Zachariah) عليه السلام

This righteous man, Prophet Zakariyya, was the father of the Prophet Yahya and the uncle of Maryam bint Imran and her son the Prophet 'Isa (peace be upon them all). He was one of the highest ranking priests of the Children of Israel. He had grown old and him and his wife did not have any children and he called out to Allah to bless him to have a child who would carry on the righteous tradition of preaching the truth and worshipping Allah, (Subhaanahu wa Ta`Ala). His desire to be blessed with a righteous child became strong after being given the responsibility to care for Maryam bint Imran, Prophet 'Isa's mother. He saw how Allah had favored her, provided for her needs and was thankful for having been allowed to be chosen to care for her. Allah ﷻ said about him,

(Remember Zachariah, when he cried to his Lord, "My Lord, do not leave me childless, though You are the best of heirs." We answered him and We gave him John, and cured his wife of barrenness; they were always keen to do good deeds. They called upon Us out of longing and awe, and humbled themselves before Us.) (Qur'an 21:89-90)

He also said

(Kaf Ha Ya 'Ayn Sad. This is an account of your Lord's grace towards His servant, Zachariah, when he called to his Lord secretly, saying, "Lord, my bones have weakened and my hair is ashen grey, but never, Lord, have I ever prayed to You in vain. I fear [what] my kinsmen [will do] when I am gone, for my wife is barren, so grant me a successor, a gift from You to be my heir and the heir of the family of Jacob. Lord, make him well pleasing. "Zachariah, We bring you good news of a son whose name will be John—We have chosen this name for no one before him." He said, "Lord, how can I have a son when my wife is barren, and I am old and frail?" He said, "This is what your Lord has said: 'It is easy for Me: I created you, though you were nothing before.'" He said, "Give me a sign, Lord." He said, "Your sign is that you will not [be able to] speak to anyone for three full [days and] nights." He went out of the sanctuary to his people and signalled to them to praise Allah morning and evening.) (Qur'an 19:1-11)

Another beautiful thing about the Prophet Zakariyya is that within his house and under his care grew the Blessed Prophets Yahya and 'Isa ibn Maryam bint Imran (peace be upon them all). Just imagine the high level of Faith and Taqwaa that came from out of this Blessed man to be entrusted with the care and upbringing of such great Prophets and Maryam.

Prophet Yahya (John The Baptist) عليه السلام

Prophet Yahya (peace be upon him) was born as a result of Allah answering the prayer of his father the Prophet Zakariyya. He was a truly devout and upright Prophet who had surpassed the priests of the temple. He was endowed with superior intelligence and made a person of great love and concern for the creation. Allah ﷻ says,

(The angels called out to him, while he stood praying in the sanctuary, "God gives you news of John, confirming a Word from God. He will be noble and chaste, a prophet, one of the righteous.") (Qur'an 3:39)

He ﷻ also says,

(Zachariah, We bring you good news of a son whose name will be John—We have chosen this name for no one before him.'.... [We said], 'John, hold on to the Scripture firmly.' While he was still a boy, We granted him wisdom, tenderness from Us, and purity. He was devout, kind to his parents, not domineering or rebellious. Peace was on him the day he was born, the day he died, and it will be on him the day he is raised to life again.) (Qur'an 19:7, 12-15)

Prophet ʿIsa (Jesus) عليه السلام

Isa ibn Maryam is the fourth of the "Ulil ʿAzim". The grandmother of Prophet ʿIsa ibn Maryam and her husband Imran wanted children. So Maryam's mother made duʿa to Allah and pledged to dedicate her child to His service if He ﷻ would allow her to have a child. Allah answered her prayer and blessed her with a child, but while she thought she would be graced with a boy, she was given a beautiful girl instead whom she named Maryam. Allah ﷻ said about this series of events,

(Imran's wife said, "Lord, I have dedicated what is growing in my womb entirely to You; so accept this from me. You are the One who hears and knows all," but when she gave birth, she said, "My Lord! I have given birth to a girl"—God knew best what she had given birth to: the male is not like the female- "I name her Mary and I commend her and her offspring to Your protection from the rejected Satan." Her Lord graciously accepted her and made her grow in goodness, and entrusted her to the charge of Zachariah. Whenever Zachariah went in to see her in her sanctuary, he found her supplied with provisions. He said, "Mary, how is it you have these provisions?" and she said, "They are from God: God provides limitlessly for whoever He will.") (Qur'an 3:35-37)

Allah also says about Isa ibn Maryam (peace be upon them both)

(The angels said to Mary: "Mary, Allah has chosen you and made you pure: He has truly chosen you above all women. Mary, be devout to your Lord, prostrate yourself in worship, bow down with those who pray." This is an account of things beyond your knowledge that We reveal to you [Muhammad]: you were not present among them when they cast lots to see which of them should take charge of Mary, you were not present with them when they argued [about her]. The angels said, "Mary, Allah gives you news of a Word from Him, whose name will be the Messiah, Jesus, son of Mary, who will be held in honour in this world and the next, who will be one of those brought near to Allah. He will speak to people in his infancy and in his adulthood. He will be one of the righteous." She said, "My Lord, how can I have a son when no man has touched me?" [The angel] said, "This is how Allah creates what He will: when He has ordained something, He only says, 'Be', and it is. He will teach him the Scripture and wisdom, the Torah and the Gospel, He will send him as a messenger to the Children of Israel: 'I have come to you with a sign from your Lord: I will make the shape of a bird for you out of clay, then breathe into it and, with Allah's permission, it will become a real bird; I will heal the blind and the leper, and bring the dead back to life with Allah's permission; I will tell you what you may eat and what you may store up in your houses. There truly is a sign for you in this, if you are believers. I have come to confirm the truth of the Torah which preceded me, and to make some things lawful to you which used to be forbidden. I have come to you with a sign from your Lord. Be mindful of Allah, obey me, Allah is my Lord and your Lord, so serve Him-, that is a straight path.'") (Qur'an 3:42-51)

We should all be familiar with the major details of this blessed story as well, but there are a couple of points that we want to make sure you are aware of.

✦ Prophet 'Isa (peace be upon him) was conceived in a virgin birth.

Denying either his miraculous birth or his Mother being a virgin is Kufr. Allah ﷻ says,

(And mention [O Muhammad] in the Book [the story of] Mary, when she withdrew from her family to a place toward the east. And she took, in seclusion from them, a screen.
Then We sent to her Our Angel, and he represented himself to her as a well-proportioned man. She said, "Indeed, I seek refuge in the Most Merciful from you, [so leave me], if you are fearful of Allah." He replied, "I am only a messenger of your Lord to give you [news of] a pure boy." She said, "How can I have a boy while no man has touched me and I have not been unchaste?" He said, "Thus [it will be]. Your Lord says 'It is easy for Me and We will make him a sign to the people and a mercy from Us. It is a matter already decreed.'"
So she conceived him and she withdrew with him to a remote place.... Then she brought him to her people, carrying him [in hand]. They said "O Mary, you have certainly done a thing unprecedented. O sister of Aaron, your father was not a man of evil, nor was your mother unchaste." So she pointed to him. They said, "How can we speak to one who is

a child in the cradle?" [Jesus] said, "Indeed, I am a servant of Allah. He has given me the Scripture and made me a prophet.") (Qur'an 19:16-30)

What is being said here is clear. Anyone who claims that Isa ibn Maryam was not born of a virgin birth is suggesting that Allah conveniently left out her marriage from the story. And they are also denying the clear charge of adultery that was laid at Maryam's feet. Had she been married without her people's knowledge, she would have merely informed them of this fact.[7] Instead, she simply pointed to her infant child who spoke up on her behalf. In case that was not clear enough, Allah ﷻ also said,

(Verily, the similitude of Jesus with Allah is like the similitude of Adam. He created him from dust, then He said to him, "Be" and he was.) (Qur'an 3:59)

The analogy between Isa ibn Maryam and our Father Adam (peace be upon them both) is obvious. The suggestion that Isa was born of natural circumstances completely renders this verse obsolete since that would make Isa ibn Maryam no different than the rest of us. And while He says "Be" to anything He wishes to create, the reference to His act of creation here is to the creation of Adam without any parentage.

✦ He was neither crucified or even placed upon the cross.

Allah ﷻ says,

(And so for breaking their pledge, for rejecting God's revelations, for unjustly killing their prophets, for saying "Our minds are closed"—No! God has sealed them in their disbelief, so they believe only a little and because they disbelieved and uttered a terrible slander against Mary, and said, "We have killed the Messiah, Jesus, son of Mary, the Messenger of God." They did not kill him, nor did they crucify him, though it was made to appear like that to them; those that disagreed about him are full of doubt, with no knowledge to follow, only supposition: they certainly did not kill him. There is not one of the People of the Book who will not believe in [Jesus] before his death, and on the Day of Resurrection he will be a witness against them.) (Qur'an 4:155-159)

---

[7] We also believe in the "Perpetual Virginity" of Maryam for this same reason, *i.e.*, Allah does not mention her ever having a husband in the Qur'an. Her alleged marriage to Joseph is only established through the New Testament, which is not a reliable source of information. As we mentioned, our Prophet ﷺ ordered us to neither believe in nor deny it. However, this is not a point of kufr, only the virgin birth of her son.

In this verse, Allah denies both claims that Isa ibn Maryam was murdered by his people or placed upon the cross. In fact, Allah clearly says that it was only made to appear to people that he was crucified, so the belief that some people have that Isa ibn Maryam was in actuality crucified, but simply made to appear dead and taken down from the cross while he was in an unconscious state opposes what Allah (Glorified & Exalted) states about the situation.

✦ He is alive in Heaven and we are awaiting his return to kill the Dajjal and bring about righteous rule under the banner of Islam. He will marry and have children and be buried alongside our Prophet Muhammad ﷺ and his Two (2) Companions, Abu Bakr and Umar, may Allah be pleased with them both.

Allah ﷻ says

(He said: "I am indeed a servant of Allah: He hath given me revelation and made me a prophet; made me blessed wherever I may be. He commanded me to pray, to give alms as long as I live, to cherish my mother. He did not make me domineering or graceless. Peace was on me the day I was born, and will be on me the day I die and the day I am raised to life again.' Such was Jesus, son of Mary. [This is] a statement of the Truth about which they are in doubt.) (Qur'an 19:30-34)

It has also been related to us through the Hadith, such as

Abu Huraira narrated that the Prophet Mohammad ﷺ said: **'There is no prophet between me and him (*i.e.*, `Isa). He shall descend, so recognize him when you see him. He is a man of medium height, [his complexion] is between reddish and white, he will be in two yellowish garments. His head looks as if it is dripping water even though it is not wet. He will fight people in the way of Islam, will break the cross, kill the swine, and abolish the Jizyah. Allah will put an end to all religions except Islam during his time. He will slay the Antichrist and he will stay on Earth for forty years. Then, he will die and the Muslims will perform the funeral prayer over him.'** (Abu Dawud, Ahmad)

We pray that if Allah allows us to be alive at the time of his descent that we are able to heed his call and follow him and Imam Mahdi.

Prophet Muhammad ibn ʿAbdullah ﷺ

He is the last of the Ulil ʿAzim in appearance, but the first of them in rank. The Messenger of Allah ﷺ is the epitome of righteousness, virtue, character, manners, intelligence, and all the qualities that we are asked to cultivate, display, and have been commanded to imitate. He is the unquestioned leader of the entire creation with no equal. He is the Beloved of Allah, Subhaanahu wa Taʿala. His name is Abu al-Qasim Muhammad ibn Abdullah ibn Abd al-Muttalib ibn Hashim ﷺ. The entire creation has been told of his coming since the first Messenger our Father Adam (peace be upon him) and each successive prophet and Messenger since has been charged with preparing humanity to accept his call. Those people who refuse to respond to his call are doomed to face Allah's punishment in the Hellfire, for all eternity, while those who accept his call shall benefit from His Mercy and Favor by being granted entrance into Paradise. Allah ﷻ says,

(Allah took a pledge from the prophets, saying, "If, after I have bestowed Scripture and wisdom upon you, a messenger comes confirming what you have been given, you must believe in him and support him. Do you affirm this and accept My pledge as binding on you?" They said, "We do." He said, "Then bear witness and I too will bear witness." Those who turn away after this are the ones who break pledges. Do they seek anything other than submission to Allah? Everyone in the heavens and earth submits to Him, willingly or unwillingly; they will all be returned to Him. Say [Muhammad], "We [Muslims] believe in Allah and in what has been sent down to us and to Abraham, Ishmael, Isaac, Jacob, and the Tribes. We believe in what has been given to Moses, Jesus, and the prophets from their Lord. We do not make a distinction between any one among them. It is to Him that we devote ourselves." If anyone desires a religion other than Islam (submission to Allah), never will it be accepted of him; and in the Hereafter He will be in the ranks of those who have lost (all spiritual good). Why would Allah guide people who deny the truth, after they have believed and acknowledged that the Messenger is true, and after they have been shown clear proof? Allah does not guide evildoers such people will be rewarded with rejection by Allah, by the angels, by all people, and so they will remain, with no relief or respite for their suffering. Except for those that repent after that, and make amends; for verily Allah is Oft-Forgiving, Most Merciful.) (Qur'an 3:81-89)

There were two pledges that Allah contracted with humanity: one taken from all the Children of Adam and the other taken by all of the Prophets.

Allah ﷻ says,

> (When your Lord took out the offspring from the loins of the Children of Adam and made them bear witness about themselves, He said, "Am I not your Lord?" and they replied, "Yes, we bear witness." So you cannot say on the Day of Resurrection, "We were not aware of this," or "It was our forefathers who, before us, ascribed partners to God, and we are only the descendants who came after them: will you destroy us because of falsehoods they invented?" In this way We explain the messages, so that they may return (to the right path).) (Qur'an 172-174)

This was the general covenant we all took, to recognize our Lord and not ascribe partners to Him. But the Prophets and Messengers (peace be upon them) took another covenant that applied exclusively to them. Allah says about this,

> (We took a solemn pledge from the prophets and from you (Muhammad), from Noah, from Abraham, from Moses, from Jesus, son of Mary. We took a solemn pledge from all of them. Allah will question [even] the truthful about their sincerity, and for those who reject the truth He has prepared a painful torment.) (Qur'an 33:7-8)

The Prophet is the "Door of Allah". Following him ﷺ is the guaranteed path to Allah's Love, Forgiveness, and success in this World and the Next. Refusing to follow him ﷺ is the path that leads to Allah's Hatred, Wrath, and misery in this World and the Next.

Allah ﷻ says,

> (The Messenger of Allah is an excellent model for those of you who put your hope in Allah and the Last Day and remember Him often.) (Qur'an 33:21)

He ﷻ also says,

> (Say [O Prophet], "Allah knows everything that is in your hearts, whether you conceal or reveal it; He knows everything in the heavens and earth; Allah has power over all things." On the Day when every soul finds all the good it has done present before it, it will wish all the bad it has done to be far, far away. Allah warns you to beware of Him, but Allah is compassionate towards His servants. Say, "If you love Allah, follow me, and Allah will love you and forgive you your sins; Allah is Most Forgiving, Most Merciful." Say: "Obey Allah

and His Messenger": But if they turn back, Allah loveth not those who reject Faith.) (Qur'an 3:29-32)

And He ﷻ says

(Whoever obeys the Messenger obeys Allah. If some pay no heed, We have not sent you to be their keeper.) (Qur'an 4:80)

As well as,

([S]o take what the Messenger assigns to you, and deny yourselves that which he withholds from you. And fear Allah; for Allah is strict in Punishment.) (Qur'an 59:7)

And,

(When Allah and His Messenger have decided on a matter that concerns them, it is not fitting for any believing man or woman to claim freedom of choice in that matter. Whoever disobeys Allah and His Messenger is far astray.) (Qur'an 33:36)

It has also been narrated in the Hadith

Narrated Abu Huraira: **Allah's Messenger ﷺ said, "All of my Umma will enter Paradise except those who refuse."** They said, **"O Allah's Messenger ﷺ! Who will refuse?"** He said, **"Whoever obeys me will enter Paradise, and whoever disobeys me is the one who refuses."** (Bukhari)

◆ He is the Khatam al-Nabiyyin, the Seal on the line of Prophets, as Allah ﷻ says

(Muhammad is not the father of any of your men, but (he is) the Messenger of Allah, and the Seal of the Prophets: and Allah has full knowledge of all things.) (Qur'an 33:40)

As we mentioned, every Messenger is necessarily a Prophet, but not every Prophet is a Messenger. And so our leigelord Muhammad ﷺ being the "Seal of the Prophets" necessarily means that he is also the "Seal of the Messengers" by definition. Thus, anyone who claims to believe that he is the Seal of the Prophets, but claim that another Messenger was sent after him has committed Kufr and their Islam has been negated absolutely. And even though we affirm that Isa ibn Maryam (peace be upon him) will descend in the Last Days, he will not return as a

Messenger, but a major sign of the End of Times and a follower of our Prophet ﷺ as he himself promised his Lord ﷻ.

✦ He ﷺ is the Master of the Children of Adam and all the Prophets and Messengers will stand under his banner on the Day of Judgement:

Narrated Abu Sa'eed: The Messenger of Allah ﷺ said: **"I am the master of the children of Adam on the Day of Judgement, and I am not boasting. The Banner of Praise will be in my hand, and I am not boasting. There will not be a Prophet on that day, not Adam nor anyone other than him, except that he will be under my banner. And I am the first one for whom the earth will be opened for, and I am not bragging."** (Tirmidhi)

✦ He has been granted the Great Intercession, and he will also have a special Intercession for those of us from his Umma who committed major sins. He will also bring the Muslims from out of the Hellfire.

Imran bin Husain narrated that the Prophet ﷺ said: **"A group from my Ummah will depart from the Fire through my intercession, and they will be called the Jahannamiyyin."** (Tirmidhi)

Narrated Abu Hurairah: Regarding Allah's saying: (It may be that your Lord will raise you to a praised station) (Qur'an 17:79) that the Messenger of Allah ﷺ was asked about it and he said: **"It is the intercession."** (Tirmidhi)

It was narrated that Jabir said: I heard the Messenger of Allah ﷺ say: **"My intercession on the Day of Resurrection will be for those among my nation who committed major sins."** (Ibn Majah)

✦ He responds to the greetings (salams) of his Umma from his grave, by Allah's Permission:

Narrated Abu Hurayrah: The Prophet ﷺ said: **"If any one of you greets me, Allah returns my soul to me and I respond to the greeting."** (Abu Dawud)

Allah commands us to send blessings upon him ﷺ and informs us that He and His Angels do as well. We are rewarded for doing so by Allah Himself. It is one of the greatest acts of worship that we can perform, the way to attain wilaya (sainthood) and increase our rank in

OUR BELOVED PROPHETS

Paradise. And since our greetings are conveyed to and returned by him ﷺ, we should have as much presence of heart as we can muster when we are sending our salawat upon him ﷺ. We should give our salams to the Prophet ﷺ with full knowledge and realization that our greeting will be conveyed to him during the tashahhud of the ritual prayer in particular. A single salam sent upon the Prophet ﷺ is rewarded at least 10 times over. Allah ﷻ says,

(Allah and His angels send blessings on the Prophet: O ye that believe! Send blessings on him and give him greetings of peace.) (Qur'an 33:56)

And in the Hadith:

Anas bin Malik said: The Messenger of Allah ﷺ said: **"Whoever sends salah upon me once, Allah ﷻ will send salah upon him tenfold, and will erase ten sins from him, and will raise him ten degrees in status."** (Nasa'i)

And so we should make a routine of sending salawat upon him in the morning and evening, daily, weekly, whatever we can manage. Anyone who claims that doing so is bid`a is completely ignorant of the Shari`a.

He ﷺ also said,

It was narrated from Abu Darda' that the Messenger of Allah ﷺ said: **"Send a great deal of blessing upon me on Fridays, for it is witnessed by the angels. No one sends blessing upon me but his blessing will be presented to me, until he finishes them."** A man said: "Even after death?" He said: **"Even after death, for Allah has forbidden the earth to consume the bodies of the Prophets, so the Prophet of Allah is alive and receives provision."** (Ibn Majah)

And we should avail ourselves of this opportunity as well. The period between Thursday's Maghrib to Friday's Maghrib is considered a blessed time to send salawat upon him. A recommended form of the salawat that is easy to say is:

اَللَّهُمَّ صَلِّ عَلَى سَيِّدِنَا مُحَمَّدٍ وَ عَلَى آلِهِ وَ سَلِّم

(O Allah! Send your blessings on our leigelord Muhammad and his family and grant them peace.)
[Allāhumma ṣalli ʿala sayyidina Muḥammadin wa ʿala ālihi wa sallam]

Or for those who have the aspiration (himma) Imam Nawawi recommends the following phrase that combines the wording of numerous ahadith into one:

اَللَّهُمَّ صَلِّ عَلَى سَيِّدِينَ مُحَمَّدٍ عَبْدِكَ وَ رَسُولِكَ النَّبِيِّ وَ الْأُمِّيَّ وَ عَلَى آلِهِ وَ وَ صَحْبِهِ وَ سَلَّم

(O Allah! Send your blessings on our leigelord Muhammad, Your slave and Your Messenger, the Primordial Prophet, and upon his family and Companions and grant them peace.)
[Allāhumma ṣalli 'ala sayyidina Muḥammadin 'abdika wa rasūlika wa 'ala ālihi wa ṣaḥbihi wa sallam]

It is specifically recommended to send salawat after Salat al-Asr on the Day of Jumu'a based upon the Prophet's ﷺ declaration that there is a certain time on Friday that **"[If a Believer] asks something from Allah, then Allah will definitely meet his demand,"** which he indicated was a short amount of time with his hands ﷺ. (Bukhari) Most scholars said that this time was the time after the `Asr prayer until sunset. And so we should take advantage of this period of time especially in order that it be recorded in our account that we ended the blessed day of Friday by sending greetings upon the Messenger of Allah ﷺ. If that is not encouragement enough, in another famous hadith the Prophet ﷺ explained that **"The person closest to me on the Day of Judgment is the one who sent the most salawat upon me."** (Tirmidhi)

The Prophet ﷺ also recommend us to send prayers upon him after the Adhan when he said,

> Narrated 'Abdullah bin 'Amr: The Messenger of Allah ﷺ said: **"If you hear the Muadhdhin then say as he says. Then send Salat upon me, because whoever sends Salat upon me, Allah will send Salat upon him ten times due to it. Then ask Allah that He gives me 'Al-Wasilah,' because it is a place in Paradise which is not for anyone except for a slave from the slaves of Allah, and I hope that I am him. And whoever asks that I have Al-Wasilah, then (my) intercession will be made lawful for him."** (Tirmidhi)

And it is recommended to say:

اَللَّهُمَّ رَبَّ هَذِهِ الدَّعْوَةِ التَّامَّةِ وَ الصَّلَاةِ الْقَائِمَةِ، آتِ مُحَمَّداً الْوَسِيلَةَ وَ الْفَضِيلَةَ، وَ ابْعَثْهُ مَقَاماً مَّحْمُوداً الَّذِي وَ عَدْتَهُ.

(O Allah! Lord of this perfect call and established prayer, grant Muhammad status and virtue and resurrect him to the praiseworthy station that You have promised him.)
[Allāhumma Rabba hādhihi-d-da'wati-t-tammati wa-ṣ-ṣalāti-l-qā'imah, āti Muḥammadan-il-wasilata wa-l-faḍīlah, wa-b'athhu maqāma-m-maḥmūdan-illadhī wa 'adtah.]

OUR BELOVED PROPHETS

And which one of us is worshipping Allah so perfectly that we are not in need of the intercession of our Prophet ﷺ? Regarding the station of the Messenger ﷺ with his Lord, Allah ﷻ says

(All the messengers We sent were meant to be obeyed, in accordance with the will of Allah. If only they had come to you (Prophet) when they wronged themselves, and asked Allah's forgiveness, and the Messenger had asked forgiveness for them, they would have found Allah indeed Oft-returning, Most Merciful.) (Qur'an 4:64)

Allah ﷻ connects His forgiveness of the Mushrik Arabs and Hypocrites to their humbling themselves before the Prophet, seeking Allah's forgiveness and asking the Prophet ﷺ to seek forgiveness on their behalf. He ﷻ also says

(Believers, respond to Allah and His Messenger, when he (the Prophet) calls you to that which will give you life; and know that Allah comes in between a man and his heart, and that you will be gathered to Him.) (Qur'an 8:24)

There is so much more that could be said about the Prophet ﷺ. We could go on forever and not do him justice. So this will have to suffice for now. We encourage everyone to read as much as they can about our Prophet ﷺ, his life, his special qualities and the example he set forth for us, in order to increase our love for him and desire to follow his Sunna. It is that which brings the hearts to life and will be our only refuge on the Day when there will be no respite. *Allahumma salli `ala Sayyidina Muhammad wa `ala Aalihi wa Sahbihi wa sallam. Subhana Rabbika Rabbi-l-Izzati `amma yarsifun. Wa salam ala Mursalin. Wa-l-hamdlillahi Rabbi-l-alamin.*

COURSE ASSIGNMENTS YOU MUST COMPLETE

The final deadline to submit the exam and assignments is **June 30th** for the Spring Term and **December 31st** for the Fall Term.

Please note:

- Include your full name and ID number on all assignments.
- Submit the exam and written assignments all together in one envelope.
- We request that you write all assignments in print, and do not use cursive handwriting. Please try to write as clearly as possible to make it easier to read.
- Use blue or black ink only.
- If a page limit is given, you must keep within this limit. We cannot guarantee your full assignment will be graded if you fail to do so.
- All assignments including the exam are "open book" and so you may use your book and notes.
- There is no time limit for the exam.

TAYBA FOUNDATION
IMAN 100 Exam
100 Questions

Remember:
- NEVER GUESS. If you are not sure, then leave it blank, which indicates "I don't know."
- All questions relate to the text, commentary or any supplementary material. These questions are not testing or referring to "general" knowledge that you may have acquired. Make sure to base your answers on the terminology you used in the text. An example would be "sunna" in the general sense as opposed to the classification used by the text, as opposed to "mandub."
- If you believe a question is incorrectly worded or confusing, please include a written explanation on a SEPARATE piece of paper and submit it along with the test sheet.
- Mark the correct answer on the test sheet with a pen or pencil. Failure to submit the test sheet in a timely manner could result in a failing grade. We advise that you keep a copy of the test sheet for yourself before mailing the original.
- Keep this Exam and only submit the test sheet along with your written assignment.
- Make sure to write the following on your test sheet: Your name, your ID number, the course title, and the Exam title (for this one it would be "IMAN 100 Exam, v5").

1. "The source and virtue of Ahlul Bayt and the Companions is the Messenger of Allah, peace and blessings be upon him. They are branches of this one source." Who made this statement?
    a. Ali ibn Abi Talib
    b. Imam Ja'far As-Sadiq
    c. Imam Nabahani
    d. Imam Abu Hanifah

2. Tasalsul means _____.
    a. To tie something
    b. Infinite Regression
    c. To be connected
    d. Circular Reasoning

3. What happens first, Hashr or Nashr?
    a. The terms are synonymous
    b. Nashr
    c. Hashr

4. Can the existence of Allah be known through rational proofs?
    a. Yes
    b. No

5. Dreams are 1/46th of prophecy. If a person is capable of giving accurate dream interpretation and also has true dreams are they considered to be part of the Prophetic Brotherhood and are recipients of Wahy?
    a. No and to believe this is Kufr
    b. Yes. But they are not permitted to declare this openly to people who may not appreciate their spiritual accomplishments.
    c. No. But their belief is not Kufr, just an ignorance misunderstanding.
    d. Yes. But they have not fully arrived at Prophethood because they have not been given a Book.

6. Allah being "The Creator" and "The Originator" means that He created the Universe, set the rules on how it operates and then set it run on auto pilot. The "Laws of Nature" explain how the world operates and Allah does not actively intervene except when sending Revelation or making miracles appear.
    a. True
    b. False

7. How many Angels accompany the Believer when they are raised from their Grave?
    a. 6.0
    b. 19.0
    c. 2.0
    d. 4.0
    e. 0.0

8. When we elect a person to be the "Amir" of our Masjid or Organization or we have Ulama' in our community, we are bound in obedience to them in carrying out our affairs.
    a. True
    b. False
    c. Only in matters that make the Deen stronger

9. Which companion narrated that the Prophet, peace and blessings be upon him, that there would be 10 signs before the Last Hour?
    a. Ali
    b. Hamza

c. Ibn Mas`ud
  d. Huzaifa

10. It is impermissible to ever make takfir (accuse someone of not being Muslim) after they have declared their Shahadah.
    a. True
    b. False

11. Anything that is added to the Deen is reprehensible Bid`a, no exceptions.
    a. True
    b. False

12. If a misguided and deviant person performs a miracle, this is known as _____.
    a. Sihr/Magic
    b. Nothing, this will never happen
    c. Mustadraj/Istidraj (deluded one/one being lead astray)
    d. Karama

13. Saa`ah is used to refer to how many things?
    a. 5.0
    b. 3.0
    c. 2.0
    d. 1.0

14. It is a form of Kufr to _____.
    a. Believe that we can perform miracles
    b. Believe that Angels are female
    c. Believe that one should visit the graves and offer Du`a for its inhabitants
    d. Believe that the Prophet hears the greetings sent to him

15. Whenever we intend to perform any type of deed, good or bad, how do the Angels know and what do they do?
    a. They call the curse of Allah upon us and they leave us
    b. They talk to us in the form of our conscience and if we listen Allah forgives us and if we do not then we will be taken to account
    c. They smell a pleasing or foul smell emitting from us based on our intentions and record them accordingly when we have acted
    d. Nothing, Angels are not like us and smells and other things do not affect them

16. Who declared that there were three (3) double orders in the Qur'an?
    a. Ibn Abbas
    b. Mother Aisha
    c. Ali
    d. Umar ibn Al-Khattab
    e. Abu Bakr As-Siddiq

17. _____ witnessed two (2) desert Arabs having a conversation that helped him to understand the meaning of Fatir?
    a. Umar
    b. Hudhayfa
    c. Abu Musa al-Asha`ri
    d. Abu Hurayrah
    e. Ibn Abbas

18. The number of things which comprises what we know to be the sunnah are _____.
    a. 2.0
    b. 5.0
    c. 3.0
    d. 7.0

19. The most important thing to ask Allah for is _____ so that we die as Muslims.
    a. Strong Faith
    b. The Best Seal
    c. Righteous Spouses and Offspring
    d. Abundance of Taqwa

20. Who taught Shaykh Rami about the constellations?
    a. Shaykh Abdullah bin Ahmedna
    b. Shaykh Katri bin Bayba
    c. Shaykh Muhammad Ali
    d. Murabit al-Hajj

21. The Evildoers will receive their Scrolls _____.
    a. Attached to a chain around their necks
    b. After they have been weighed in the Mizan and they are judged
    c. From behind their backs or in their left hand
    d. They will be slapped in their faces with them by the Angels of Punishment

22. It is Kufr to deny that there is a land called "Egypt", but not if you deny that there is a land called "Scandanavia".
    a. True
    b. False

23. Imam Qurtubi is a scholar primarily known for _____.
    a. Hadith Authentication
    b. Qur'anic Recitation
    c. History
    d. Qur'anic Commentary

24. Our belief that Muhammad ibn Abdullah is the last Prophet necessarily means he is also the last Messenger.
    a. True and therefore anyone who believes that another Messenger came is outside of the fold of Islam.
    b. True, but since it isn't explicitly stated, someone who believes in another Messenger is still considered to be Muslim.
    c. False. If the Qur'an meant that he was the final Messenger then it would have stated so explicitly.

25. Prophet Yusuf, peace be upon him, is alive in his grave.
    a. True
    b. False

26. Women being clothed and unclothed at the same time is a sign of what?
    a. A sign of our times
    b. A sign of their need for Guidance
    c. A lesser sign of the Hour
    d. A sign that the society is doomed to Hell

27. Kevin's little brother has taken a keen interest in Islam. He is very intelligent and he has been talking with his brother and asking questions for over a year. He is 10 and about to turn 11 years old in a month. Is he to be held accountable for saying his Testimony of Faith at this time?
    a. No, young boys do not commonly reach Bulugh at this age
    b. Yes, The Prophet, prayers and peace be upon him, said to beat the children if they do not pray at this age
    c. Only if he has reached puberty, otherwise he cannot be held responsible
    d. Yes, he is learning about the Deen he needs to take that step and commit himself

e. No, he is a child and no one can make him do something like this unless his parents give him permission until he is grown and of age

28. We say "'Allah creates all actions" instead of saying that "Allah creates good and evil" because:
    a. To claim that Allah creates evil is kufr.
    b. We avoiding directly saying Allah creates evil out of respect (adab).
    c. We only quote what Allah says about Himself in the Qur'an.
    d. Claiming that Allah creates evil is absurd.

29. If you are talking with a person who is unable to speak and they make a gesture to indicate that they understand and accept the truth of what you are sharing with them about Islam, does this qualify as a sound Shahadah?
    a. Yes. They clearly affirmed that they believed in Allah and His Messenger and that is sufficient.
    b. No. They need to write out their Shahadah since they are unable to speak and writing is the next closest thing to speech.

30. In terms of our belief about previous Scriptures, which of the following is the most accurate:
    a. We outright reject the Hebrew Scriptures (i.e., Torah, Psalms, Gospel, etc.)
    b. We affirm the validity of all major world religious Scriptures (i.e., Bible, Bhagavad Gita, Buddhist Sutras, etc.) as having been revealed by Allah
    c. We affirm the validity of every single line the original Scriptures mentioned explicitly in the Qur'an, but not their current versions
    d. We affirm the validity of the original major world religious Scriptures, but not their current versions

31. Which of the following is NOT one of the Major Signs of The Final Hour?
    a. Destruction of the Ka`bah
    b. The removal of the Qur'an from the Earth
    c. The Dajjal
    d. Murder becoming rampant

32. Which of the following most accurately defines what a "Companion (Sahabi)" is according to the coursebook:
    a. Someone who met the Prophet, believed in him, spent a significant amount of time with him and died while believing in him.
    b. Anyone who believed in the Prophet during his time and died while believing in

him.
c. Someone who met the Prophet, professed their belief to him and died believing in him without having ever doubted his Prophethood.
d. Someone who met the Prophet, believed in him and died while believing in him, even if they had rejected their faith at some point in time.

33. What is the Barzakh?
    a. It is an intermediate realm where the sinful people reside after death until Resurrection where they are punished as a purification of their deeds.
    b. It is the intermediate realm between death and Resurrection where all souls reside where they are both rewarded and punished for all the deeds they did in their earthly life.
    c. It is the intermediate realm between death and Resurrection where all souls reside and experience bliss or punishment according to Allah's Will.
    d. It is the intermediate realm between death and Ressurection where all souls that did an equal amount of bad and good remain in a limbo-like state unti Judgement.

34. The Qur'an clarifies the belief in the Angels in what two (2) ways?
    a. Through confirming and denying
    b. Through stories and similitudes
    c. Through the use of logic and revelation

35. What do you call the person who leaves the Salah, but still affirms it is obligatory?
    a. Fasiq (disobedient sinner)
    b. Zindiq (heretic)
    c. Kafir (unbeliever)
    d. Murtadd (apostate)

36. Naji Allah (the one who Allah saved) applies to who?
    a. Yusuf (from the well and prison)
    b. Ibrahim (from the fire)
    c. Nuh (from the flood)
    d. Yunus (from the belly of the fish)

37. Sincere repentance consists of _____ conditions.
    a. 3.0
    b. 5.0
    c. 4.0
    d. 2.0

38. In the Musannaf of `Abd ar-Razzaq, _____, and in al-Bayhaqi's, Ba`th, _____, narrates a tradition on an ayat from Suwarun al-An`am and an-Naba.
    a. Ibn `Abbas and Ibn `Umar
    b. `Amr ibn al-`As and Abu Dharr
    c. Ibn Jubayr and Abu Hurayrah
    d. Nafi` and Qatadah

39. When we experience ease or feel better because of the fact that we know that Allah's Prophets went through certain difficulties this is known as _____.
    a. Sakinah
    b. Tawfeeq
    c. Tasalli
    d. Baraka
    e. Fadl

40. Which of the following do we understand from the list of 13 Divine Attributes mentioned in the section on Allah Most High:
    a. These 13 Attributues are the only Divine Attributes that we ascribe to Allah
    b. That the Divine Attributes and Divine Names are distinct from one another, so we affirm that He has 13 Attributes and 99 Names.
    c. It is just a list derived from the Qur'an by the scholars to help us understand the most fundamental things about Allah's Oneness
    d. A and B

41. To say that some of the Prophets have a higher rank than others is Kufr because it is a denial of the Qur'an.
    a. True
    b. False

42. Allah created us with the inherent ability to create our own actions and this is the reason why we are responsible for them.
    a. True
    b. False

43. The Prophet's order to "relate traditions from the children of Israel" means that we affirm all of the stories of the Old Testament to be true, but not the New Testament
    a. True
    b. False

44. Someone who denies the existence of the Jinn or claims they are just are metaphor for natural forces is guilty of Kufr.
    a. True
    b. False

45. Which of the following most accurately describes our belief about Allah's Speech:
    a. We believe that He speaks with sounds, but only the Angels, Prophets and Messengers can hear or understand Him.
    b. His "Speech" is just a metaphor for His instilling knowledge directly into the hearts of the Prophets and Messengers.
    c. We affirm that His Speech is one of His Attributes and His Attributes are beyond our comprehension.
    d. We believe that Allah speaks through His creation because He is above needing to speak to communicate with anyone.

46. When we say that we do not distinguish between the Prophets and Messengers, we mean:
    a. We do not consider any of the Prophets or Messengers to be better than the others.
    b. We believe that they are all equal in their function of being representatives of Allah Most High.
    c. We believe that it was obligatory for everyone to follow and obey all of them in their time.
    d. We consider all the Prophets to be equal but lesser so than the Messengers, who we also consider to be equal.

47. Do Christians commit shirk when they say that Isa, upon him be peace, is the "son of God"?
    a. Yes
    b. No
    c. It depends since not all Christians are in agreement about what the term "Son of God" means

48. What are the Four (4) ways of reading upon which the Qur'an was sent down?
    a. The dialects of the Four main Arab tribal regions, Qurayshi, Yemeni, Iraqi, Shamsi
    b. According to the previous People of the Books texts, the Suhuf of Ibrahim, the Zabur of Dawud, the Tawrah of Bani Isra'il, and the Injil of Isa, upon all of them be peace
    c. Halal, Haram, Tafsir, and Mutashabih

d. We do not have this knowledge

49. If a person does not answer the questions of the grave properly they will be _____.
    a. Ripped to shreds by the Dogs of Hell
    b. Struck upside the head
    c. Taken straight to Hell without delay
    d. Tormented and burned by Munkar and Nakir

50. Prophets and Messengers were intelligent and righteous people who earned Allah's favor due to the soundness of their beliefs and their righteous actions.
    a. True
    b. False

51. The arrival of the Mahdi is confirmed by a Hadith that has reached the level of tawaatur.
    a. True
    b. False

52. If a person acquires spiritual accomplishments through being self-reflective and hard work this is known as _____.
    a. Wilaya
    b. Sabab
    c. Baraka
    d. Kasb

53. How many categories of Bid`a are there?
    a. 1.0
    b. 2.0
    c. 3.0
    d. 5.0
    e. 4.0

54. Can a person who is 17 be held responsible to pray and accept Islam as the Truth if they have not yet seen any of the signs of puberty?
    a. Yes
    b. No

55. When we take medicine for healing, drink water to quench our thirst, eat food for satiation, etc., these things are viewed as a _____.
    a. Things that Allah has placed function that benefit us by Allah's permission

indirectly
- b. A means of attaining a goal that Allah acts directly through
- c. Things that are part of the natural laws that Allah has permitted us to benefit from when necessary
- d. Frivolties that only those of weak Iman seek after

56. What are the obligatory qualities for the Prophets?
    - a. Sidq (Truthfulness), Adl (Just), Tabligh (Conveying the Message), Ihsan (Beautiful Perfomance of Deeds)
    - b. Amanah (Trustworthiness), Sidq (Truthfulness), Sadaqa (Charitable), Male
    - c. Fatana (Intelligence), Sidq (Truthfulness), Tabligh (Conveying the Message), Amanah, (Trustworthiness)
    - d. Sidq, Tawakkul (Reliance on Allah), Yaqin (Certainty), Amanah

57. The meaning of Bid`a can only be used in reference to matters relating to our practice of the Deen, so sifting flour and using utensils to eat with cannot be considered Bid`a.
    - a. True
    - b. False

58. Which of the following is true:
    - a. You should not make tawba for committing minor sins.
    - b. Intentionally commiting major sins takes someone outside the fold of Islam.
    - c. Major sins can only be wiped out through tawba.
    - d. Anyone caught committing a major sin needs to make tawba in front of the community.

59. What is the reason why we reject the notion that Prophets could be afflicted with repulsive sicknesses and physical defects?
    - a. It goes against their noble status as representatives of Allah.
    - b. It would make it reasonable for someone to reject their Message.
    - c. It would force them to rely on others, which would undermine their authority and therefore their Message.
    - d. All of the above

60. What is the lesser Final Hour?
    - a. The last year of our life
    - b. The first blowing of the horn on Yawmul Qiyamah
    - c. Death
    - d. The period of time we spend in the womb

61. What had `Izraeel wondering how to carry out Allah's order in the court of Solomon?
    a. How to take Solomon's soul and he knew who he was and had the entire creation at his command
    b. How to take the soul of a man who was supposed to die in another place who was present in the court
    c. How to take the souls of so many people at once in the court of Solomon without hurting Solomon

62. "The oppression of a _____ for one year is less harmful than the people being in anarchy for one instant."
    a. Bid`i
    b. Tyrant
    c. Sultan
    d. Kafir

63. What is a good way to learn about who Allah is?
    a. Reading more Qur'an
    b. Calling on Him by His Supreme Name
    c. Through studying the hadith of the Rasul, peace and blessings be upon him
    d. By learning the Ninety-nine Names

64. What beloved act does Shaykh Rami perform for his beloved Father?
    a. He recites Sura Ikhlas in the mornings and evenings and makes du`a before and after
    b. He visits his grave every Friday and makes du`a
    c. He started the Tayba Foundation and teaches others about the Deen because of his father's support and encouragement when he went off to study
    d. I do not know about this story

65. Faruq was smoking weed with his friends and halfway through the blunt, he started to feel bad and kept making Istighfar to himself, promising Allah that he would never do it again after this blunt was finished. Was this acceptable?
    a. Yes. He made a firm resolve not to return to the sin.
    b. No. He needs to make tawba for smoking the blunt as well as delaying his tawba.
    c. No. His tawba wasn't valid because he kept it to himself and didn't enjoin the good with his friends.
    d. Yes, but to complete his tawba he should have prayed two (2) raka`a if salat al-tawba.

66. In what sura do we find the ayah that says that the Prophet, peace be upon him does not speak of his own desire?
    a. Sura Muhammad, peace be upon him
    b. Sura al-Fath
    c. Sura al-Najm
    d. Sura al-Isra'

67. The Ulil Amr (the ones possessing command) are the people in charge of the Masjid or any type of Islamic group.
    a. True
    b. False

68. Our belief that Isa ibn Marym (AS) was not crucified means that he did not die on the cross, not that he was never placed upon it.
    a. True
    b. False

69. We acquire our actions because we have the freewill to decide whether we do good or evil. This known as _____.
    a. Taqwa
    b. Kasb
    c. Wilaya
    d. Taklif

70. "Whoever mentions that places confine him, will always be baffled and confused." Who made this statement?
    a. Abu Bakr
    b. Prophet Muhammad, peace and blessings be upon him
    c. Imam Ali
    d. Imam Tahawi
    e. Imam al-`Ashari

71. There are _____ Angels that we must know about.
    a. 25.0
    b. 10.0
    c. 5.0
    d. 19.0
    e. 3.0

72. It is a form of apostasy to tell someone to delay taking their Shahada.
    a. True
    b. False

73. It is possible for a Prophet to be physically deaf or blind.
    a. True
    b. False

74. Which if the following statements is true?
    a. We believe that the Angels are higher in rank than the Prophets and the Messengers.
    b. We believe the Messengers, then Prophets, then Companions, then the Angels are highest in rank.
    c. We believe that the Messengers, then Prophets, then Angels, then the Companions are highest in rank.
    d. We believe than the Messengers, then the Angels, then the Prophets, then the Companions, are highest in rank.

75. It is possible for someone to be buried as a non-Muslim, but in reality be a Muslim.
    a. True
    b. False

76. How do we understand the Prophet's (SAW) statement that "Abrahim never lied except for on three occasions?
    a. It is permissible to lie out of necessity so we do not consider something to be a lie when someone was forced to say it.
    b. We affirm that Prophets sometimes are forced to lie but we do not attribute lies to them out of respect (adab).
    c. This hadith is rejected since it goes against our beliefs about the Prophets being unable to tell lies.
    d. Ibrahim (AS) made truthful statements in a deceptive way and made rhetorical arguments that were obviously falsely to prove a point.

77. Which of the following best describes our belief about the Prophet's (SAW) Sunna?
    a. It is a form of Revelation similar to the Qur'an.
    b. It is Divinely-inspired, but we do not consider it to be Revelation.
    c. It is a good example to be followed, but is not Divinely-inspired.
    d. It is the best example to follow, but reflects his personal judgements.

78. Anytime that we commit a sinful action we have _____ to make tawbah until it is recorded against us.
    a. 7 days
    b. 6 months
    c. 6 hours
    d. 5 hours
    e. 6 days

79. A person becomes a Muslim when they _____.
    a. State the Shahadatayn
    b. When they start praying
    c. The moment they internally accept the Haqq
    d. Gain the acceptance of the other Muslims based on their adherence to the Deen

80. Which statement contains negation and affirmation?
    a. There is no might nor power except with Allah (la hawla wa la quwwata illa biLlah)
    b. There nothing worthy of worship except Allah and Muhammad is the Messenger of Allah (la ilaha illa Allah Muhammad Rasul Allah)
    c. Allah Decrees and does whatever He wills (Qaddar Allahu Maa Shaa'a fa`al)

81. Is it better to think about Allah's Entity or His creation?
    a. Creation
    b. Allah
    c. Both
    d. Neither, it is better to think about how we are going to gain Allah's Mercy and Favor

82. What does it mean when Allah says "We are closer to him than (his) jugular vein"?
    a. That He is in close proximity to us so that He is fully aware of all things
    b. That He is physically present everywhere in His Entity so He is aware of all of our actions
    c. That He has full knowledge of our every action that we have performed
    d. That He has full knowledge of everything concerning His creation and nothing is hidden from Him

83. Why do we make Du`a when everything is already written?
    a. To have good manners with Allah because He does not need our prayers; they

233

only help us to acknowledge His Glory
   b. So that we can have a reason to believe and Allah Loves for His slaves to call on Him
   c. Because there are things written in the Lawh al-Mahfudh that can be added or removed as a result of our Du`a
   d. Because we want Allah to have Mercy on us

84. It is reasonable to say that a Prophet of Allah would have sores with pus and blood running from them.
   a. True
   b. False

85. People will see the Signs of Allah according to their nature and state according to _____.
   a. Ibn Al-Qayyim
   b. Qadi `Iyyad
   c. Shaykh `Illish
   d. Imam Ghazzali

86. We should turn to the Torah (Tawrah) if we cannot find something in the Qur'an and the Sunnah since it is a revelation from Allah and we have been commanded to believe in all of the Revealed Texts.
   a. True
   b. False

87. Jibril is _____.
   a. The Angel of Mercy
   b. The Angel of Revelation
   c. One of the our Guardian Angels
   d. The Chief Angel of The Tablet and The Pen

88. Anyone who picked up arms against the Prophet (SAW) is excluded from being considered a Companion.
   a. True
   b. False
   c. False, but we make a clear distinction between the Companions who converted before and after the Conquest of Makka in terms of our love and respect.

89. Is it agreed upon that anyone who does not pray is a Kafir irregardless of the reason?

a. Yes
b. No

90. Ibn Abi Zayd said "Belief consists of what you say with the tongue, what you believe sincerely in the heart, and what you do with the limbs." This means which of the following:
    a. We do not affirm someone's Shahadah until they adopt all the rest of the pillars they are capable of applying.
    b. No one should be given their Shahadah until they pledge to uphold ALL of the pillars of Islam.
    c. Acting upon the other pillars is a completion of the Shahadah but their Shahadah is valid based on their belief and articulation alone.
    d. Action is necessarily a part of Iman and anyone who denies this is a heretic.

91. Iskandar is another name for _____.
    a. Al-Khadir
    b. Prophet Muhammad
    c. Dhul Qarnayn
    d. Luqman

92. To call a Muslim a Kafir is a type of ridda (apostasy).
    a. True
    b. False

93. As long as someone affirms that the Prophet Muhammad is the Messenger of Allah, they are considered Muslim, even if they reject acting on sahih Ahadith.
    a. True
    b. False

94. Is it possible for the Prophets to experience the same types of major ailments and commit sins the same as anyone else?
    a. No, they are perfect people
    b. Yes, they are human
    c. Yes, but only in certain things
    d. No, not after they become Prophets

95. Reciting the Testimony of Faith in Russian is acceptable (for those whose speak Russian).
    a. True
    b. False

96. Which passage from the Qur'an is sufficient for establishing Allah's Oneness?
    a. Qul A`udhu bi Rabbin Nas 114:1-6 (Say: I seek refuge with the Lord of Mankind)
    b. Allahu la ilaha illa huwa al-Hayyul Qayyum 2:255 (Allah, there is none worthy of worship except Him, The Ever-Living, The Self-Sustaining)
    c. Qul Huwa Allahu Ahad 112:1-4 (Say: Allah, He is One [and indivisible])
    d. Wa ilahukum ilahu Wahid 2:163 (And your God is One God)

97. If a person says "I believe in Allah and His Messenger and I know Islam to be the Truth from Allah", and this person fasts, prays, and pays his zakat, but he gambles and whenever he is asked about this he says, "I am doing something that I like to do and I am not bothering or cheating anyone, so please leave me alone!" Is this person Muslim?
    a. No, he is an Apostate (Murtad)
    b. Yes, he accepts the Kalimah, prays, etc, he has done nothing wrong. We cannot judge him
    c. It depends on whether or not he knows that he is wrong
    d. Yes. As long as he doesn't claim he is doing is halal, he is still Muslim, but is sinful (fasiq)

98. What has a specific Ajal?
    a. All created things
    b. Humans
    c. Jinn
    d. Humans and Jinn

99. Two Muslims, Mel and Corey are at visitation and they hear their homeboy Phil and the Christian Chaplain talking next to them as he makes his rounds. The Chaplain asks to pray for him and his family. Phil's family accepts but Phil politely says "I believe that God is One without any partners, and I do not believe that Jesus, peace be upon him, was the son of God and I believe that Prophet Muhammad, peace and blessings cover him, was God's Messenger and last prophet. This is the first time they ever heard him confirm The Haqq. Does this qualify as a valid Shahadah?
    a. No, it has to be in front of Muslim witnesses
    b. Yes, he publicly affirmed his Faith
    c. No, the Imam has to do it with him
    d. Yes, but he has to go back and do it in front of the Brothers

IMAN 100 Version 5 FALL 23

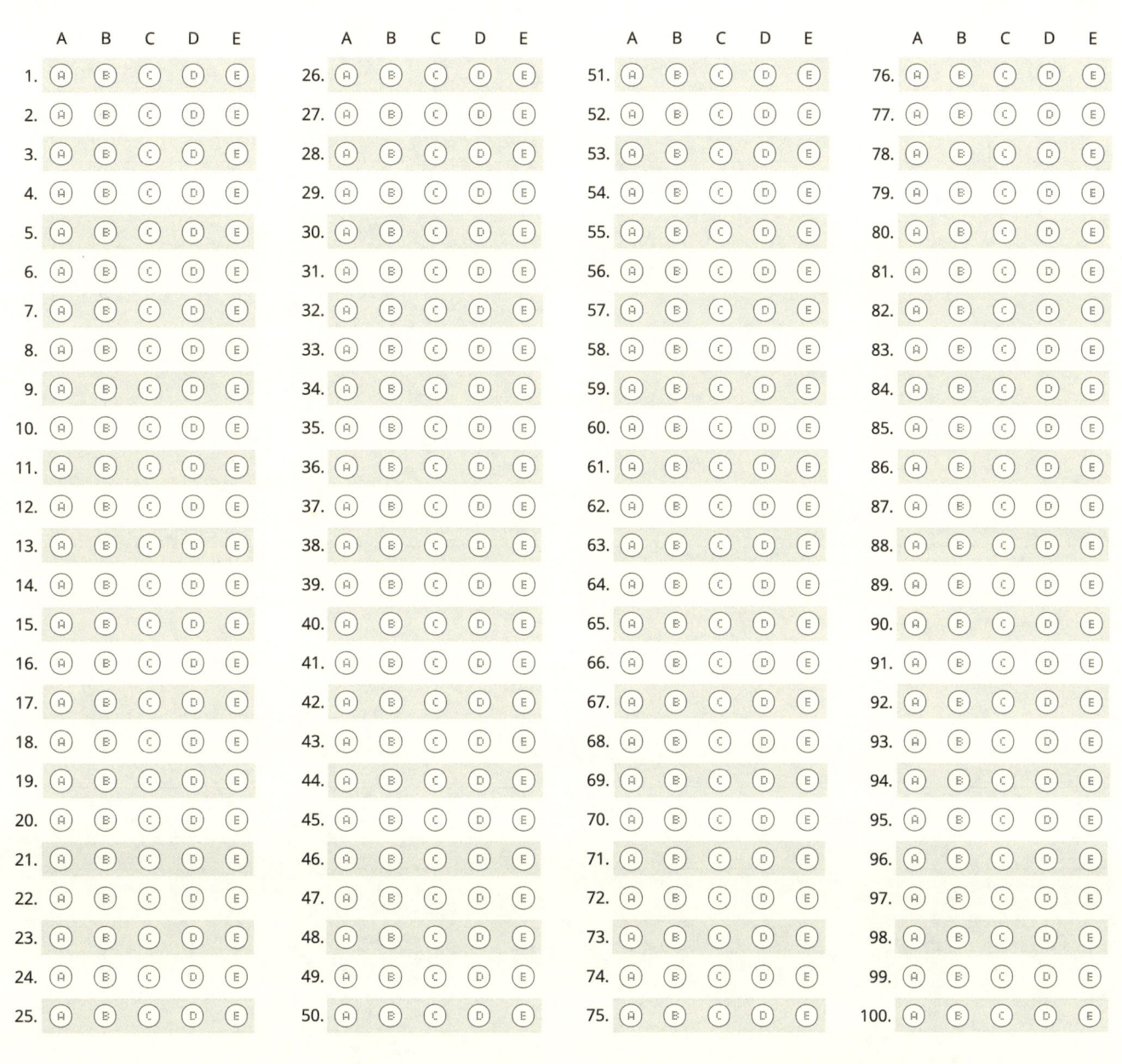

IMAN 100 Short Answer Questions Assignment

"Developing Faith in God and the matters of the unseen such as Paradise, Hell, Resurrection, Day of Judgment, Angels, Prophets, *etc.*"

This is your opportunity to share your life with us, through the lens of faith.

Faith is an evolutionary process, which is constantly fluctuating throughout our life. We experience various highs and lows that test our faith to certain degrees. In these tests, we achieve clarity both in our inner strength and our belief system. For the purpose of this assignment reflect on your journey of faith and discuss how it has grown and changed over time. This includes BEFORE your acceptance of Islam (shahada) and after (if you converted/reverted) or before and after you began practicing your faith seriously (if you were raised as a Muslim).

NOTE: This assignment is to be written as personal reflections from the perspective of your Iman. Essentially, it is *your* story about *your* faith. Please only share and discuss experiences that tie into your faith development. To help guide your thoughts and reflections, we have come up with a series of discussion questions. Your answers should be no less than half a page (½) and no more than two (2) full pages each, typed or handwritten.

Please answer the following questions:

1) Who has had a role in influencing your faith?
2) What specific experiences have tested and/or strengthened your faith?
3) Were there particular experiences that made you question your faith?
4) What series of events led you to your current state of faith?
5) What are your earliest memories of developing faith?
6) What developments of faith did you have that helped you on your road to accepting Islam?
7) Explain how your faith has been affected by your studies with Tayba Foundation, IMAN 100 in particular.

If you are not typing out your answers, please make sure to write as clearly as you can. Please do not write in cursive. Although cursive is beautiful, it is difficult to read when it is digitized. **So please write in print and make sure to write in pen, not pencil, unless you do not have**

access to a pen. <u>If your handwriting is small, please write a little larger for this paper</u>. If your instructor is unable to read your handwriting, your work may be returned ungraded and you will be asked to re-write your paper in more legible handwriting.

Course Assignments Checklist:

❏ I read/studied the coursebook before submitting my assignments.
❏ I have asked any questions I have about the course material before submitting my assignments OR the questions I have about the course material are being submitted on a separate piece of paper, separate from my written assignments (if applicable).
❏ I have read all of the assignments and understand what I need to do.
❏ I contacted Tayba to clarify any questions I might have about the assignments (if applicable).
❏ I completed all assignments using <u>blue</u> or <u>black</u> ink only.
❏ I completed the written assignment by printing clearly and legibly (if applicable).
❏ I made a copy of my written assignment for my records (recommended, but not necessary).
❏ I did not exceed the maximum number of pages permitted for each written assignment.
❏ I completed the multiple-choice exam answer bubble sheet <u>using the original bubble sheet from the coursebook</u> and then cut/neatly tore the page out to submit with my assignment packet. *Please note that if you accidentally tear your bubble sheet, you can contact our office for a replacement sheet.
❏ I made a copy of the answer bubble sheet for my records (recommended, but not necessary).
❏ I included my name and ID number on all of my assignments.
❏ I am submitting all of my assignments together in one packet.
❏ I am submitting my assignments before the deadline (June 30 for Spring/December 31 for Fall).

Your Journey
Through Tayba's Curriculum

INTRO LEVEL

IMAN100 — *Beliefs of a Muslim* → **FIQH100** — *How to Approach Studying Fiqh*

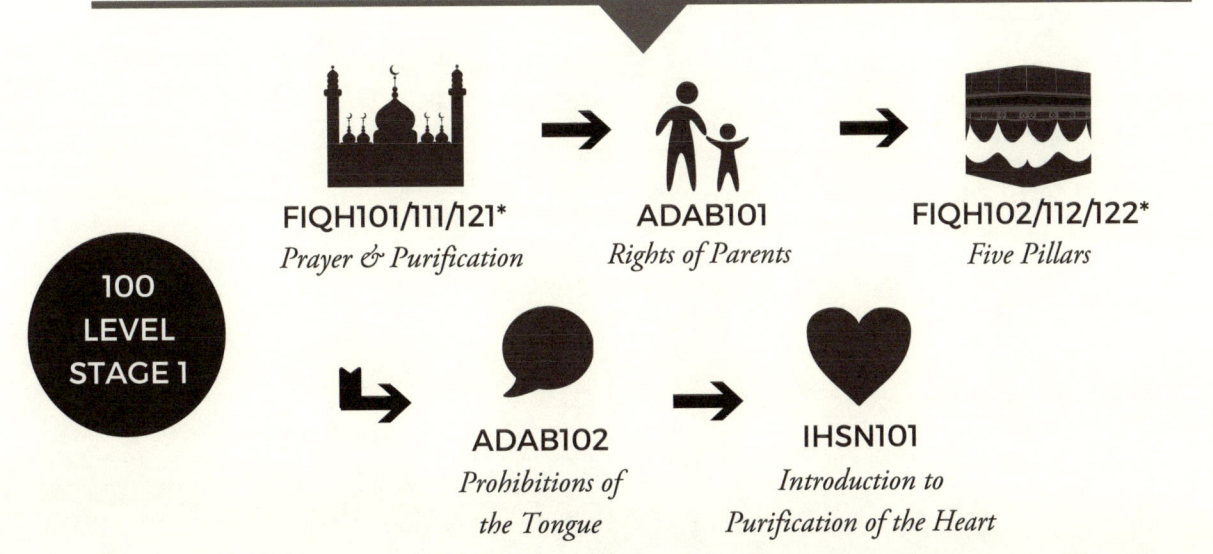

100 LEVEL STAGE 1

FIQH101/111/121* — *Prayer & Purification* → **ADAB101** — *Rights of Parents* → **FIQH102/112/122*** — *Five Pillars* → **ADAB102** — *Prohibitions of the Tongue* → **IHSN101** — *Introduction to Purification of the Heart*

*FIQH classes are offered in the Maliki, Hanafi & Shafii schools of Islamic Law.

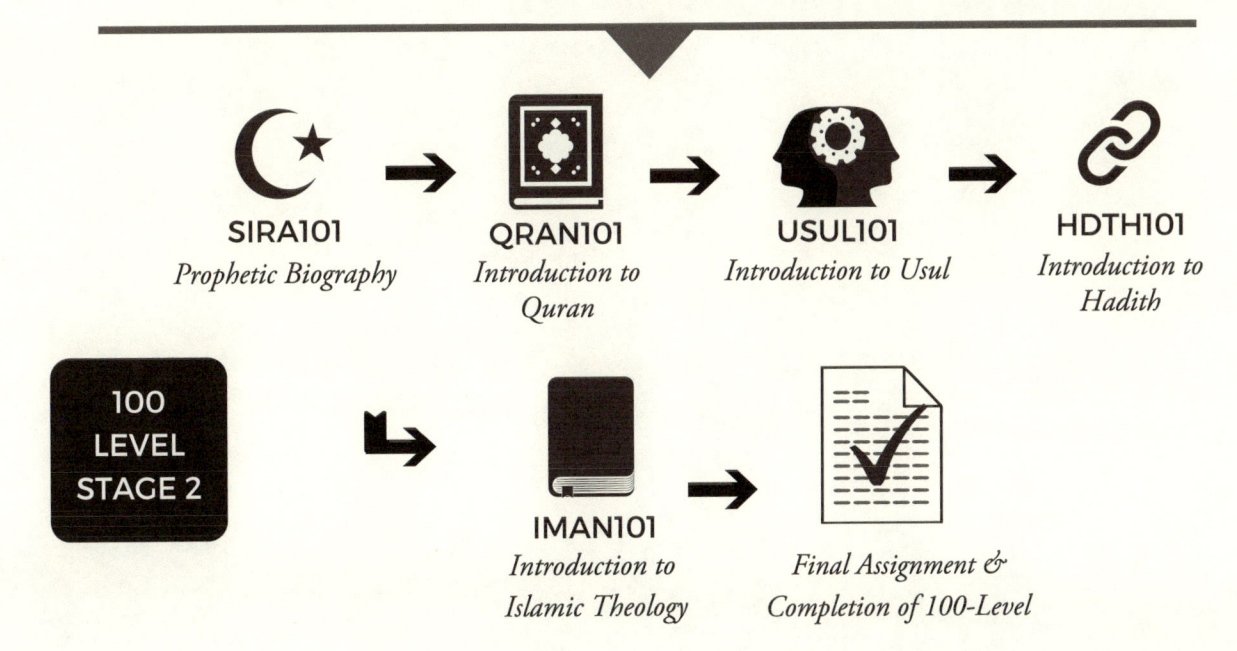

100 LEVEL STAGE 2

SIRA101 — *Prophetic Biography* → **QRAN101** — *Introduction to Quran* → **USUL101** — *Introduction to Usul* → **HDTH101** — *Introduction to Hadith* → **IMAN101** — *Introduction to Islamic Theology* → *Final Assignment & Completion of 100-Level*

A GENERAL MESSAGE TO ANYONE WHO FINDS THIS BOOK

If you have found or have been given this book and would like to become a Tayba Foundation student, please complete the application form below and return it to us.

Thanks to our generous donors, our courses are available to those impacted by incarceration at no cost.

TAYBA FOUNDATION
Freedom Through Education

COMPLETE, SIGN & RETURN PAGES 1 & 2 TO:
Tayba Foundation
P.O. Box 1154
Portsmouth, NH 03802-1154
510-952-9683

TAYBA FOUNDATION STUDENT APPLICATION FORM
(CORRESPONDENCE PROGRAMS)
PLEASE WRITE CLEARLY IN INK (NO PENCIL) AND SIGN TO AVOID DELAYS IN YOUR ADMISSION PROCESS

Full legal name: _____

Preferred name (if applicable): _____

Prison ID No: _____ Birth Date (MM/DD/YYYY): _____

Institution Name: _____

Exact address <u>where you receive books</u>: _____
Dorm/Unit # _____ City: _____ State: _____ Zip Code: _____

Exact address <u>where you receive letters</u> (if different from above): _____
Dorm/Unit # _____ City: _____ State: _____ Zip Code: _____

Expected Parole Date: (MM/DD/YYYY): _____
Expected Release Date: (MM/DD/YYYY): _____

Check if you have access to:

[ ] Phone [ ] Tablet [ ] Email (Please identify: Ex: JPay, Corrlinks, *etc.*) _____

*Note that for those of you who have access to Corrlinks, you will need to add **instructors@taybafoundation.org** to your contacts list and we will accept your request. Unfortunately, we are unable to receive student email through the GettingOut service at this time.

I am interested in taking courses in:
[ ] Islamic Studies   [ ] Life Skills   [ ] Both

The following five items (**A-E**) will not affect your admission in any way. This data assists Tayba Foundation in applying for grants to continue offering our services at low or no cost to our student population.

A. [ ] Raised Muslim   [ ] Converted in prison   [ ] Converted in Society
B. Years as a Muslim (if converted) _____

C. Gender: [ ] Male [ ] Female **D.** Ethnicity (optional)_____

E. Highest level of education: [ ] Some high school [ ] High school [ ] GED

[ ] Some College [ ] AA [ ] BA/BS [ ] MS [ ] PhD

Please note that it is **extremely important for you to keep us updated with any changes in your address/unit, etc.** so we can ensure your books and course materials are sent to the correct address. It is your responsibility to ensure that the mailroom can/will accept mail/shipments from Tayba Foundation.

By signing and submitting this application form, you are agreeing to participate in the entire Tayba Curriculum, or as much of the curriculum as possible, in the order set out by Tayba, which is outlined in the graphic found below. As Tayba adds new courses and/or changes existing courses, Tayba reserves the right to update the order of the curriculum path. By signing and submitting this application form, you are authorizing Tayba Foundation to accept and use financial aid available on your behalf to cover the monthly cost of your subscription. Full details of Tayba's Financial Aid Policy found on the reverse side of this page. Please review them before signing. By signing and submitting this application form, you are agreeing to abide by the Guidelines for Students that was sent with this application.

By my signature below, I acknowledge and accept Tayba Foundation's Financial Aid Policy and Guidelines for Students. I certify that the information contained in this application form is true and complete.
*Signature:*_____ *Date:* _____

Facility Authorization required:

Please note that it is **your responsibility** to ensure you have taken all of the proper measures to receive approval from your facility to receive Tayba Distance Learning Correspondence Course books. Your Chaplain, Education Director or Warden, etc can sign off on their approval below, under your signature.

[ ] I certify that I have filled out any necessary paperwork that may be required by my facility for me to participate in Tayba's Distance Learning Correspondence Programs.

Facility Authorization section:

I, [name and title] _____, hereby

grant permission for [prisoner's name/ID] _____ to

participate in Tayba Foundation's Distance Learning Correspondence Courses. He/she has completed the necessary paperwork required by our facility. And he/she has my permission to receive Tayba coursebooks, correspondence, and any additional educational resource materials required to complete his/her course(s).

Signature of facility authority: _____ Date: _____

TAYBA FOUNDATION FINANCIAL AID POLICY

Financial Aid Policy: Tuition with Tayba Foundation's distance learning programs and access to Tayba Foundation services costs $100 (one hundred) dollars per month. To date, we have been successful in finding financial aid for all our students. By submitting this form, you are authorizing Tayba Foundation to accept and use financial aid available on your behalf to cover this monthly cost. **No cash will be sent to you.** The monthly subscription cost will include, but is not limited to, books and other relevant educational resources, as well as shipping costs and sales tax. This will also allow access to any newsletters you sign up for, Life Skills courses, our Reentry coaching and planning, and our peer mentor services. Tayba receives grants and donations for our program from a number of sources. If you choose not to use Tayba's financial aid, please enclose a check or money order to cover the cost of $100.00 (one hundred) dollars per month.

If you wish to cancel your access at any time, please submit your notice to Tayba Foundation in writing. If we do not receive any communication from you for a period of twelve (12) months, we will consider you "inactive." If any communications Tayba sends you is returned to us (Return To Sender - RTS), we will attempt to resend. If we are not able to send to a new address, we will consider your subscription inactive. Should you become inactive in distance learning programs or other Tayba Foundation services, your access will be put on hold and Tayba Foundation will cease to collect the $100 per month financial aid on your behalf. You can reactivate your subscription to Tayba Foundation's services by mail, email or phone, letting us know that you would still like to be on our mailing list and remain eligible for our educational programs and other services. Note that Tayba Foundation's distance learning programs follow a set learning schedule of semesters. Tayba Foundation's services are not unlimited. However, we have been able to accommodate all reasonable requests for services to date. If you wish to cancel your access at any time, please submit your notice to Tayba Foundation in writing. If we do not receive any communication from you for a period of twelve (12) months, we will consider you "inactive."

TAYBA FOUNDATION ISLAMIC STUDIES CURRICULUM

Tayba's Curriculum Path

1. Essential Track — Average of 18+

2. Intermediate Track — Average of 5+ years

3. Arabic Language Studies

4. Advanced Track Course

Essential Track:
8 foundational courses with essential information for every Muslim, in easy-to-read texts in colour, with many opportunities to check one's understanding. Courses include enrichment and reflection exercises.

Intermediate Track:
Course List:
- 'Aqida (Iman 100, 101)
- Fiqh (FIQH 100, 101, 102)
- Adab (ADAB 100, 101, 102)
- Sira 101
- Qur'an 101
- Uṣul 101
- Hadith 101
- Iman 101

Arabic Language Studies:
Arabic Studies program offers learning from the very beginner level (Arabic alphabet) to Intermediate Arabic, including assessments.

Advanced Track Course:
Course List:
- 'Aqida (iman 201)
- Ihsan 201
- Individualized further study

TAYBA FOUNDATION
Freedom Through Education

KEEP THE REMAINING PAGES OF THIS APPLICATION FORM FOR YOUR RECORDS

TAYBA FOUNDATION GUIDELINES FOR STUDENTS

The superiority of knowledge has been clearly established through the Qur'ān and the sayings of the Prophet Muhammad ﷺ. Those that aid in the pursuit of knowledge are given a great reward. So, it is an honor for our organization to facilitate education for those who are seekers of knowledge. To ensure that the education process remains unhindered for our students, teachers and the organization, we expect all those who participate in the Distance Learning Program to understand and abide by these guidelines. Failure to comply with these guidelines will result in expulsion from the Distance Learning Program.

1. **Education is our goal and security is our primary concern.**
   a. Students must fully comply with prison regulations and protocols at all times.
   b. No material of the Tayba Foundation shall be used by students to legitimize otherwise illegal activity.
   c. Adherence to the laws of the land is a duty on all. Our obedience to established laws comes from our obedience to our Lord. All students will be expected to obey the laws and not do anything to circumvent said laws.
   d. No student shall be engaged in any illegal activity. We have a zero tolerance policy in this regard.
   e. In those cases where the material is sent to the chaplain, it is the responsibility of the student to contact the chaplain about
      access to the material. Students may use legal remedies available to them to ensure compliance with the free practice of
      their religion, but the Tayba Foundation will not be responsible for taking these actions.

2. **Tayba Foundation Correspondence Courses are not meant to be used to undermine other established programs.**
   a. All students must respect the programs of other Muslims and other faith groups.
   b. Students will not make blanket references to staff, volunteers, or other incarcerated prisoners such as "kāfir/infidel,"
      "fāsiq/deviant", "bid'i/innovator." This behavior will not be tolerated.
   c. No material from the Tayba Foundation is to be used to challenge established programs whether they are administered by prison staff, chaplains, volunteers or other incarcerated prisoners.
   d. Students will recognize and respect all established authority figures. This includes, but is not limited to Imams, chaplains, prison administration, and prison staff.
   e. Tayba Foundation will not attempt to resolve issues with staff or other incarcerated prisoners. Students will have to contact appropriate advocacy organizations to find meaningful resolutions to infringement of rights: CAIR, Muslim Advocates, ACLU, etc. In some cases, Tayba can assist the student in finding an appropriate advocacy organization.

3. **Tayba Foundation is non-political.**
   a. We believe that the path to changing our societies is through education and the root of all problems lies in ignorance. Therefore, our solution to the problems comes through educational means and not political means.
   b. Students will not use Tayba Foundation material for political motives.

4. **Tayba Foundation Courses are not meant in any way to be a movement. We are an educational and charitable organization that aims to facilitate educational programs.**
   a. Our course material is not to be used to form any type of unauthorized organization.
   b. Students are not to participate in any group or movement that is illegal or questionable.
   c. Students will not use Tayba Foundation material as part of any unauthorized group.

5. **The Tayba Foundation supports unity.**

a. Tayba Foundation does not condone use of our material to divide or cause discord within the inmate population or the prison staff. Students must only use our material for the purposes of learning and not create political or social division.

b. All students will learn to recognize and respect valid differences of opinion.

c. All students will engage in discussion about the religion in the best of manners. The Qur'ān obliges us to this in the verse, "Do not debate with them except in the best of manners."

d. The Tayba Foundation's courses are not meant to replace all programs that an inmate may be participating in as our courses are meant to enhance the inmate's learning.

e. Students should continue any vocational training they are engaged in. A strong work ethic is a must for all Muslims, especially our students.

f. Students should participate in rehabilitation programs suggested to them by their counselors or administration.

6. **All students will follow their institutional guidelines in regards to all communication with Tayba Foundation.**

a. Students will not jeopardize Tayba Foundation programs by attempting to communicate in a manner with us that is not allowed by their respective institution's guidelines.

b. All communication with Tayba Foundation must be in accordance with federal, state and local laws. The Tayba Foundation operates out of Alameda County in California.

c. Students will not attempt to use Tayba Foundation to relay messages to persons not associated with the organization. This includes other incarcerated prisoners, family, or friends.

d. Correspondence with Tayba Foundation must only pertain to its educational program.

7. **Students will maintain the highest standard of conduct.**

a. Students will adhere to the highest standards of ethics and moral behavior.

b. Tayba Foundation expects all students to behave with integrity and honesty in all their interactions with their prison staff, fellow incarcerated prisoners, family, and community, as well as with Tayba staff.

c. Tayba Foundation will not be responsible for any inappropriate behavior on the part of its students.

d. Tayba Foundation strongly condemns religious extremism, intolerance, and any form of terrorism. Students must act in accordance with Tayba's stance on such issues.

Made in the USA
Columbia, SC
19 July 2025